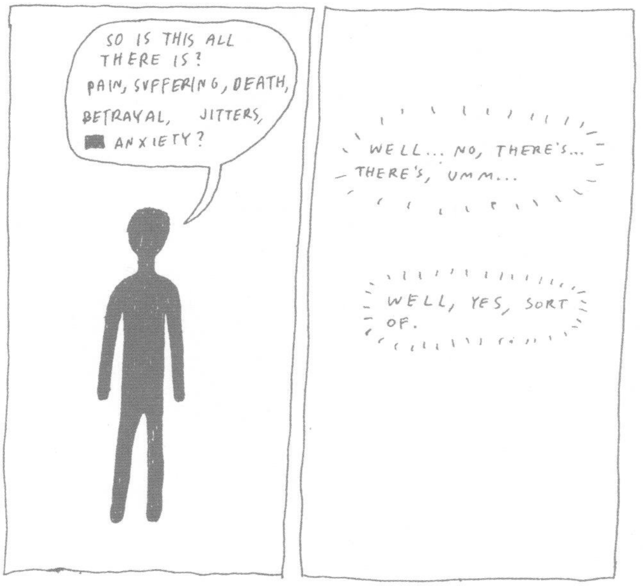
SO IS THIS ALL THERE IS? PAIN, SUFFERING, DEATH, BETRAYAL, JITTERS, [redacted] ANXIETY?
WELL... NO, THERE'S... THERE'S, UMM...
WELL, YES, SORT OF.

FANTAGRAPHICS BOOKS INC.

FANTAGRAPHICS BOOKS INC.
7563 LAKE CITY WAY NE
SEATTLE, WASHINGTON 98115
www.fantagraphics.com

DESIGNER: ANDERS NILSEN
PRODUCTION: PAUL BARESH
PROMOTION: JACQUELENE COHEN
VP/ASSOCIATE PUBLISHER/EDITOR: ERIC REYNOLDS
PRESIDENT/PUBLISHER: GARY GROTH

ISBN 978-1-68396-563-3
LIBRARY OF CONGRESS CONTROL NUMBER
FIRST PRINTING: JUNE 2022
PRINTED IN CHINA

SEE ALSO:
www.andersbrekhusnilsen.com
AND @andersbrekhus

FOR CHERYL

the end

anders nilsen

CONTENTS

PROLOGUE

YOU CAN'T TELL WHERE YOU ARE ANYMORE. SOMETIMES IT SEEMS LIKE A HOSPITAL BED, SOMETIMES YOU IMAGINE YOU ARE A GIANT FLIGHTLESS BIRD. YOU FEEL BLOATED, LIKE A WATER BALLOON. THERE ARE WIRES ATTACHED TO YOU AND TUBES COMING OUT OF EVERYWHERE.

THE LIGHT IS BAD. IT'S GREENISH AND THERE'S TOO MUCH OF IT.

GROUPS OF MEDICAL STUDENTS COME BY TO SEE IF THEY CAN FIGURE OUT WHAT YOUR PROBLEM IS.

I'M ALIVE, YOU THINK, THAT'S MY PROBLEM. I'M STILL ALIVE.

THEY TAKE TURNS POKING YOU. THEY STARE IN AWED SILENCE. THEY'RE NERVOUS. EVENTUALLY THEY FILE BACK OUT AND GO DOWN TO THE CAFETERIA TO EAT FROZEN PEAS AND TALK ABOUT T.V.

AND YOU AND I GO BACK TO FLOATING TOGETHER ABOVE THE BED. YOU STARE AT THE CEILING, AND SLEEP. I HOLD YOUR HANDS. I WATCH YOU BREATH AND TRY AND THINK OF SOMETHING I CAN DO TO HELP YOU.

PEOPLE KEEP BRINGING YOU FOOD EVEN THOUGH YOU CAN'T EAT IT. YOU'RE NOT HUNGRY AND ANYWAY IT ALL TASTES LIKE GROUND UP CHALK. BUT IT TAKES TOO MUCH EFFORT TO EXPLAIN THAT. SO YOU JUST TURN YOUR HEAD AND LOOK OUT THE WINDOW.

THE END IS HERE, THEY SAY, THERE'S NOTHING MORE TO BE DONE AND YOU NOD AND CRY, BUT YOU COULD HAVE TOLD THEM THAT YOURSELF.

AND THEN YOU START FEELING LIKE A TURKEY AGAIN, AND THE TV AND YOUR DREAMS START MIXING TOGETHER.

AND WE FLOAT ABOVE THE BED, HOLDING HANDS. YOU STARE OUT THE WINDOW AND I STARE AT YOU AND TRY TO THINK OF SOMETHING I CAN DO TO MAKE IT BETTER.

THERE'S SURGERY, GALLONS OF BLOOD, BEEPING MACHINES AND BLINKING LIGHTS. THERE'S SHIT AND URINE AND PUS AND MORE BLOOD. ALL THE PEOPLE WHO COME TO VISIT, YOU KIND OF WISH THEY WOULD GO AWAY. EXCEPT ME. YOU GET MAD WHEN I LEAVE.

SO WE FLOAT ABOVE THE BED TOGETHER. YOU STARE AT THE CEILING AND I STARE AT YOU, AND I TRY TO THINK OF SOMETHING I CAN DO.

I SLEEP ON THE FLOOR NEXT TO YOU IF THEY LET ME, OR BENT UP ON A CHAIR IN THE WAITING ROOM IF THEY DON'T. I'D CRAWL INTO BED WITH YOU, BUT THERE ARE TOO MANY WIRES AND TUBES. I'D GIVE YOU MY BODY AND DIE MYSELF IF I COULD, BUT THE DOCTORS DON'T KNOW HOW TO DO THAT, SO YOU DIE.

AND WE FLOAT ABOVE THE BED TOGETHER. I CLOSE YOUR EYES. I HOLD YOUR HEAD IN MY HANDS AND YOUR HEART IN MY HEART AND I LOOK AT YOU AND I AM FLOATING ABOVE THE BED ALONE. AND THERE'S NOTHING I CAN DO AT ALL BECAUSE YOU'RE GONE.

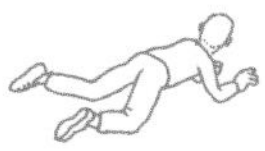

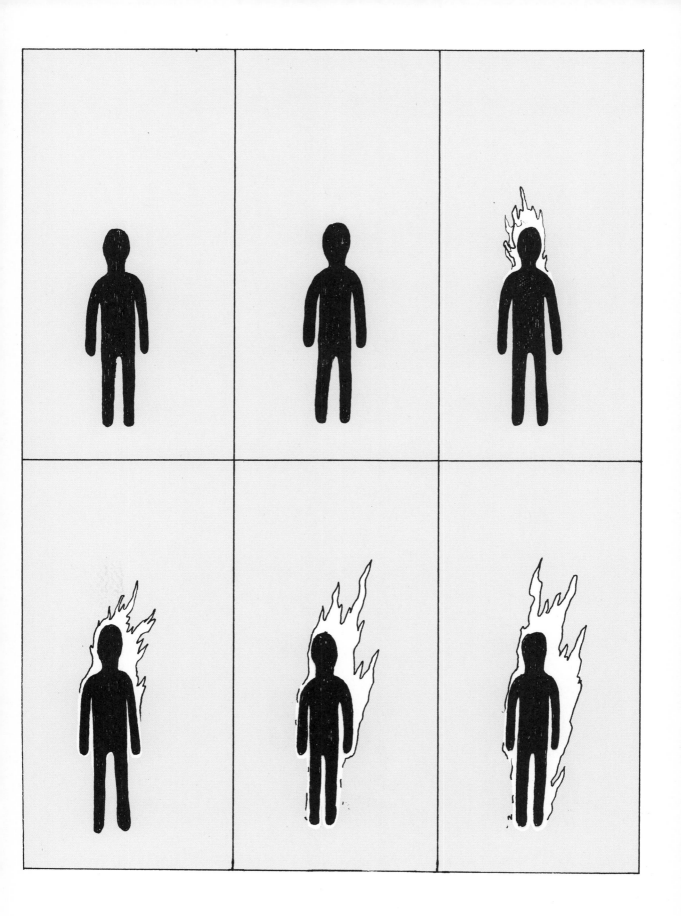

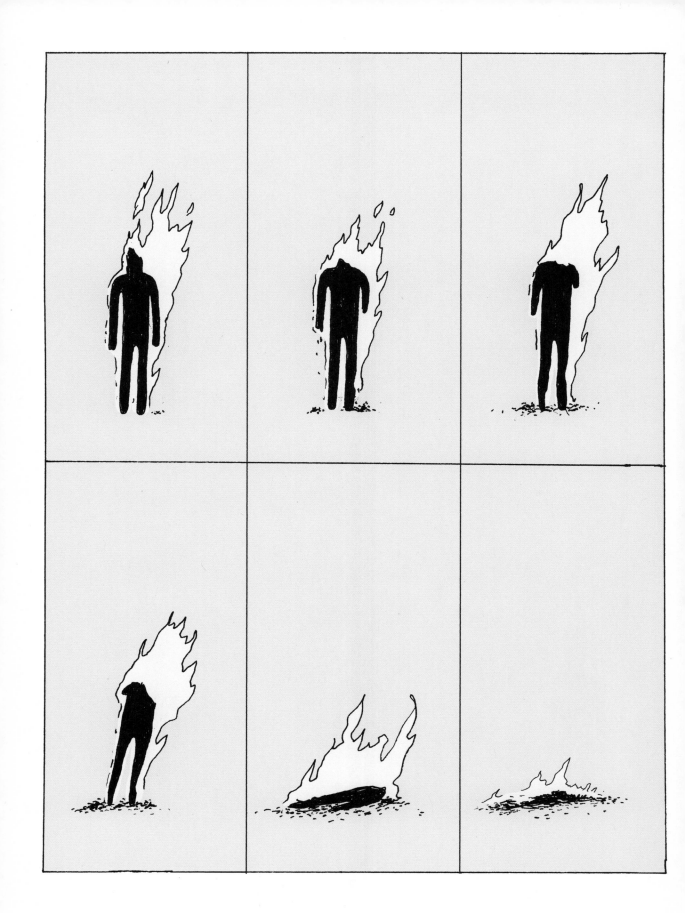

SINCE YOU'VE BEEN GONE I CAN
DO WHATEVER I WANT ALL THE TIME.

ME CRYING WHILE
TRYING TO EAT LUNCH
AND READ A BOOK

ME CRYING WHILE
DOING THE DISHES

ME CRYING WHILE TRYING TO
WORK ON THE COMPUTER

ME TRYING TO HOLD IT
TOGETHER ON THE TRAIN
IN FRANCE

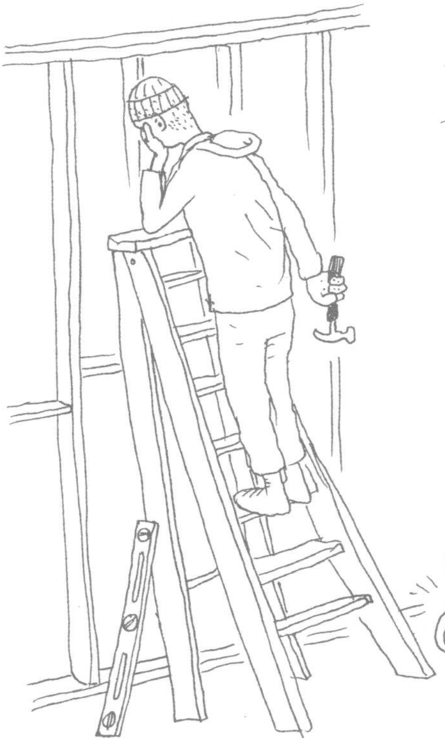

ME CRYING WHILE TRYING TO BUILD A WALL - BECAUSE OF A JOHNNY CASH SONG

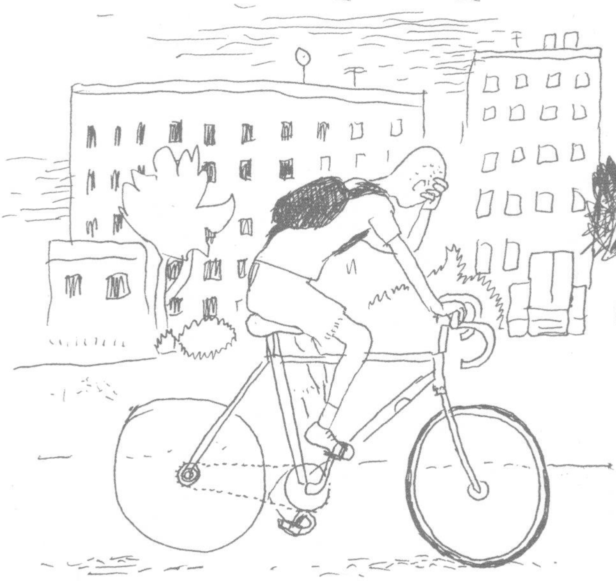

ME TRYING TO HOLD IT TOGETHER ON MY BIKE ON THE WAY PAST CABRINI GREEN

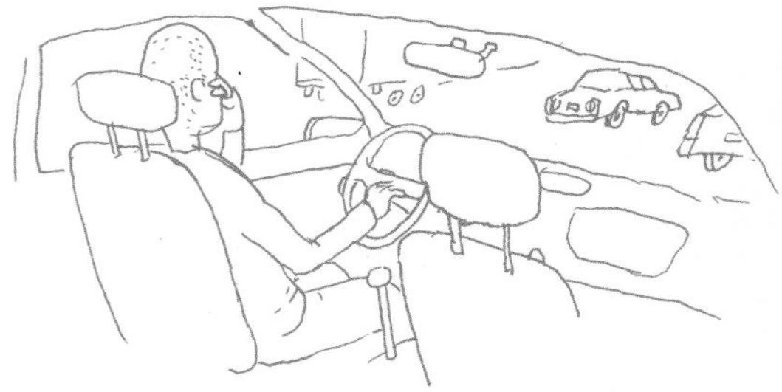

ME TRYING TO HOLD IT TOGETHER WHILE MERGING ON 90-94

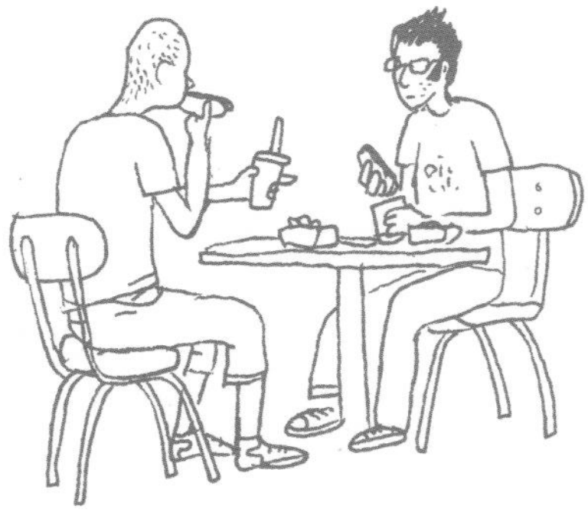

ME EATING TOFU DOGS WITH KEITH

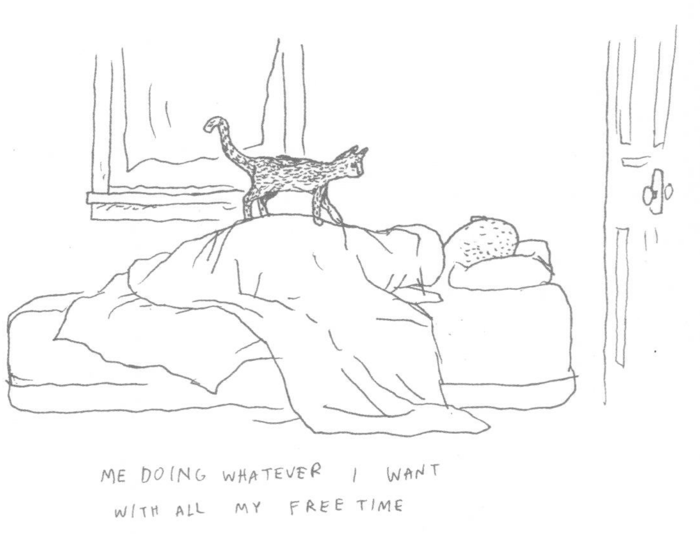

ME DOING WHATEVER I WANT WITH ALL MY FREE TIME

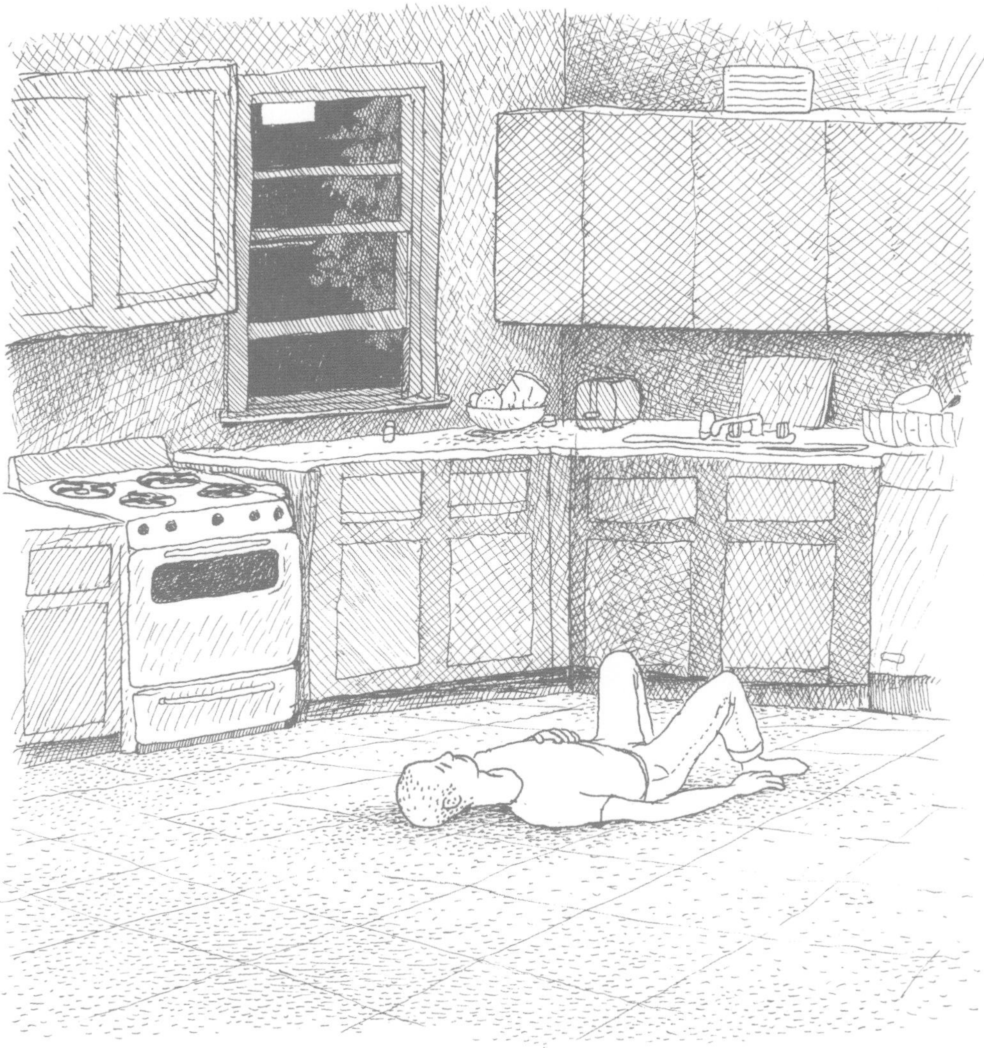

ME LYING ON THE KITCHEN FLOOR

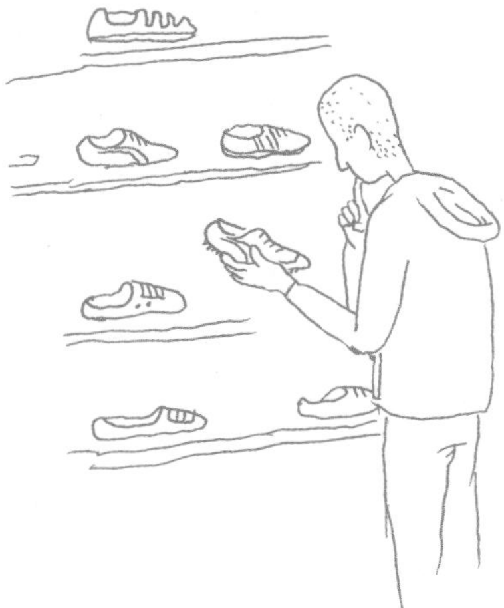

ME BUYING SHOES IN SPAIN

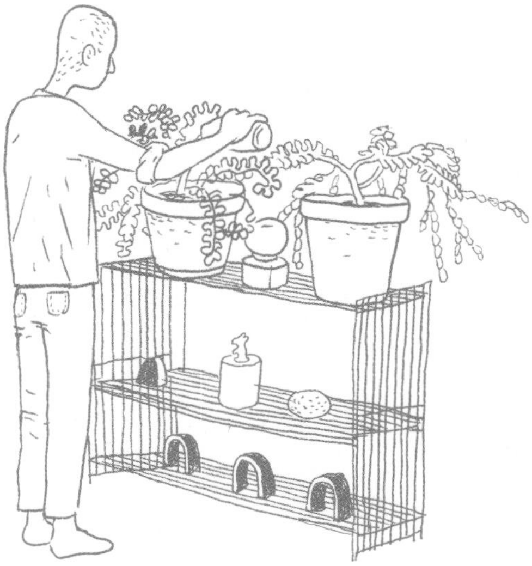

ME WATERING YOUR PLANTS

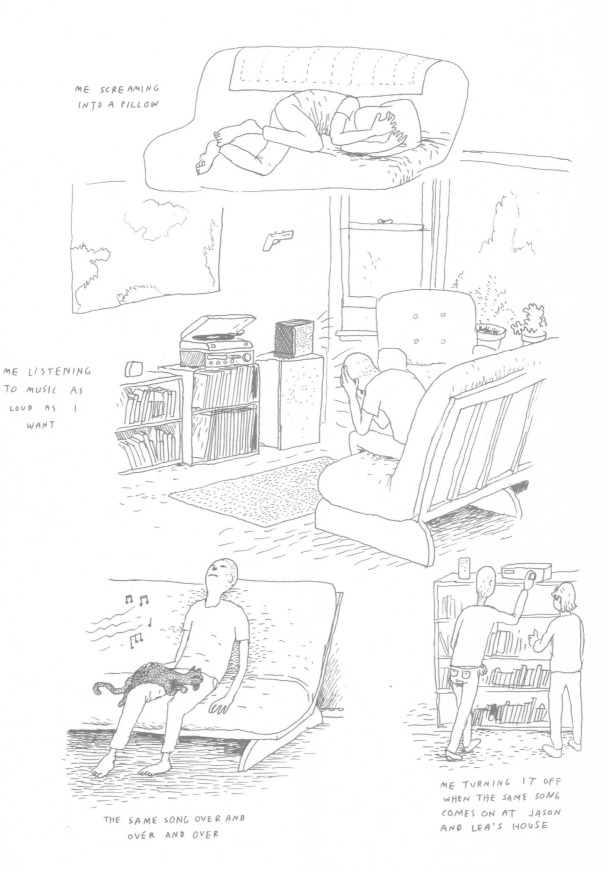

ME SCREAMING
INTO A PILLOW

ME LISTENING
TO MUSIC AS
LOUD AS I
WANT

THE SAME SONG OVER AND
OVER AND OVER

ME TURNING IT OFF
WHEN THE SAME SONG
COMES ON AT JASON
AND LEA'S HOUSE

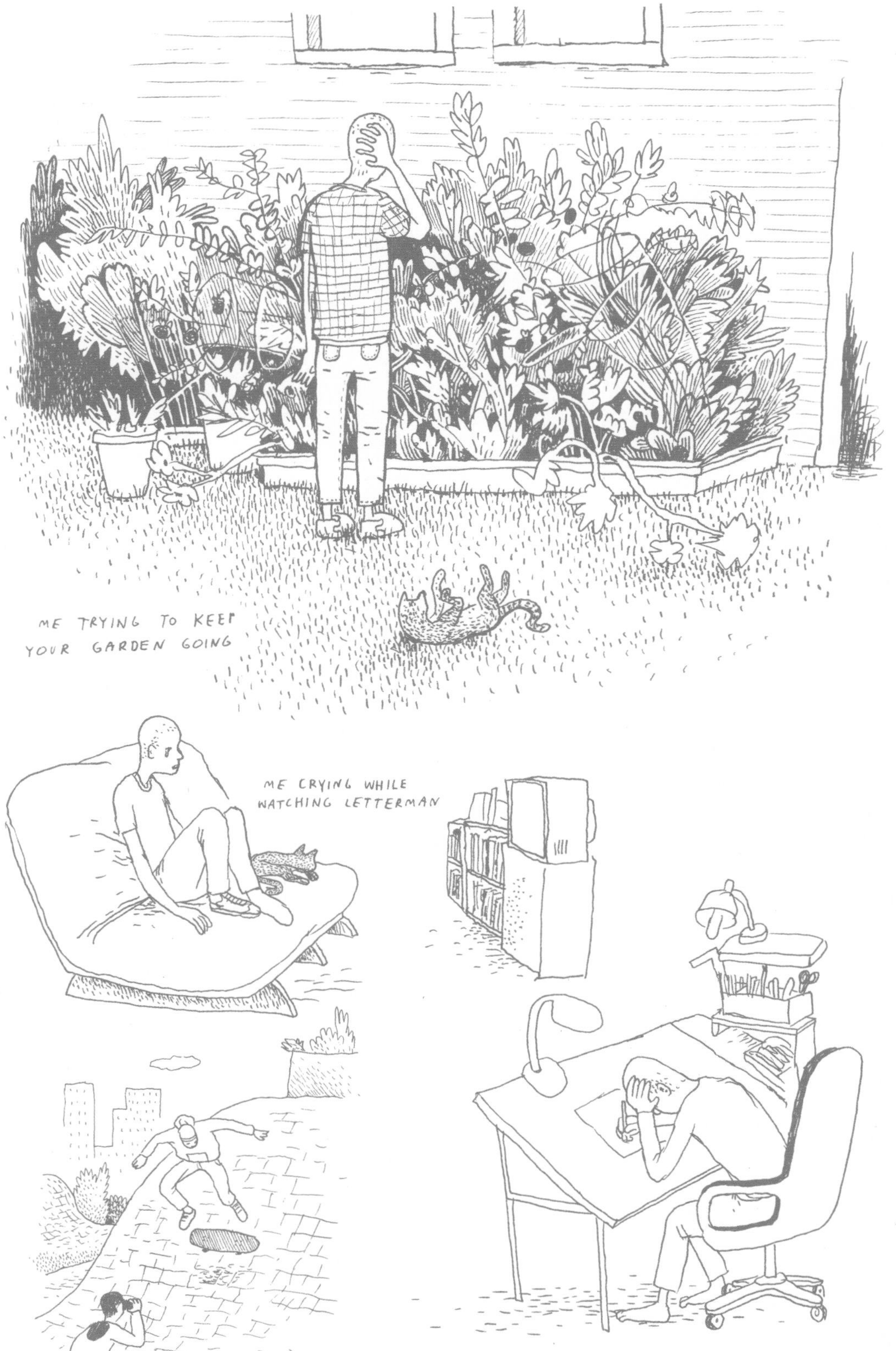
ME TRYING TO KEEP YOUR GARDEN GOING
ME CRYING WHILE WATCHING LETTERMAN
ME SKATEBOARDING WITH RYAN IN BILBAO
ME CRYING WHILE I DRAW PICTURES OF BIRDS

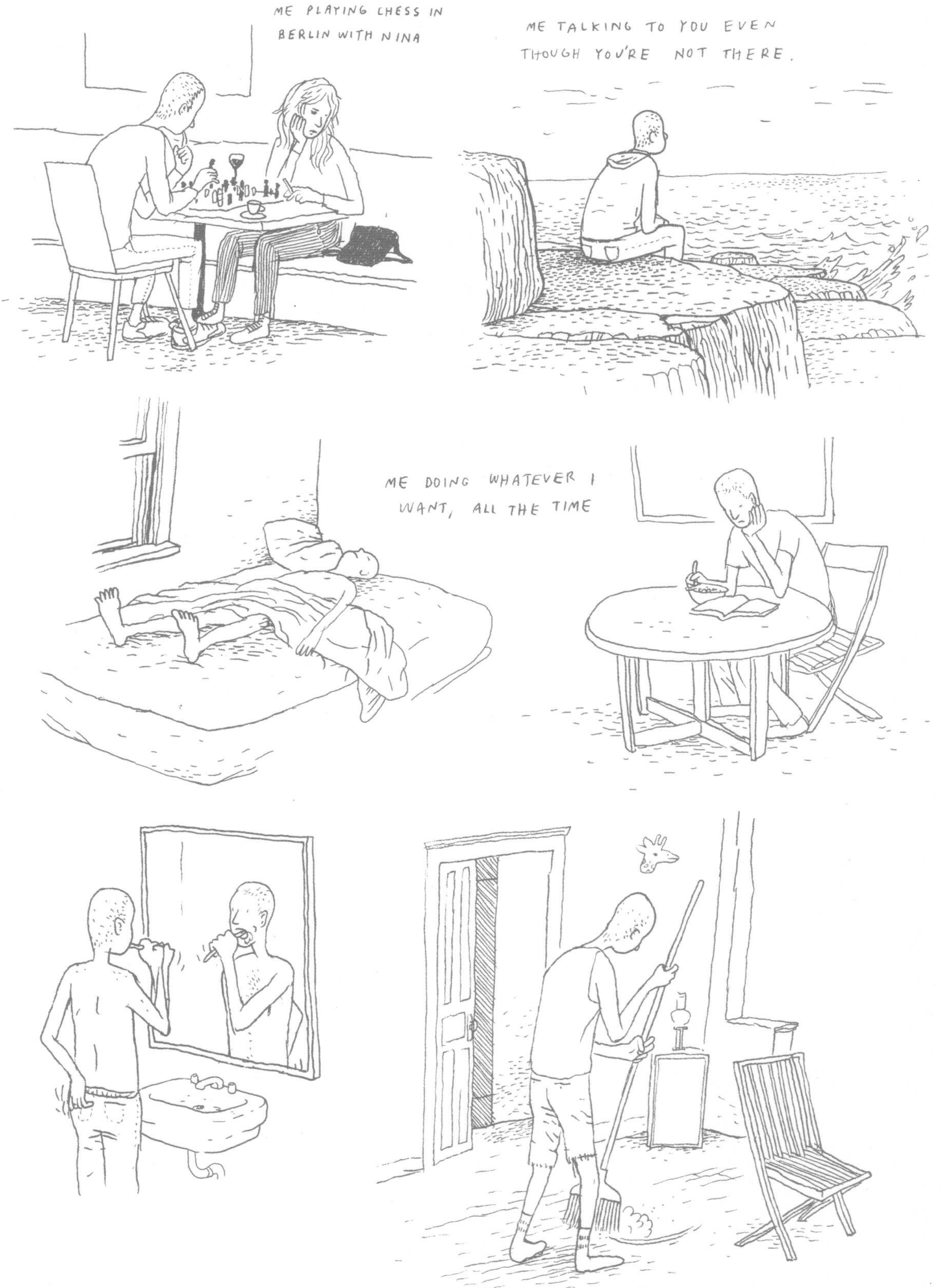
ME PLAYING CHESS IN BERLIN WITH NINA
ME TALKING TO YOU EVEN THOUGH YOU'RE NOT THERE.
ME DOING WHATEVER I WANT, ALL THE TIME

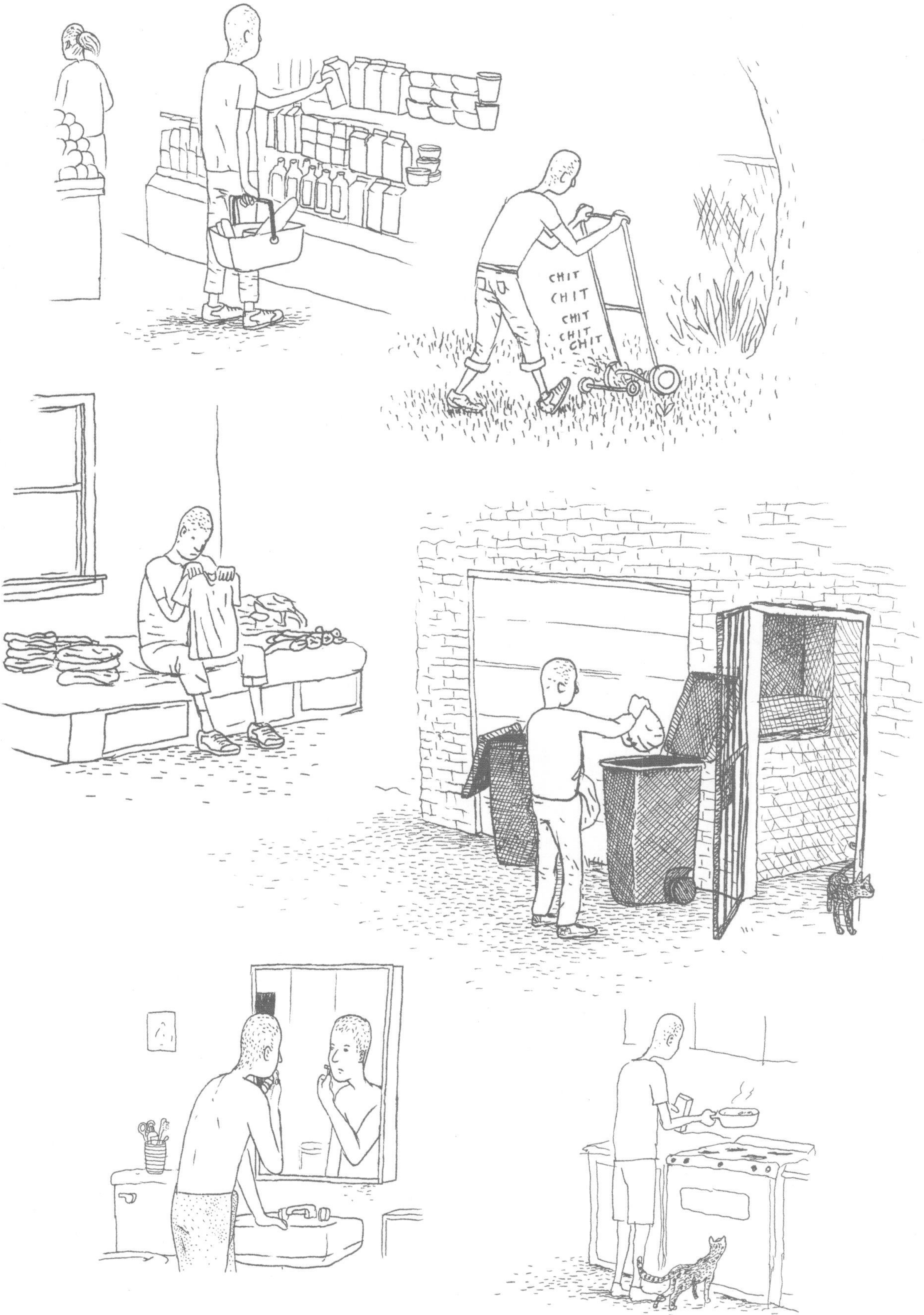
CHIT
CHIT
CHIT
CHIT
CHIT

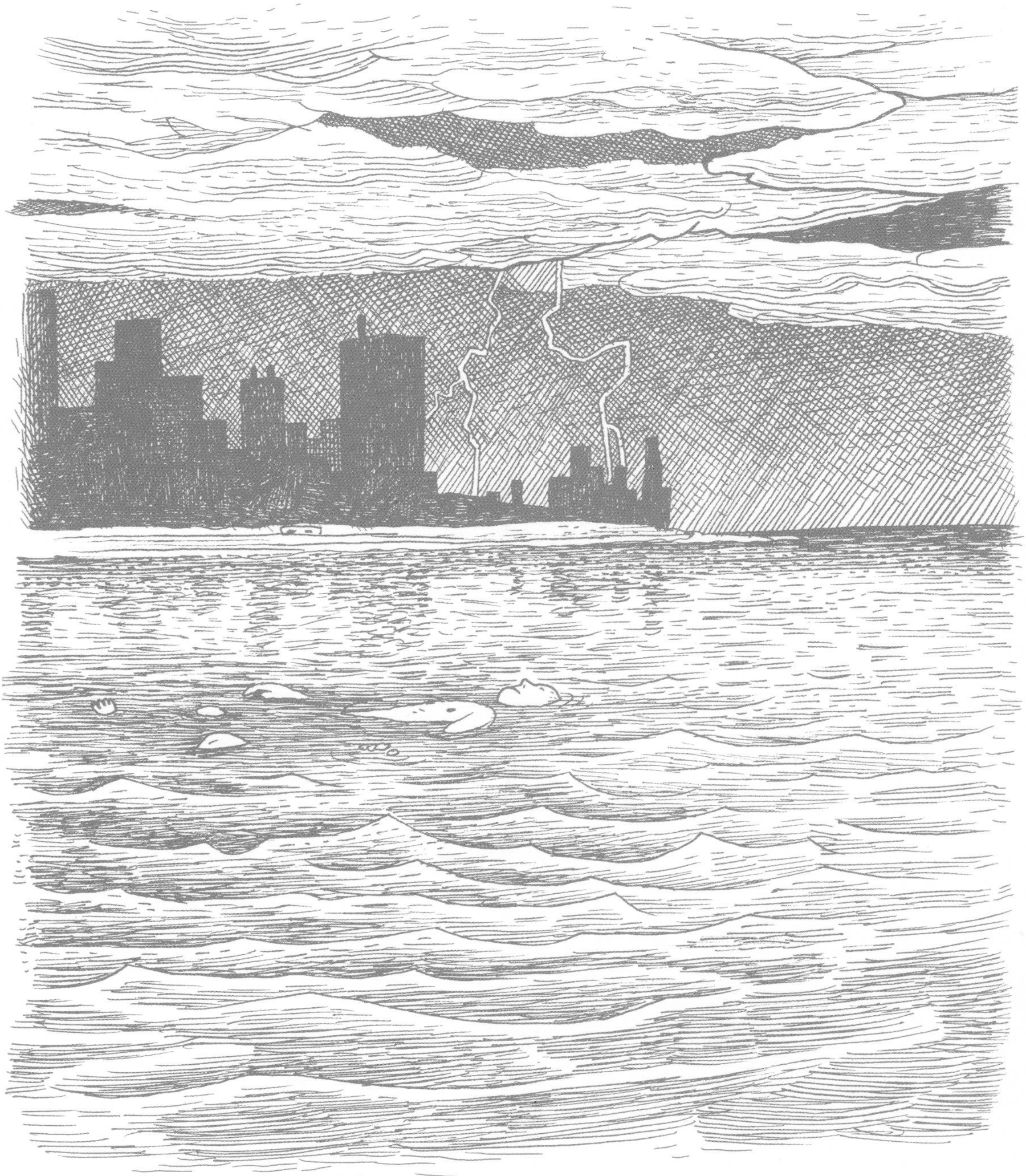

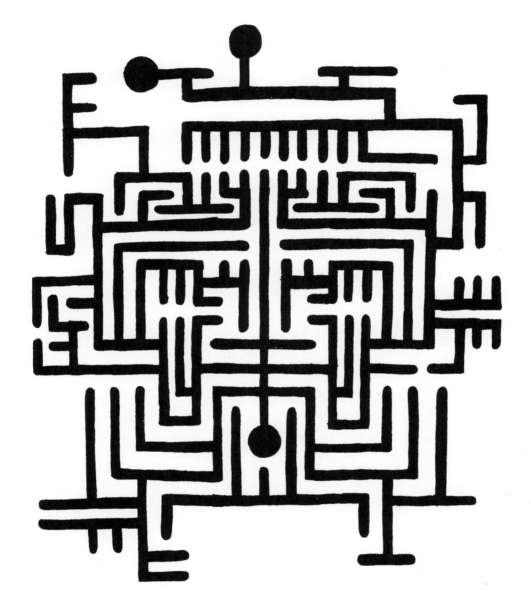

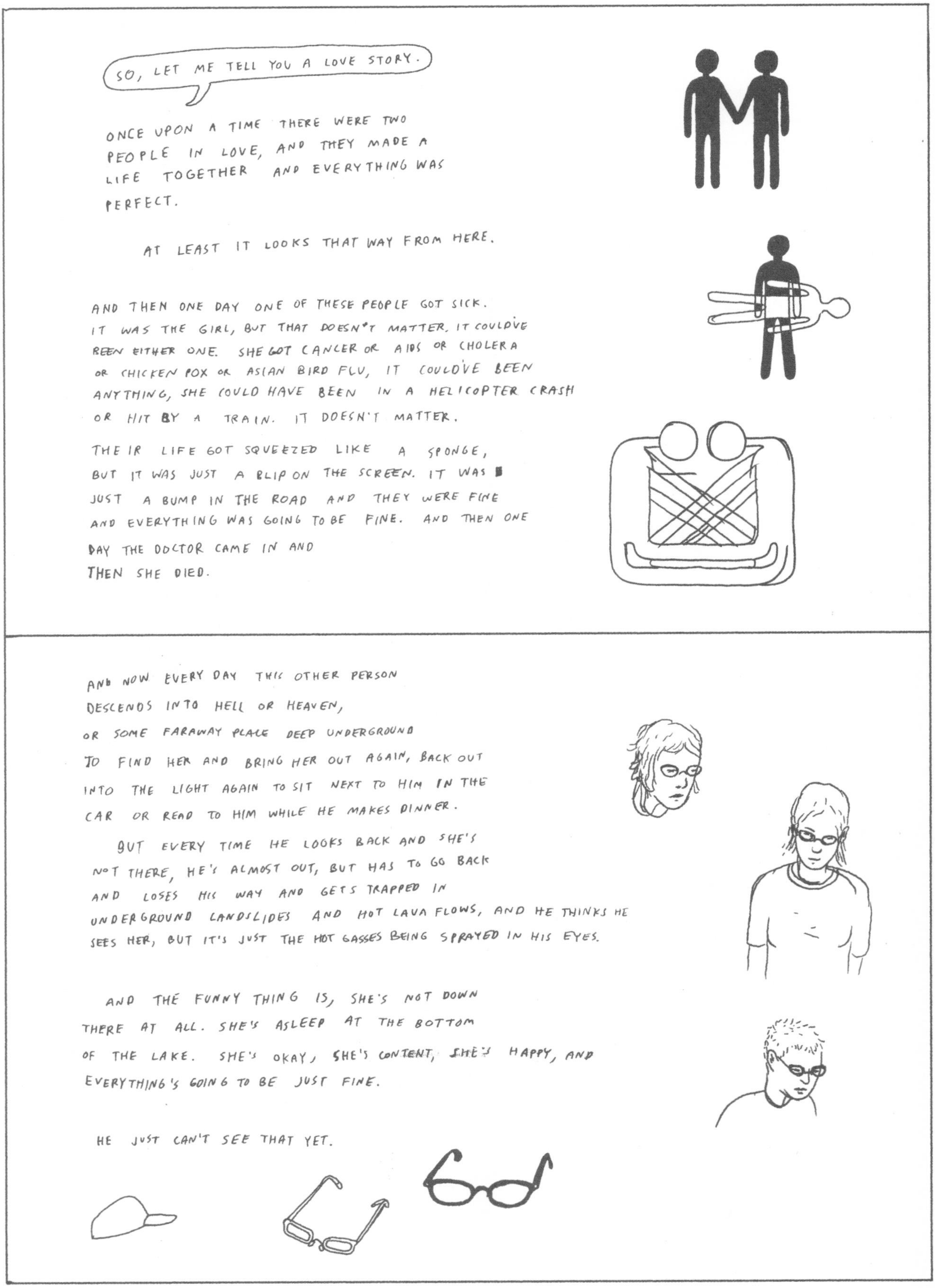
SO, LET ME TELL YOU A LOVE STORY.
ONCE UPON A TIME THERE WERE TWO PEOPLE IN LOVE, AND THEY MADE A LIFE TOGETHER AND EVERYTHING WAS PERFECT.
AT LEAST IT LOOKS THAT WAY FROM HERE.
AND THEN ONE DAY ONE OF THESE PEOPLE GOT SICK. IT WAS THE GIRL, BUT THAT DOESN'T MATTER. IT COULD'VE BEEN EITHER ONE. SHE GOT CANCER OR AIDS OR CHOLERA OR CHICKEN POX OR ASIAN BIRD FLU, IT COULD'VE BEEN ANYTHING, SHE COULD HAVE BEEN IN A HELICOPTER CRASH OR HIT BY A TRAIN. IT DOESN'T MATTER.
THEIR LIFE GOT SQUEEZED LIKE A SPONGE, BUT IT WAS JUST A BLIP ON THE SCREEN. IT WAS JUST A BUMP IN THE ROAD AND THEY WERE FINE AND EVERYTHING WAS GOING TO BE FINE. AND THEN ONE DAY THE DOCTOR CAME IN AND
THEN SHE DIED.
AND NOW EVERY DAY THIS OTHER PERSON DESCENDS INTO HELL OR HEAVEN, OR SOME FARAWAY PLACE DEEP UNDERGROUND TO FIND HER AND BRING HER OUT AGAIN, BACK OUT INTO THE LIGHT AGAIN TO SIT NEXT TO HIM IN THE CAR OR READ TO HIM WHILE HE MAKES DINNER.
BUT EVERY TIME HE LOOKS BACK AND SHE'S NOT THERE, HE'S ALMOST OUT, BUT HAS TO GO BACK AND LOSES HIS WAY AND GETS TRAPPED IN UNDERGROUND LANDSLIDES AND HOT LAVA FLOWS, AND HE THINKS HE SEES HER, BUT IT'S JUST THE HOT GASSES BEING SPRAYED IN HIS EYES.
AND THE FUNNY THING IS, SHE'S NOT DOWN THERE AT ALL. SHE'S ASLEEP AT THE BOTTOM OF THE LAKE. SHE'S OKAY, SHE'S CONTENT, SHE'S HAPPY, AND EVERYTHING'S GOING TO BE JUST FINE.
HE JUST CAN'T SEE THAT YET.

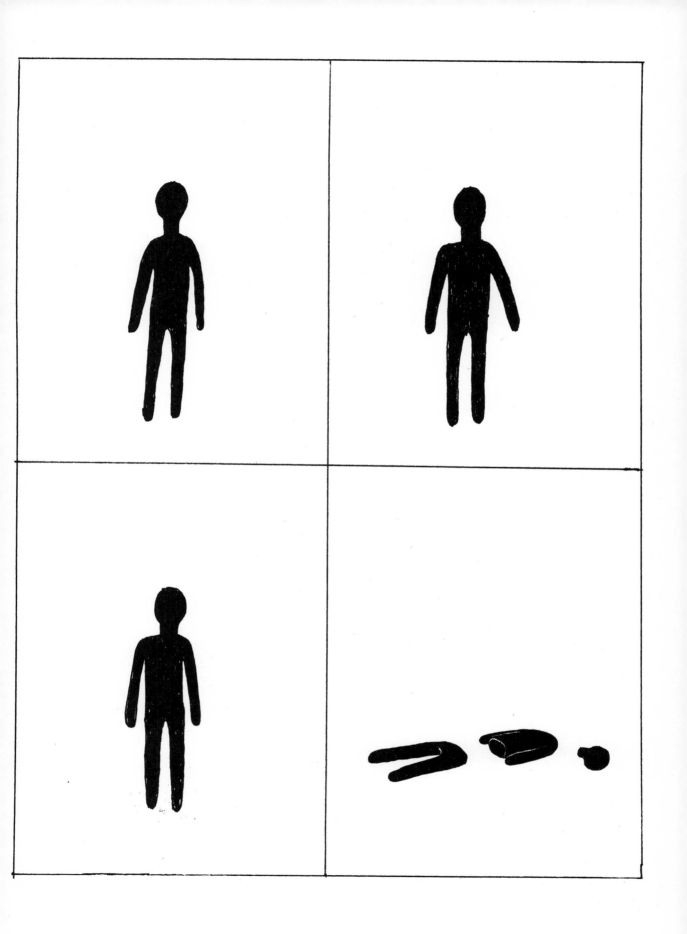

NO MATTER HOW LONG I WALK AROUND
BLINDFOLDED WITH MY HANDS OUTSTRETCHED
MY FINGERS WILL NEVER TOUCH YOUR FACE

WHERE ARE YOU?

I WANT YOU HERE

LIKE TRYING REPEATEDLY TO HANG
A SHIRT UP ON A WALL WHEN THERE IS
NO PEG

PICKING IT UP AND TRYING AGAIN
PICKING IT UP AND TRYING AGAIN

I REALLY JUST DON'T WANT TO CONTINUE
IN THIS WORLD WITHOUT YOU IN IT
I JUST WANT YOU BACK AND IT'S NOT
SATISFYING EVEN TO KEEP SAYING THAT

I HAVE TWO LIVES

THEY STARTED AS ONE, THEN SPLIT AT
A CERTAIN POINT. I'M IN ONE NOW AND THE
OTHER IS CLOSED TO ME. I DO OCCASIONALLY
GET A GLIMPSE OF IT, THOUGH: THE WARM
LIGHT THROUGH THE CURTAINS, THE CHILDREN
AND SAFETY. IT'S A COMPLICATED LIFE, THAT
ONE. IT'S NOT EASY, BUT THIS ONE ISN'T
EASY EITHER. IN THIS ONE THE LONGING
IS SHARPER. SO I WIPE A GAP INTO THE
FROST ON THE WINDOWPANE AND WATCH
AWHILE. I'M SORRY I CAN'T GO INSIDE.

I CAN SEE THE OTHER LIFE IN BEAUTIFUL SAELEE
AND OBLIVIOUS SOUTHER. IN PURPOSEFULLY PATIENT
ULLA AND EAGER JESS. IN THE MOVING FORWARD
OF LIFE AND LOVE AND FRUSTRATION. THE KNOWING
OF ANOTHER PERSON. IN CARLEEN'S ANNOYANCE THAT

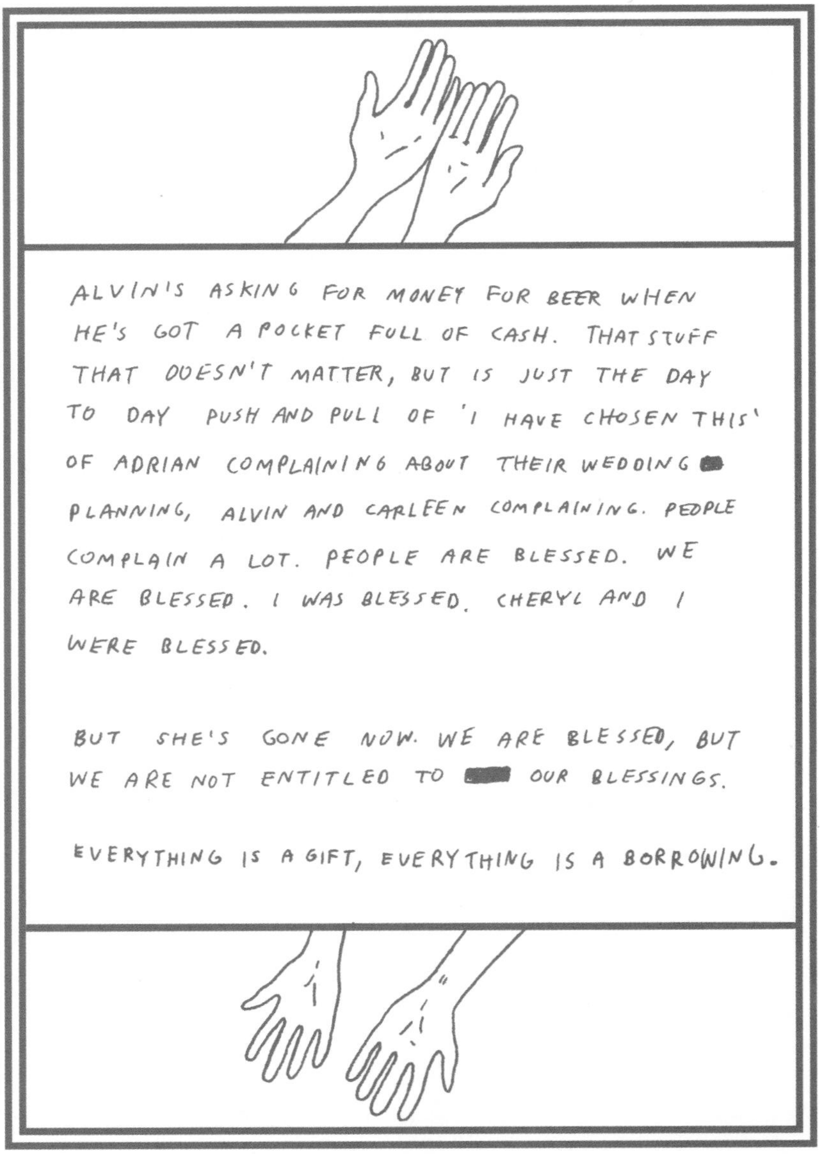
ALVIN'S ASKING FOR MONEY FOR BEER WHEN HE'S GOT A POCKET FULL OF CASH. THAT STUFF THAT DOESN'T MATTER, BUT IS JUST THE DAY TO DAY PUSH AND PULL OF 'I HAVE CHOSEN THIS' OF ADRIAN COMPLAINING ABOUT THEIR WEDDING [redacted] PLANNING, ALVIN AND CARLEEN COMPLAINING. PEOPLE COMPLAIN A LOT. PEOPLE ARE BLESSED. WE ARE BLESSED. I WAS BLESSED. CHERYL AND I WERE BLESSED.
BUT SHE'S GONE NOW. WE ARE BLESSED, BUT WE ARE NOT ENTITLED TO [redacted] OUR BLESSINGS.
EVERYTHING IS A GIFT, EVERYTHING IS A BORROWING.

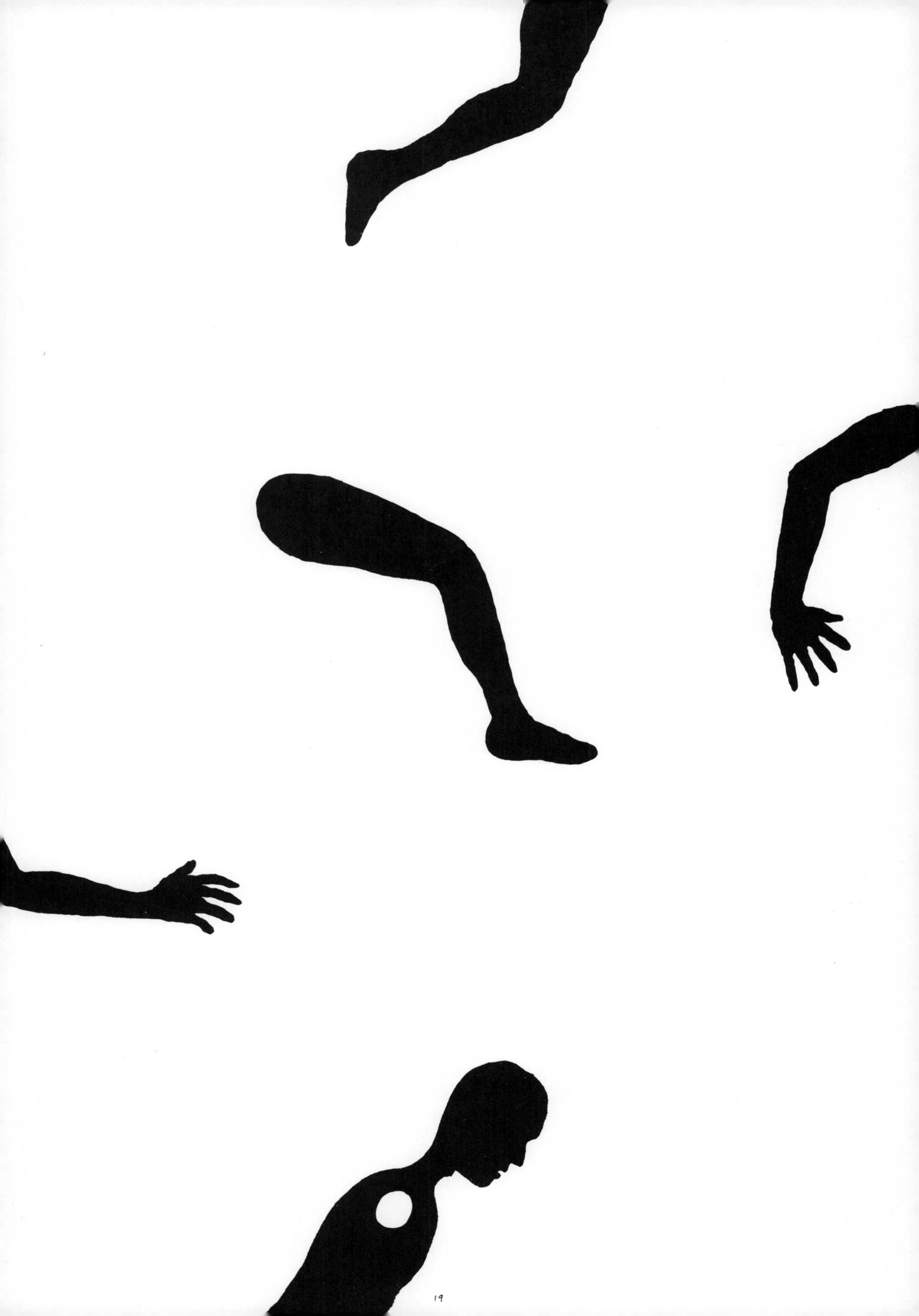

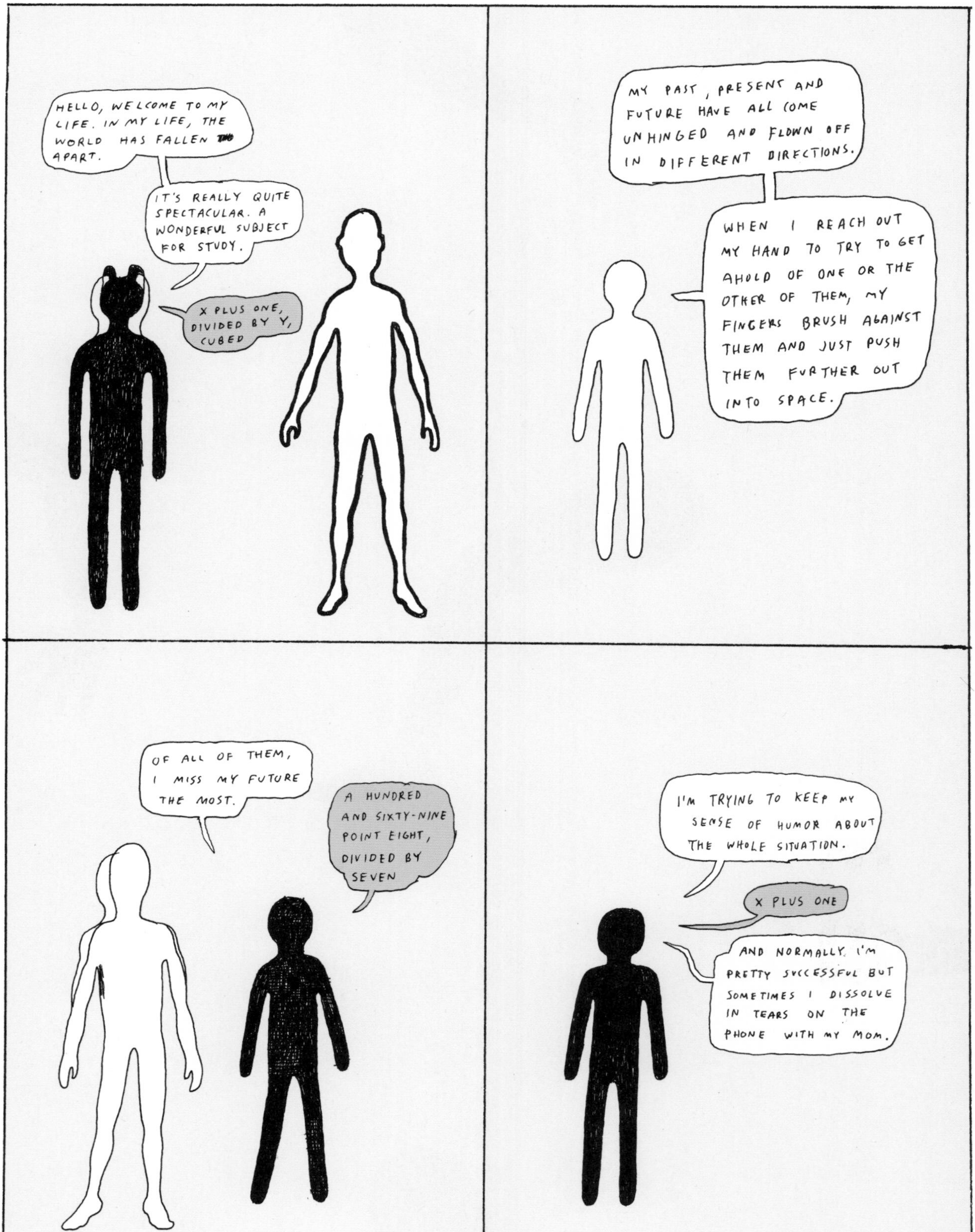
HELLO, WELCOME TO MY LIFE. IN MY LIFE, THE WORLD HAS FALLEN APART.
IT'S REALLY QUITE SPECTACULAR. A WONDERFUL SUBJECT FOR STUDY.
X PLUS ONE, DIVIDED BY Y, CUBED
MY PAST, PRESENT AND FUTURE HAVE ALL COME UNHINGED AND FLOWN OFF IN DIFFERENT DIRECTIONS.
WHEN I REACH OUT MY HAND TO TRY TO GET AHOLD OF ONE OR THE OTHER OF THEM, MY FINGERS BRUSH AGAINST THEM AND JUST PUSH THEM FURTHER OUT INTO SPACE.
OF ALL OF THEM, I MISS MY FUTURE THE MOST.
A HUNDRED AND SIXTY-NINE POINT EIGHT, DIVIDED BY SEVEN
I'M TRYING TO KEEP MY SENSE OF HUMOR ABOUT THE WHOLE SITUATION.
X PLUS ONE
AND NORMALLY I'M PRETTY SUCCESSFUL BUT SOMETIMES I DISSOLVE IN TEARS ON THE PHONE WITH MY MOM.

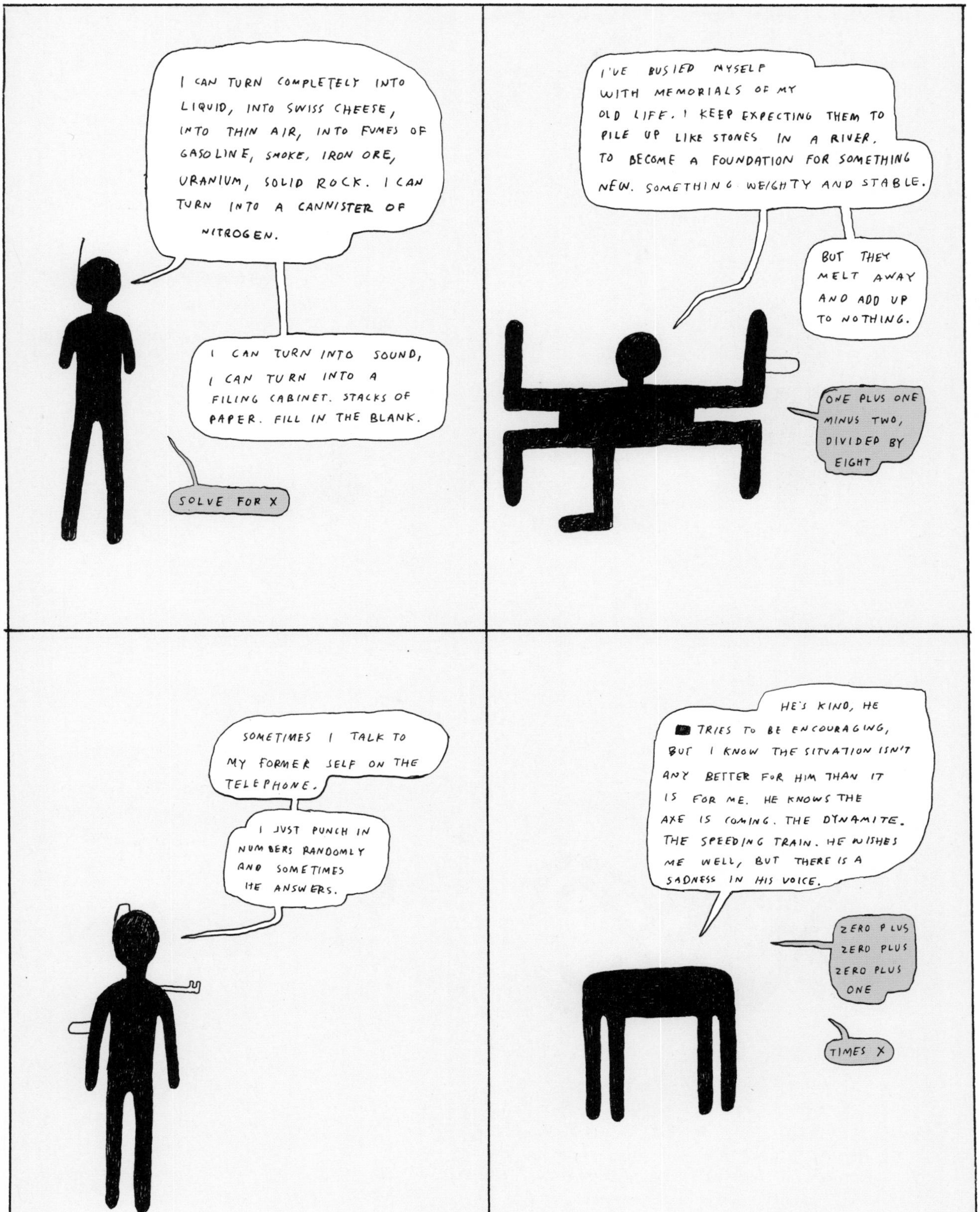

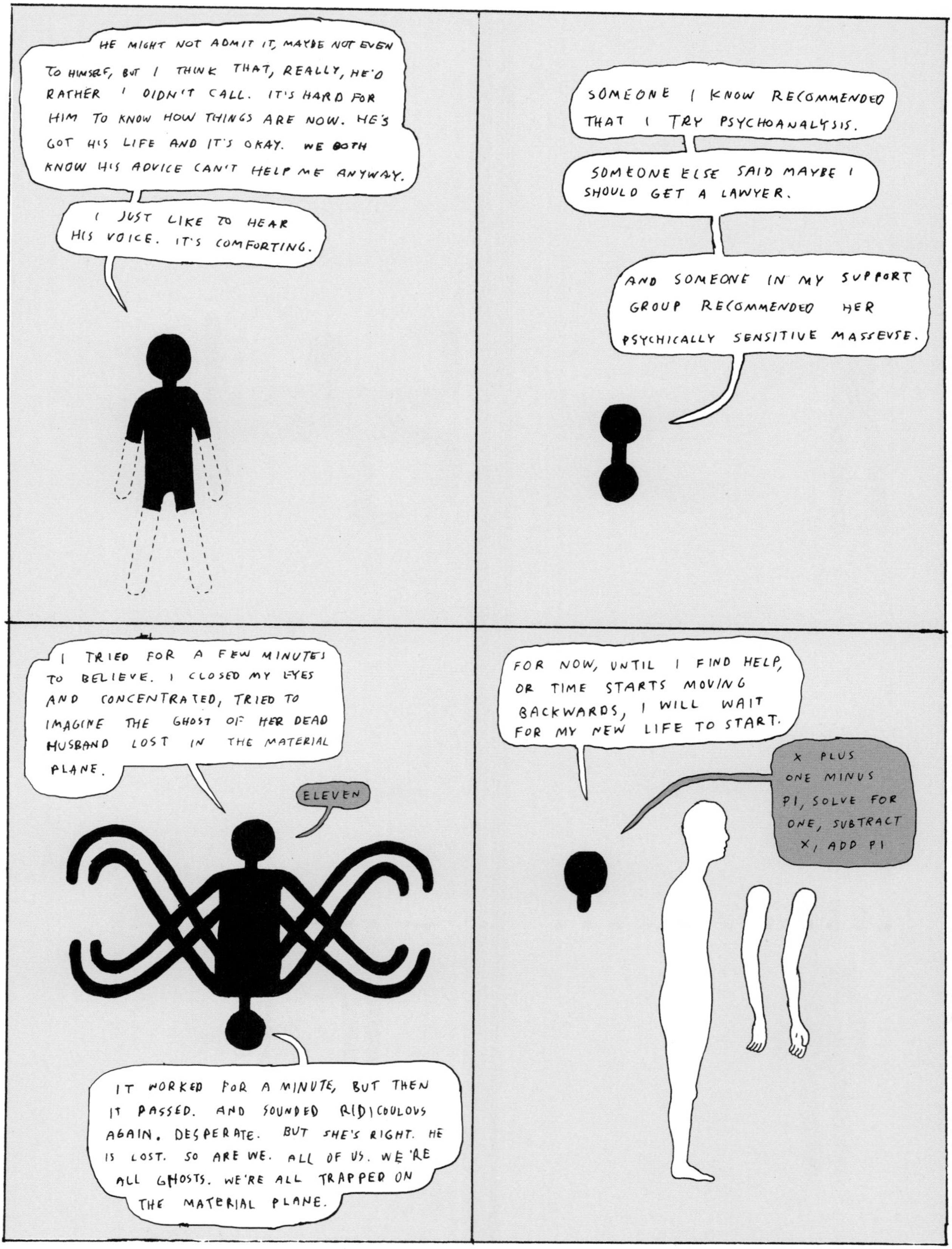
HE MIGHT NOT ADMIT IT, MAYBE NOT EVEN TO HIMSELF, BUT I THINK THAT, REALLY, HE'D RATHER I DIDN'T CALL. IT'S HARD FOR HIM TO KNOW HOW THINGS ARE NOW. HE'S GOT HIS LIFE AND IT'S OKAY. WE BOTH KNOW HIS ADVICE CAN'T HELP ME ANYWAY.
I JUST LIKE TO HEAR HIS VOICE. IT'S COMFORTING.
SOMEONE I KNOW RECOMMENDED THAT I TRY PSYCHOANALYSIS.
SOMEONE ELSE SAID MAYBE I SHOULD GET A LAWYER.
AND SOMEONE IN MY SUPPORT GROUP RECOMMENDED HER PSYCHICALLY SENSITIVE MASSEUSE.
I TRIED FOR A FEW MINUTES TO BELIEVE. I CLOSED MY EYES AND CONCENTRATED, TRIED TO IMAGINE THE GHOST OF HER DEAD HUSBAND LOST IN THE MATERIAL PLANE.
ELEVEN
IT WORKED FOR A MINUTE, BUT THEN IT PASSED. AND SOUNDED RIDICULOUS AGAIN. DESPERATE. BUT SHE'S RIGHT. HE IS LOST. SO ARE WE. ALL OF US. WE'RE ALL GHOSTS. WE'RE ALL TRAPPED ON THE MATERIAL PLANE.
FOR NOW, UNTIL I FIND HELP, OR TIME STARTS MOVING BACKWARDS, I WILL WAIT FOR MY NEW LIFE TO START.
X PLUS ONE MINUS PI, SOLVE FOR ONE, SUBTRACT X, ADD PI

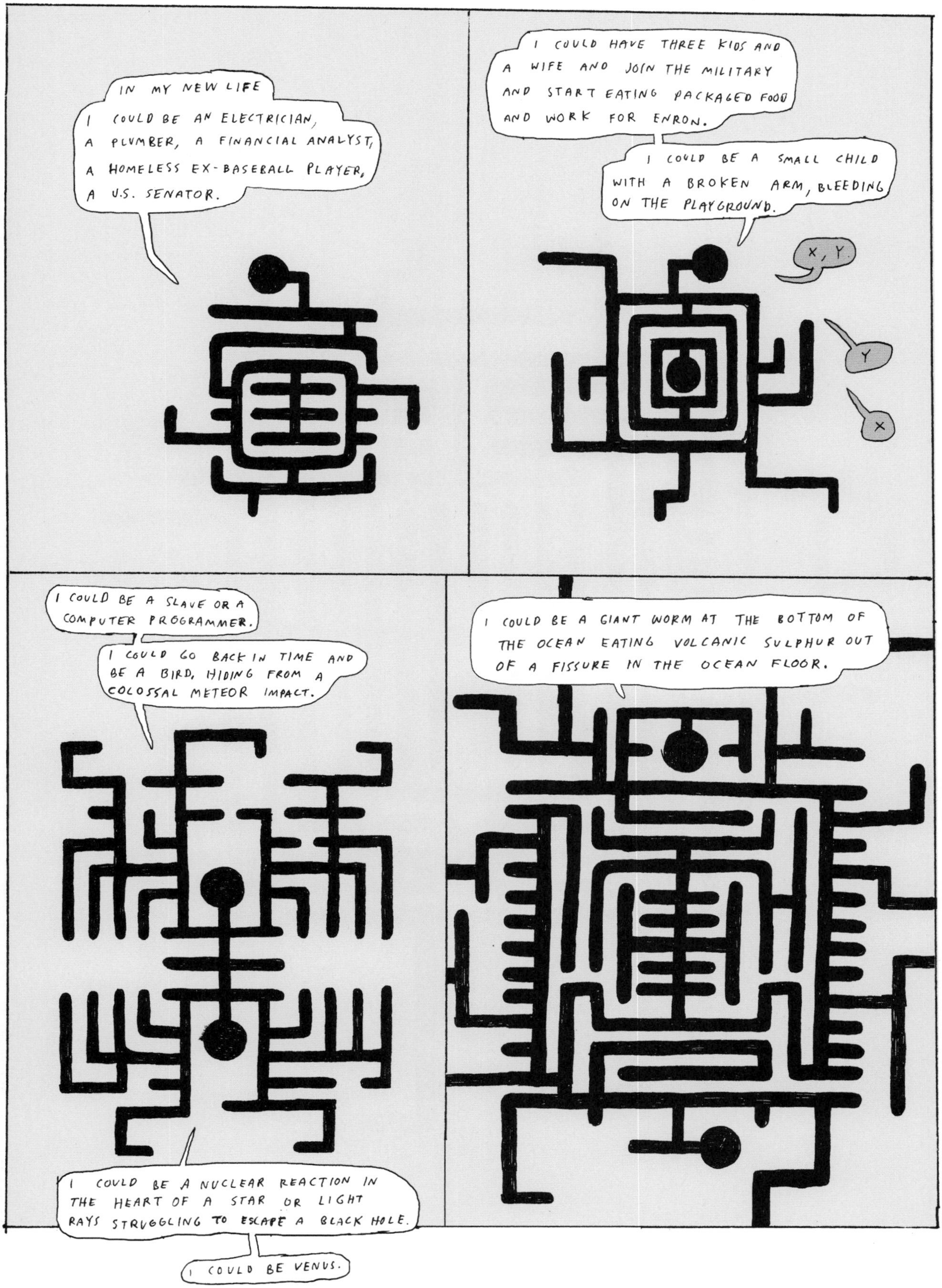
IN MY NEW LIFE
I COULD BE AN ELECTRICIAN, A PLUMBER, A FINANCIAL ANALYST, A HOMELESS EX-BASEBALL PLAYER, A U.S. SENATOR.
I COULD HAVE THREE KIDS AND A WIFE AND JOIN THE MILITARY AND START EATING PACKAGED FOOD AND WORK FOR ENRON.
I COULD BE A SMALL CHILD WITH A BROKEN ARM, BLEEDING ON THE PLAYGROUND.
X, Y.
Y
X
I COULD BE A SLAVE OR A COMPUTER PROGRAMMER.
I COULD GO BACK IN TIME AND BE A BIRD, HIDING FROM A COLOSSAL METEOR IMPACT.
I COULD BE A NUCLEAR REACTION IN THE HEART OF A STAR OR LIGHT RAYS STRUGGLING TO ESCAPE A BLACK HOLE.
I COULD BE VENUS.
I COULD BE A GIANT WORM AT THE BOTTOM OF THE OCEAN EATING VOLCANIC SULPHUR OUT OF A FISSURE IN THE OCEAN FLOOR.

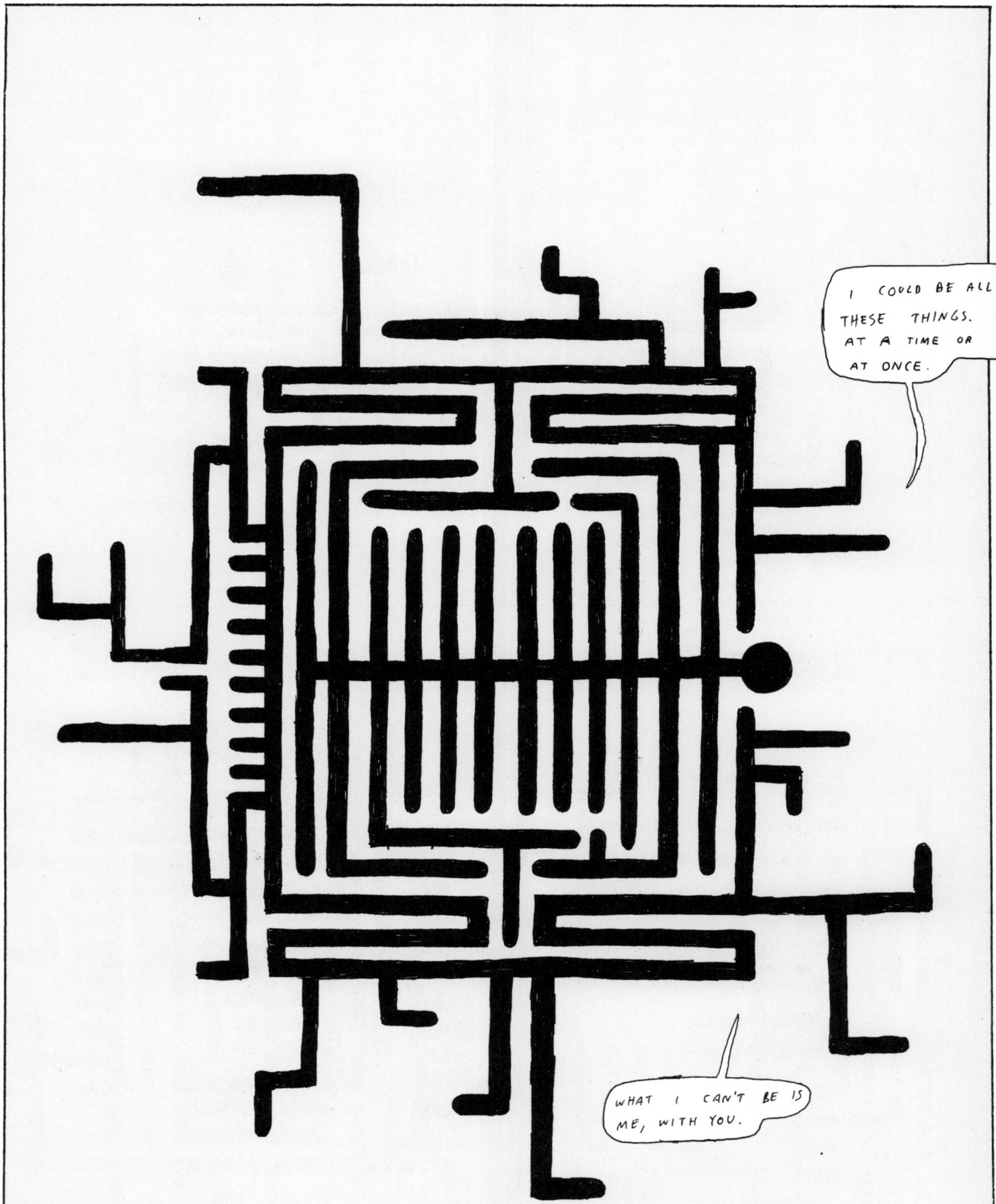
I COULD BE ALL THESE THINGS. AT A TIME OR AT ONCE.
WHAT I CAN'T BE IS ME, WITH YOU.

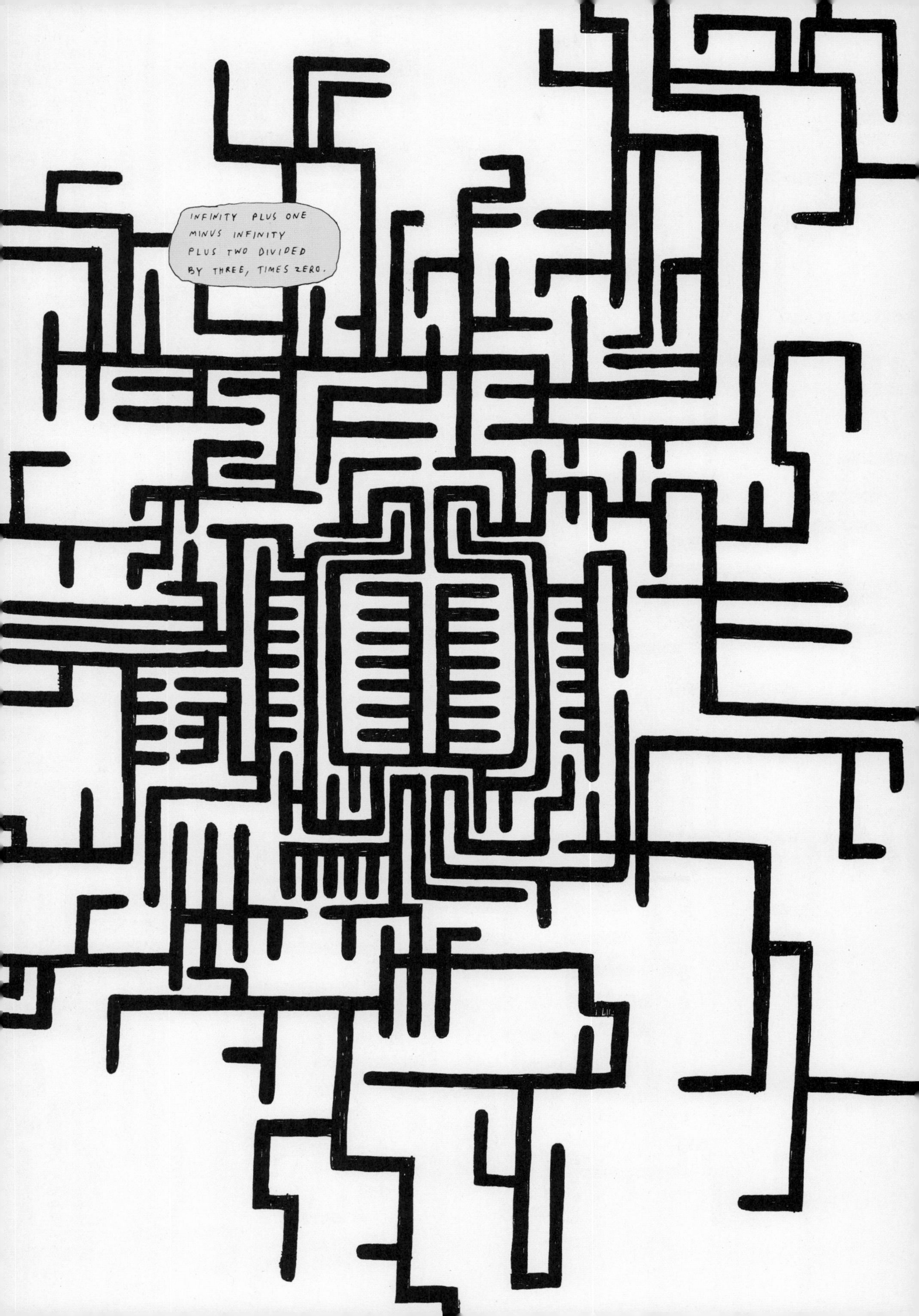
INFINITY PLUS ONE MINUS INFINITY PLUS TWO DIVIDED BY THREE, TIMES ZERO.

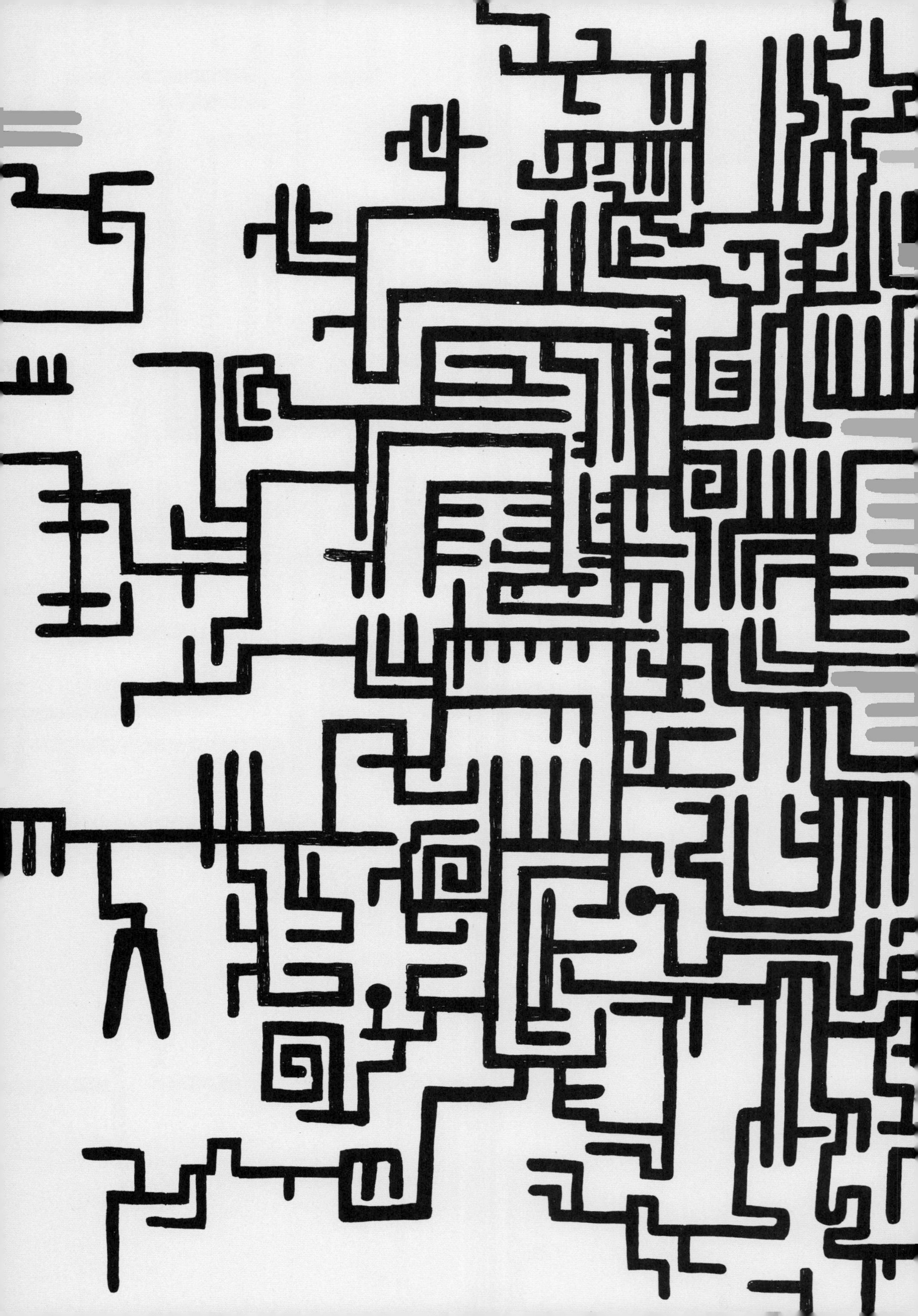

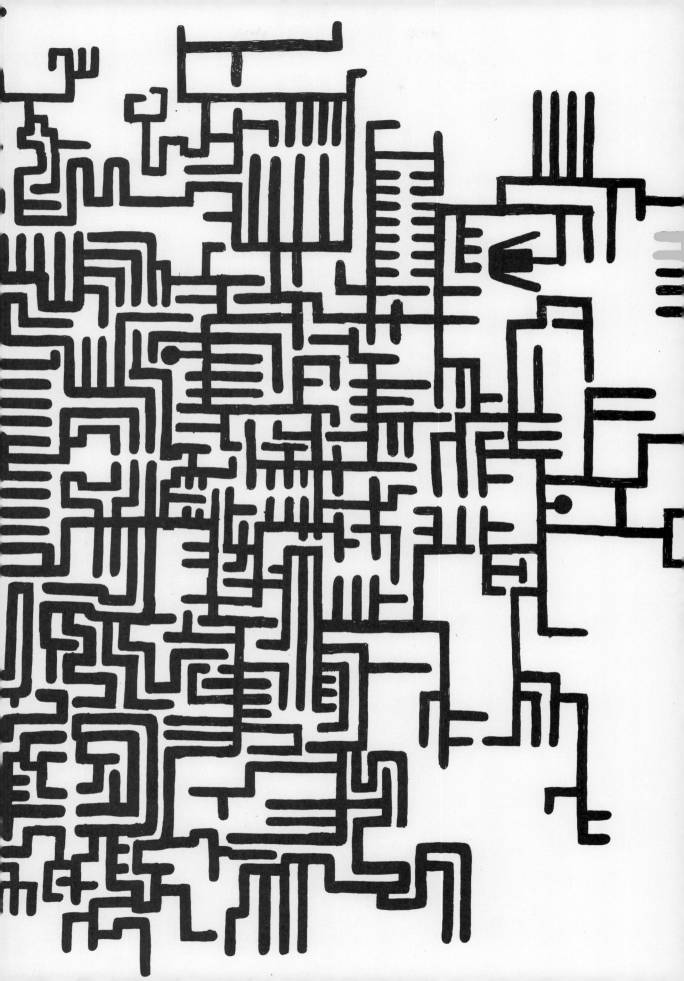

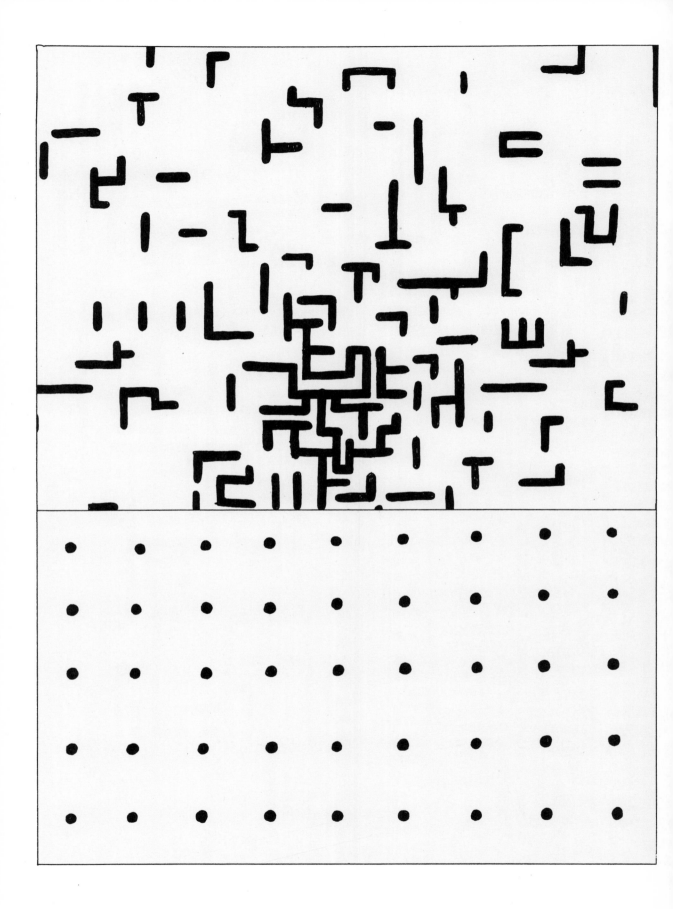

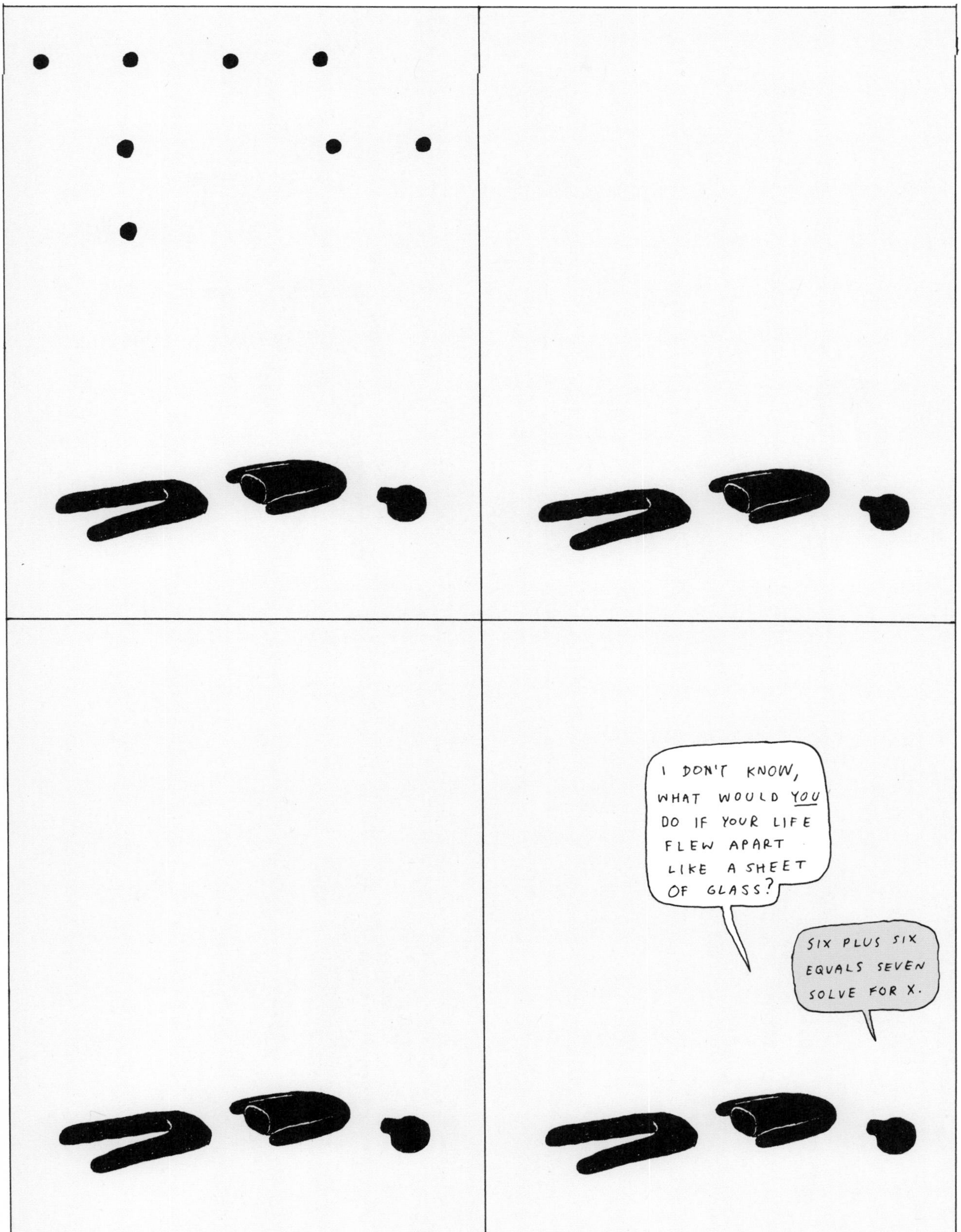
I DON'T KNOW, WHAT WOULD YOU DO IF YOUR LIFE FLEW APART LIKE A SHEET OF GLASS?
SIX PLUS SIX EQUALS SEVEN SOLVE FOR X.

WOULD YOU FIND SOMEONE TO TELL ABOUT IT? MAYBE HOLD ON TO THEIR ARM IN CASE THEY TRY TO GET AWAY AND JUST SAY OVER AND OVER HOW IT JUST... FLEW APART.
IT JUST...
...FLEW APART.
OR WOULD YOU TRY TO MAKE A MAP OF THE WHOLE PROCESS, TRY TO CAREFULLY, ACCURATELY DELINEATE THE MILEAGE BETWEEN EACH EVENT, THEN POINT AND SAY, "AND THAT'S WHERE EVERYTHING WAS GOING TO BE JUST FINE, AND THAT'S WHERE THE FISSURES STARTED TO APPEAR, BUT WE STILL TRIED TO MAINTAIN HOPE..."
"AND THAT'S WHERE IT JUST... FLEW APART...
IT JUST...
...FLEW APART."
Y.

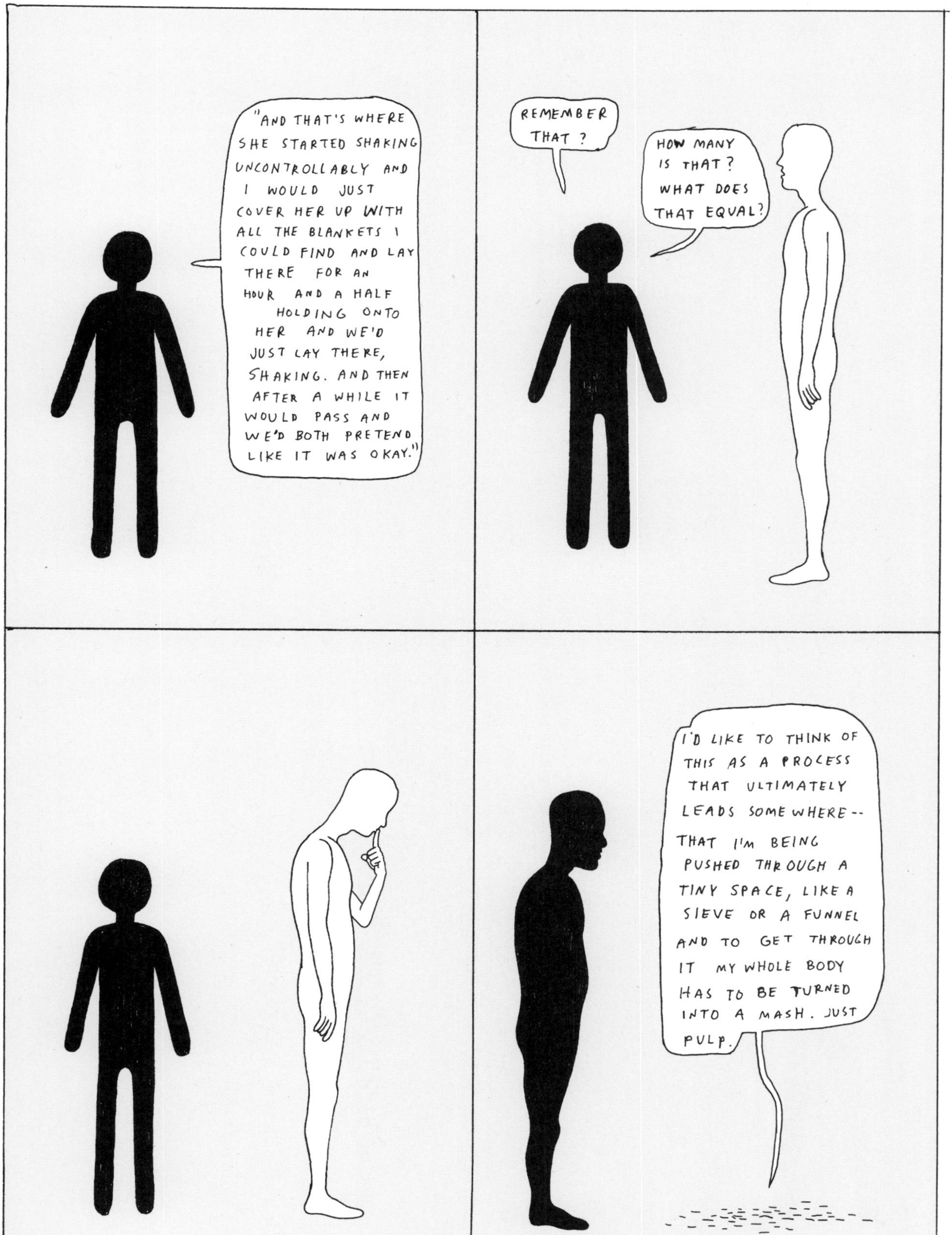
"AND THAT'S WHERE SHE STARTED SHAKING UNCONTROLLABLY AND I WOULD JUST COVER HER UP WITH ALL THE BLANKETS I COULD FIND AND LAY THERE FOR AN HOUR AND A HALF HOLDING ONTO HER AND WE'D JUST LAY THERE, SHAKING. AND THEN AFTER A WHILE IT WOULD PASS AND WE'D BOTH PRETEND LIKE IT WAS OKAY."
REMEMBER THAT?
HOW MANY IS THAT? WHAT DOES THAT EQUAL?
I'D LIKE TO THINK OF THIS AS A PROCESS THAT ULTIMATELY LEADS SOMEWHERE-- THAT I'M BEING PUSHED THROUGH A TINY SPACE, LIKE A SIEVE OR A FUNNEL AND TO GET THROUGH IT MY WHOLE BODY HAS TO BE TURNED INTO A MASH. JUST PULP.

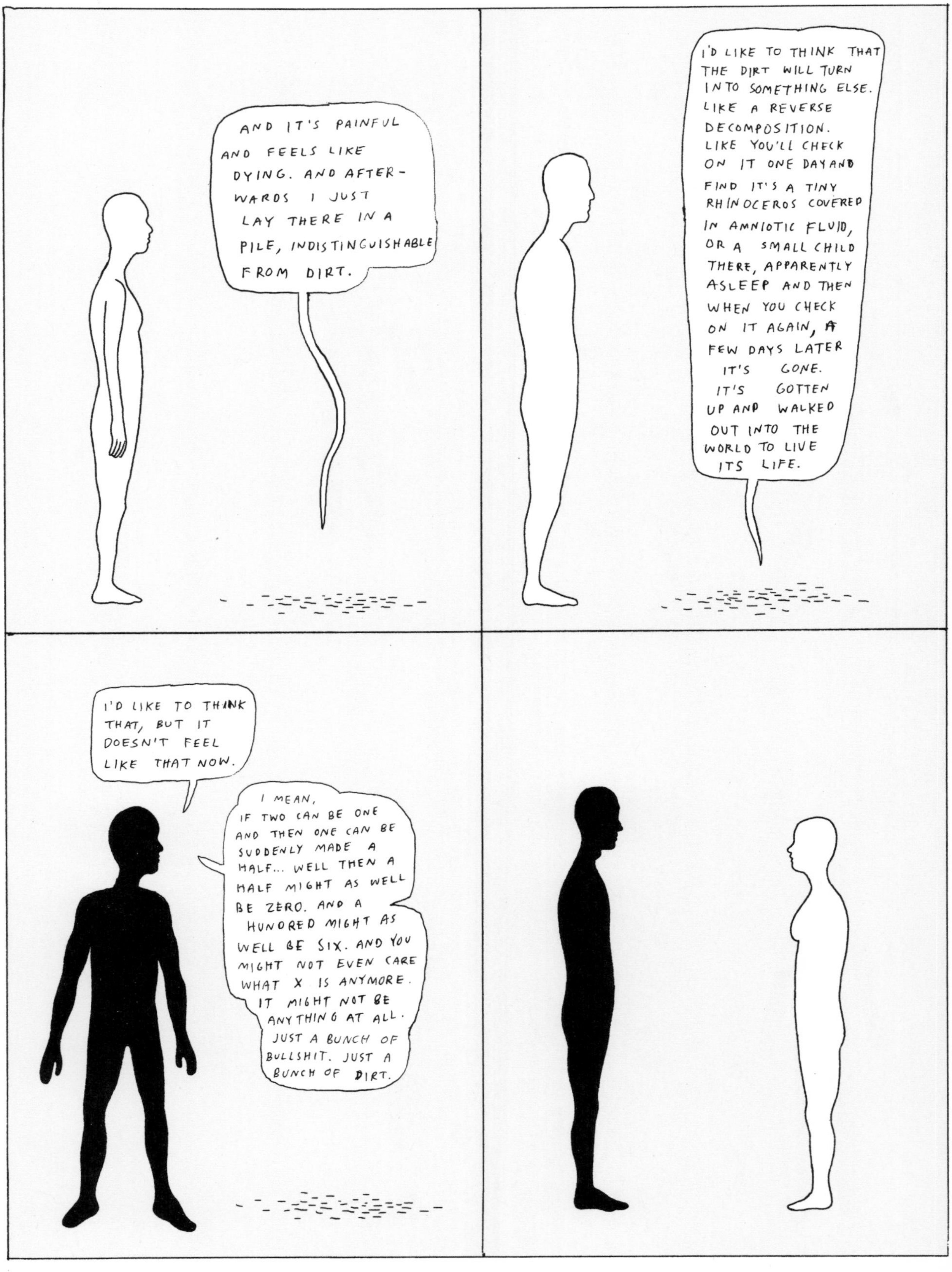
AND IT'S PAINFUL AND FEELS LIKE DYING. AND AFTER-WARDS I JUST LAY THERE IN A PILE, INDISTINGUISHABLE FROM DIRT.
I'D LIKE TO THINK THAT THE DIRT WILL TURN INTO SOMETHING ELSE. LIKE A REVERSE DECOMPOSITION. LIKE YOU'LL CHECK ON IT ONE DAY AND FIND IT'S A TINY RHINOCEROS COVERED IN AMNIOTIC FLUID, OR A SMALL CHILD THERE, APPARENTLY ASLEEP AND THEN WHEN YOU CHECK ON IT AGAIN, A FEW DAYS LATER IT'S GONE. IT'S GOTTEN UP AND WALKED OUT INTO THE WORLD TO LIVE ITS LIFE.
I'D LIKE TO THINK THAT, BUT IT DOESN'T FEEL LIKE THAT NOW.
I MEAN, IF TWO CAN BE ONE AND THEN ONE CAN BE SUDDENLY MADE A HALF... WELL THEN A HALF MIGHT AS WELL BE ZERO. AND A HUNDRED MIGHT AS WELL BE SIX. AND YOU MIGHT NOT EVEN CARE WHAT X IS ANYMORE. IT MIGHT NOT BE ANYTHING AT ALL. JUST A BUNCH OF BULLSHIT. JUST A BUNCH OF DIRT.

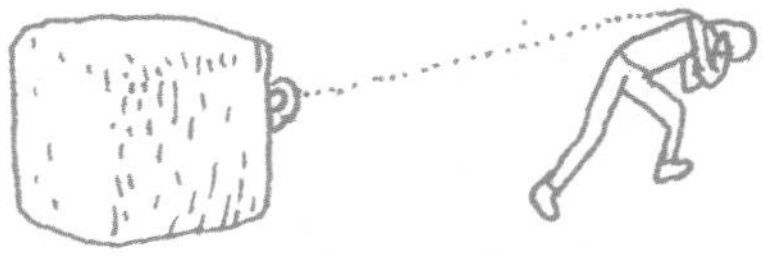

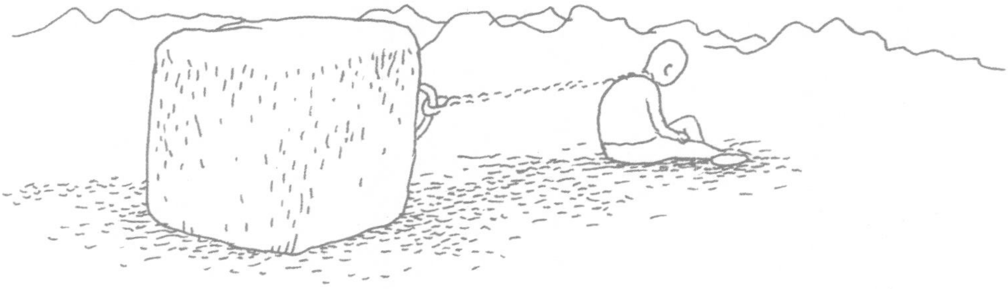

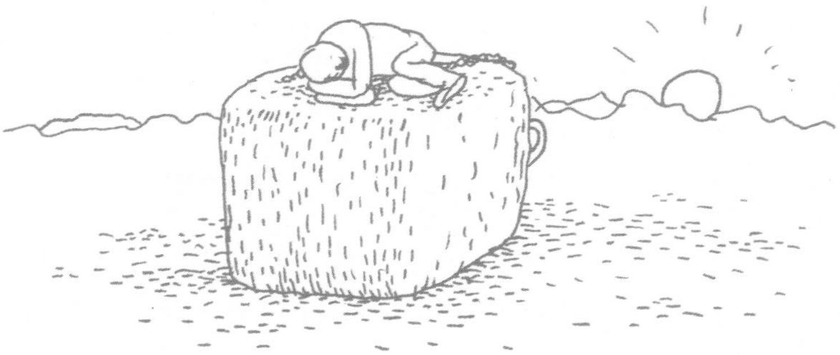

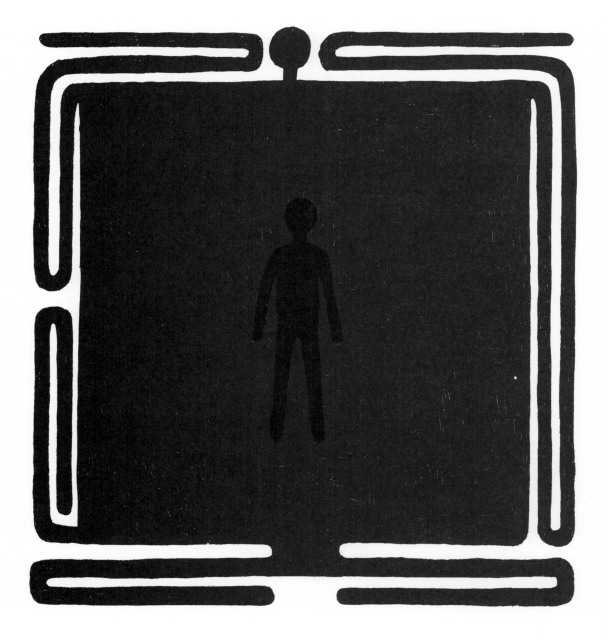

sitting eating at Lula
Wednesday night after group,
after a long bike-ride by the
lake. Malaika asked about Cheryl's
artwork - the felt silverwave coverings.
½ hour later a guy comes up to me
on his way out:

   "I couldn't help over-hearing - is
that stuff yours?"

   "no it... was my girlfriend's"
   "oh, well tell her it's fantastic!"

I feel like all of this has come home to me today differently than before: That it's cruel.

I wish there was some wall to beat down, some person to petition, a bureaucracy to try to navigate. Someone to sue, to threaten, to impress upon, to beat. But there is only the open air. It can neither resist nor acquiesce. Just that question, everyday, every horr:

WHERE ARE YOU ?

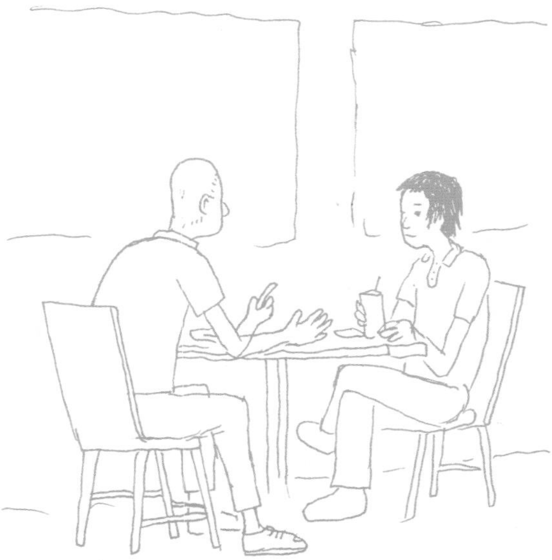
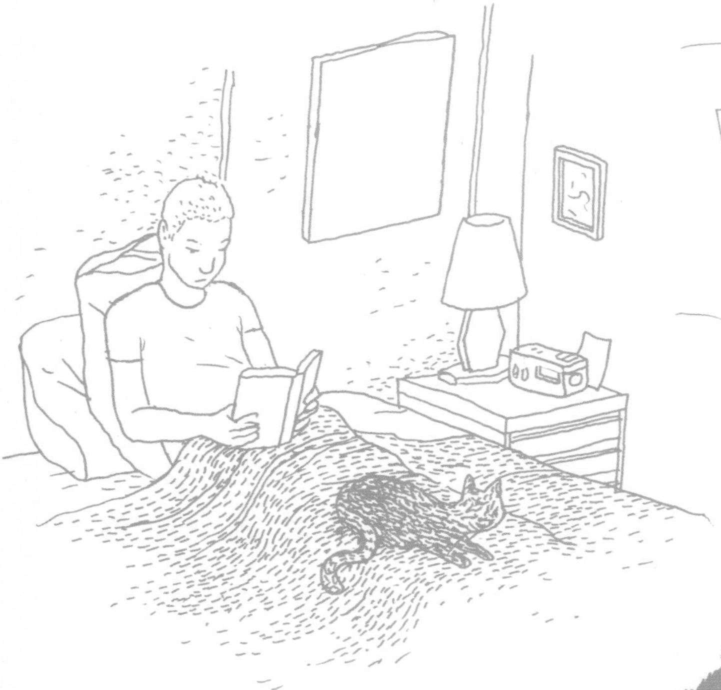
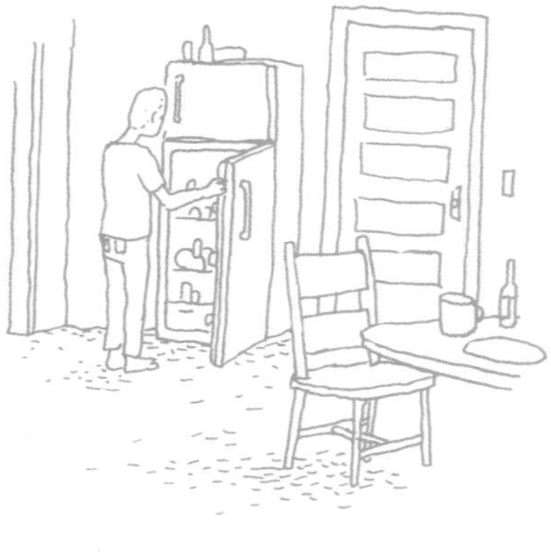
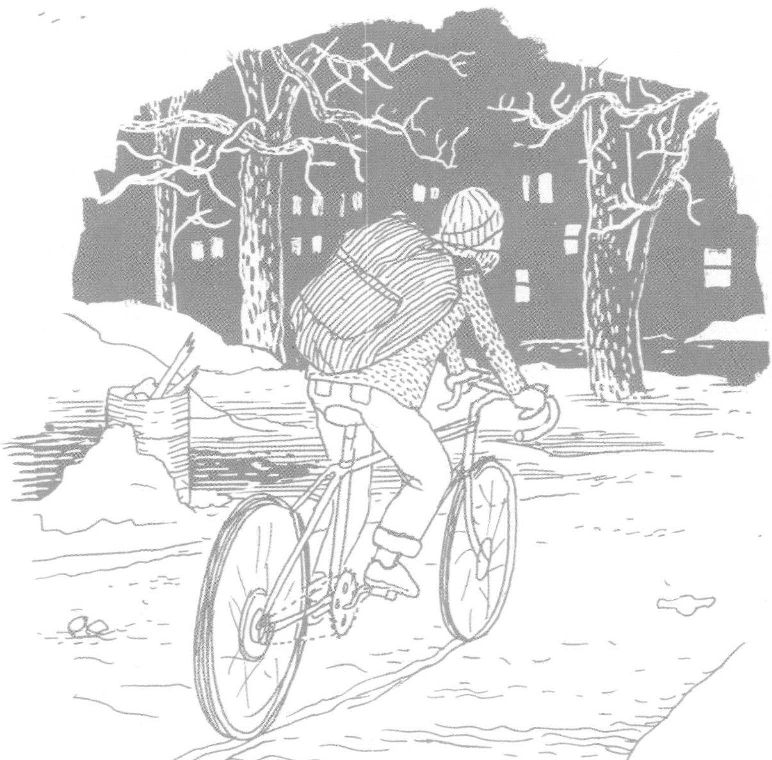

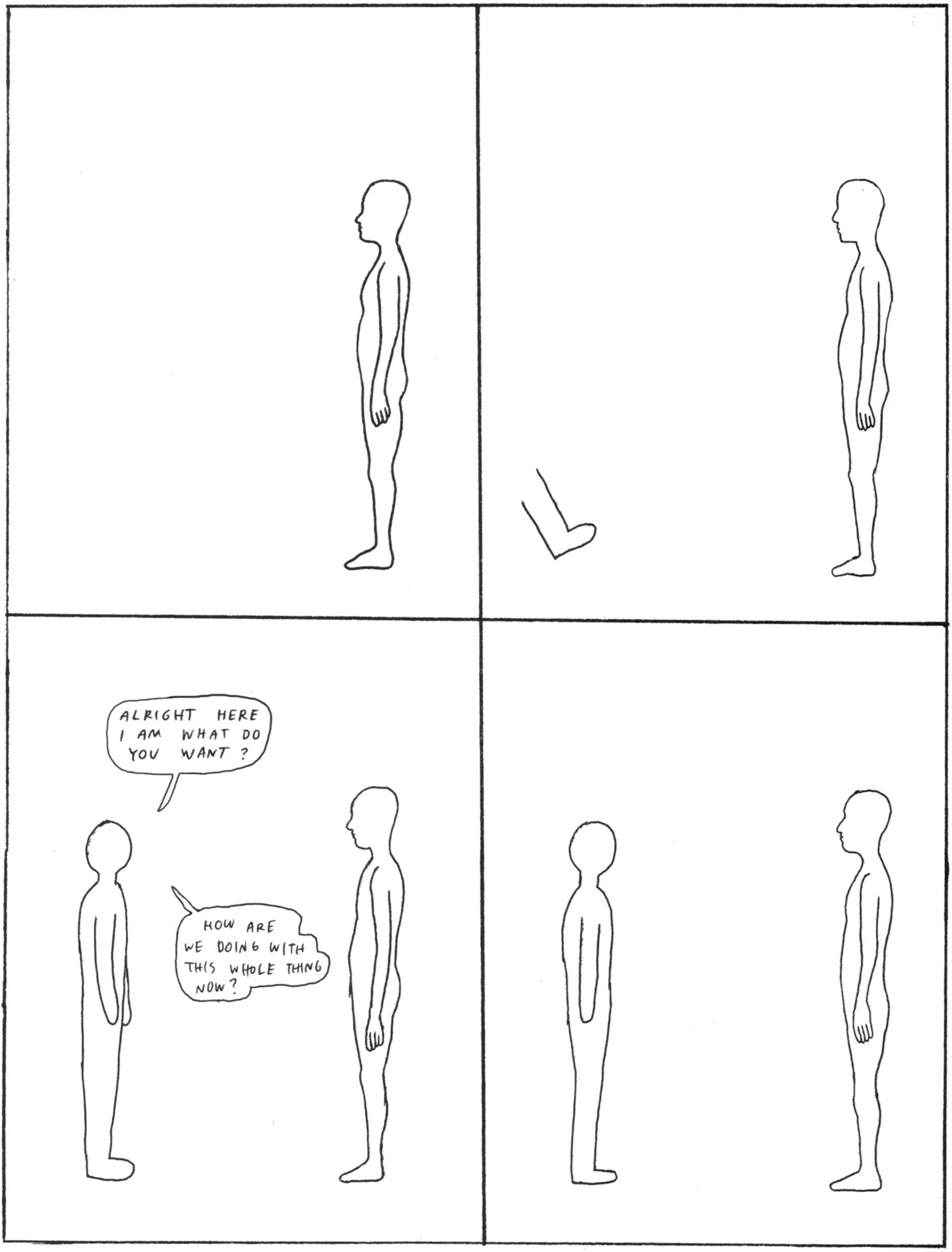
ALRIGHT HERE I AM WHAT DO YOU WANT ?
HOW ARE WE DOING WITH THIS WHOLE THING NOW ?

YOU STILL DON'T KNOW?
WHY DID YOU ASK ME HERE, THEN?
WHY DO YOU KEEP CALLING ME?
YOU'VE HAD A LOT OF TIME TO THINK ABOUT ALL OF THIS.
YOU NEED TO STOP STALLING.
AND GET ON WITH IT.
YOU NEED TO GET OVER THE WHOLE THING.
YOU NEED TO STOP PUTTING IT ALL ON OTHER PEOPLE.

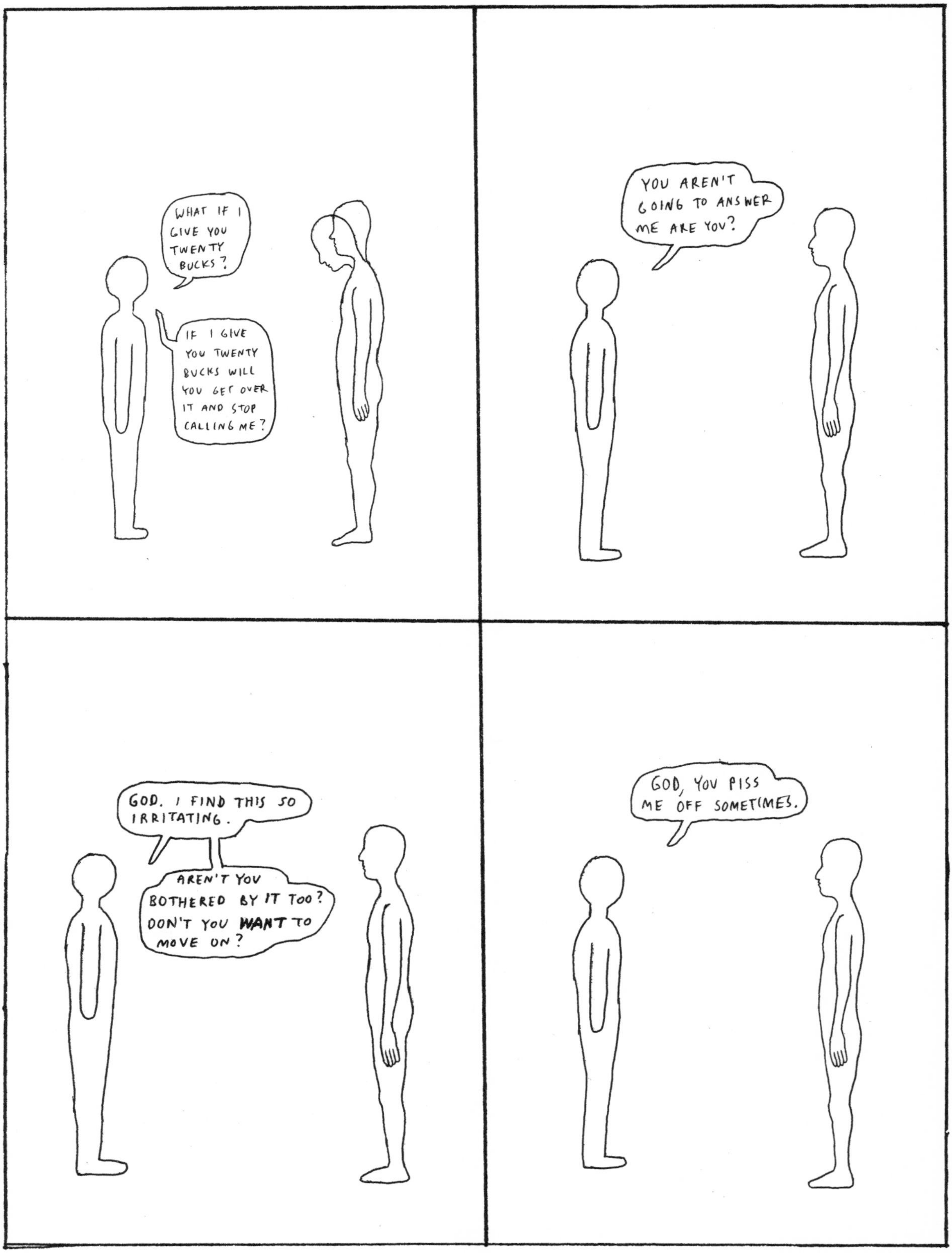
WHAT IF I GIVE YOU TWENTY BUCKS?
IF I GIVE YOU TWENTY BUCKS WILL YOU GET OVER IT AND STOP CALLING ME?
YOU AREN'T GOING TO ANSWER ME ARE YOU?
GOD. I FIND THIS SO IRRITATING.
AREN'T YOU BOTHERED BY IT TOO? DON'T YOU WANT TO MOVE ON?
GOD, YOU PISS ME OFF SOMETIMES.

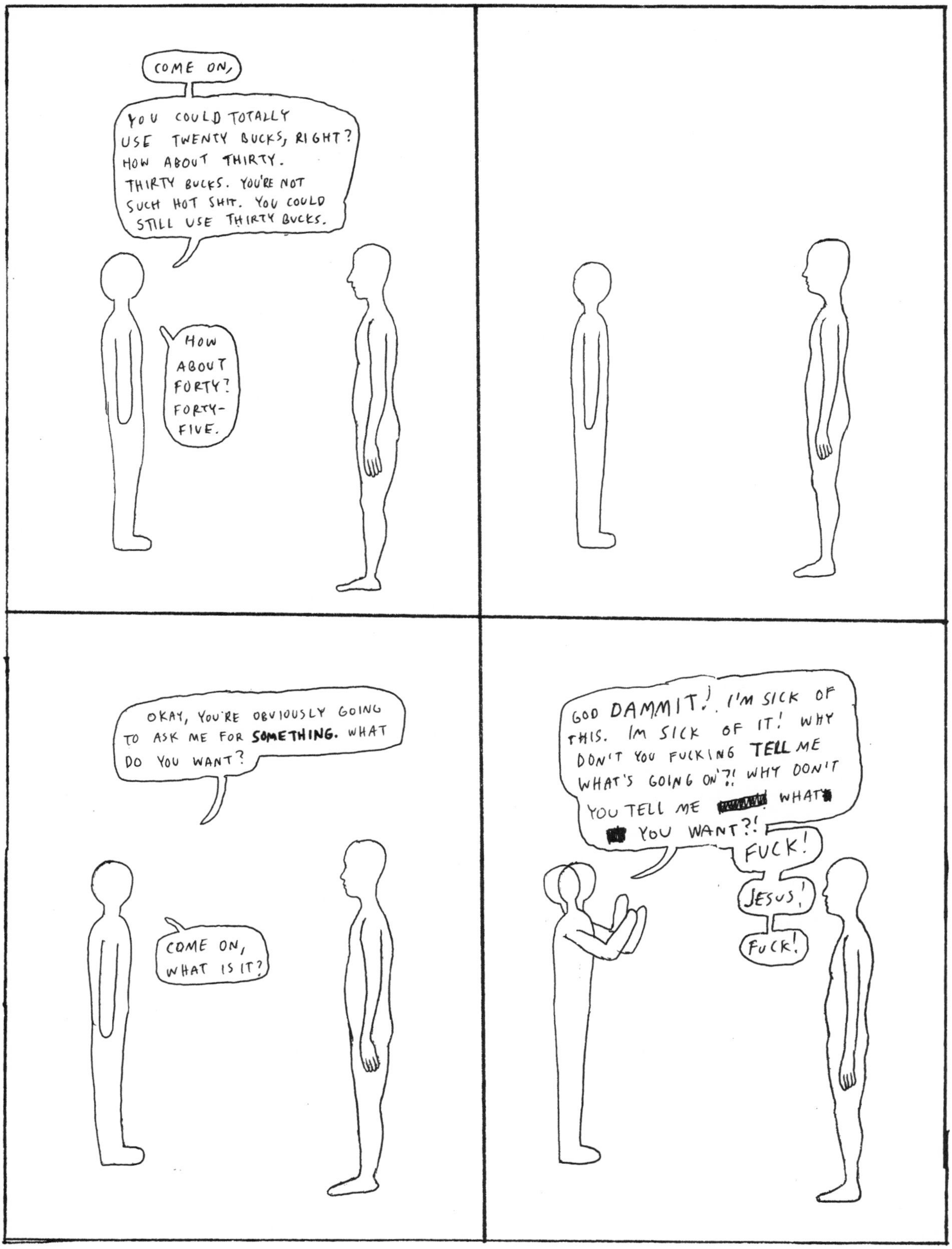

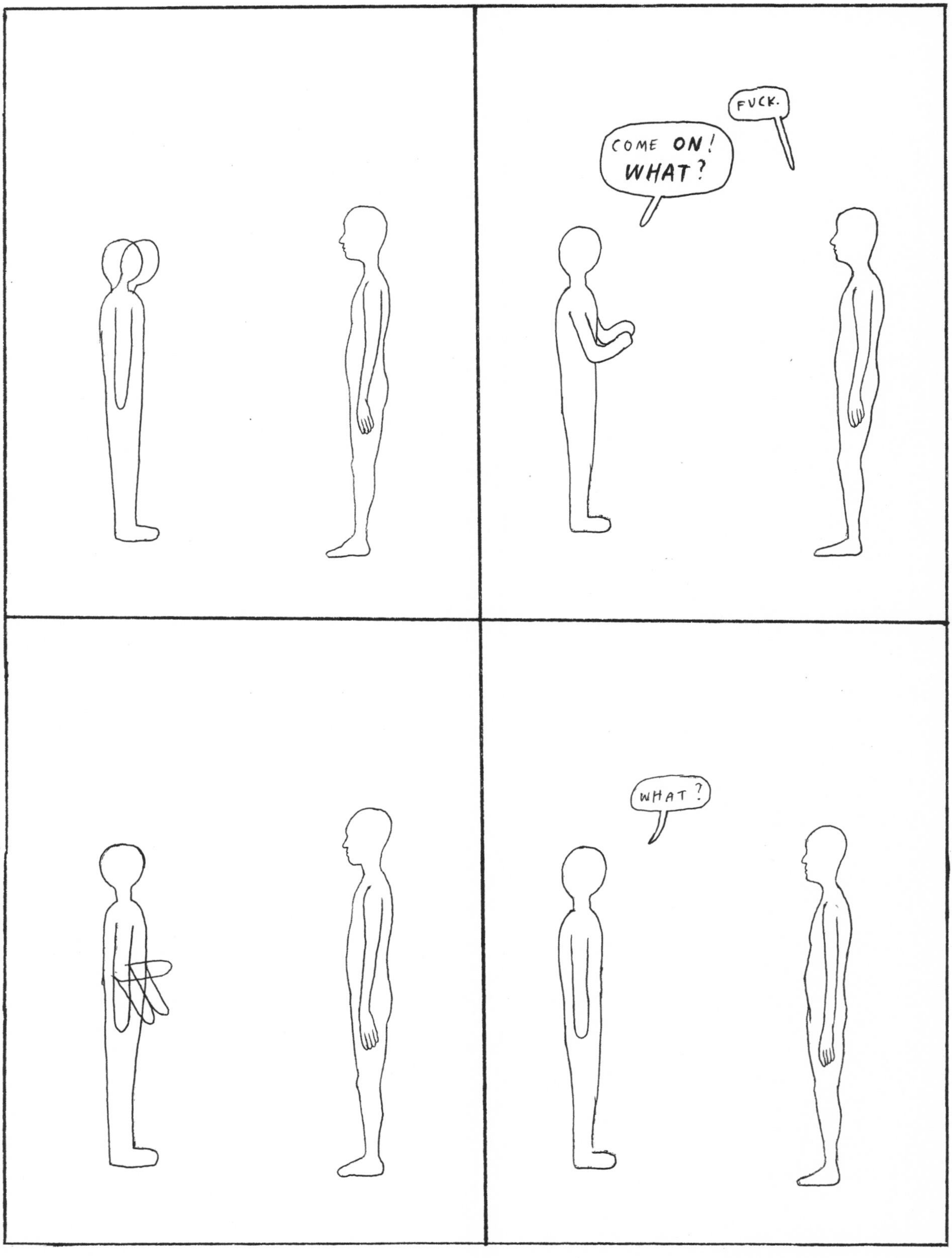
COME ON! WHAT?
FUCK.
WHAT?

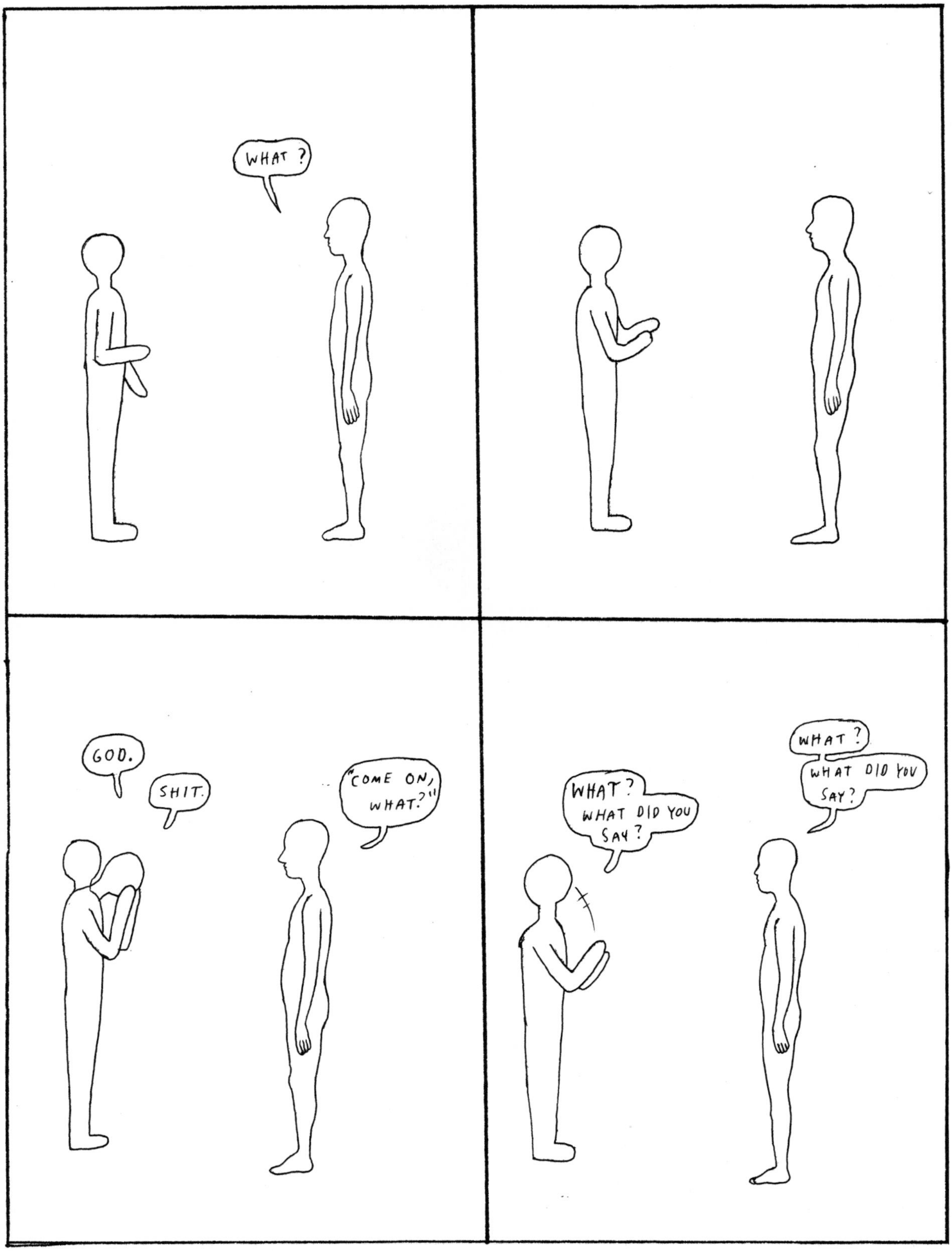
WHAT ?
GOD.
SHIT.
"COME ON, WHAT?"
WHAT? WHAT DID YOU SAY?
WHAT ?
WHAT DID YOU SAY?

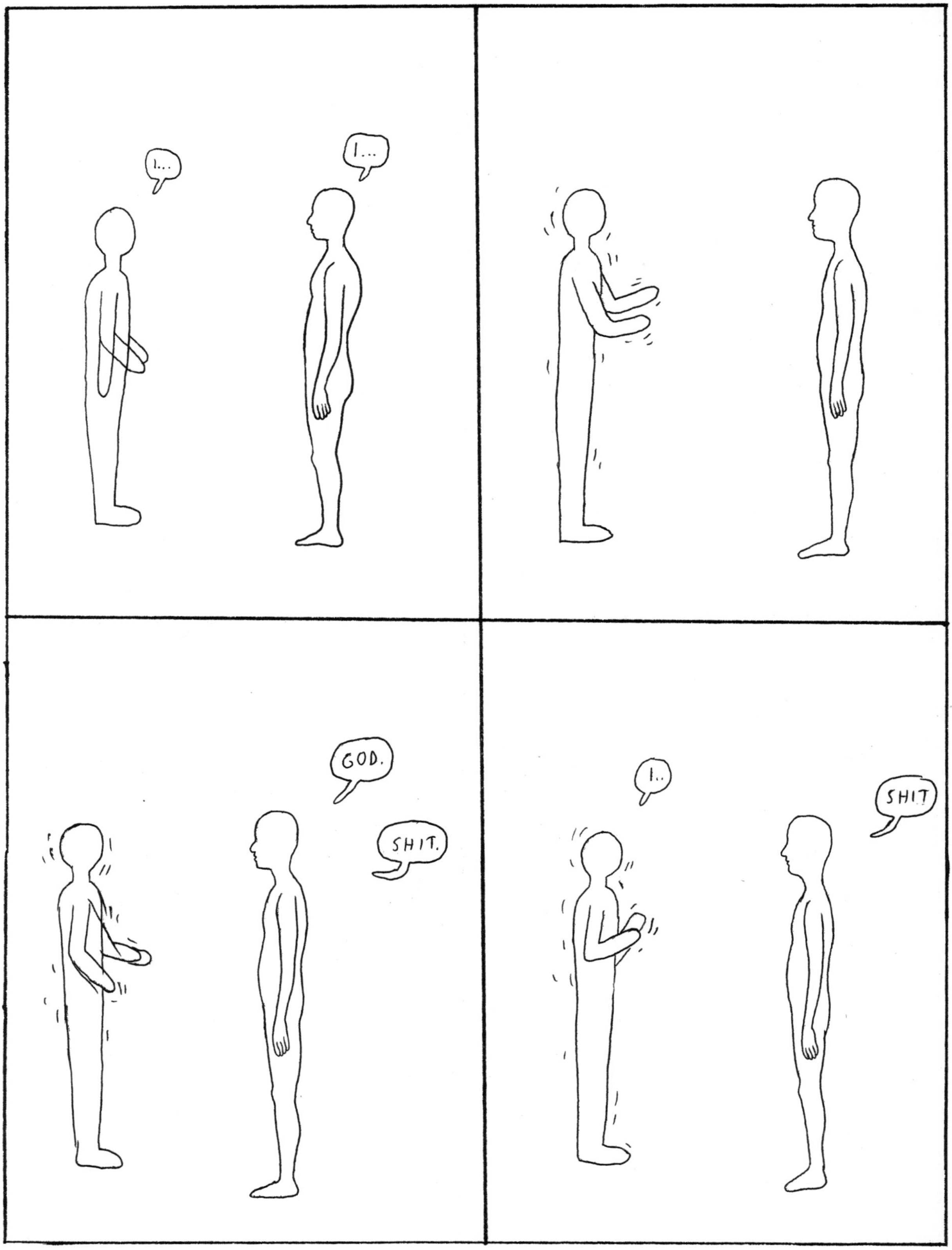
I...
I...
GOD.
SHIT.
I..
SHIT

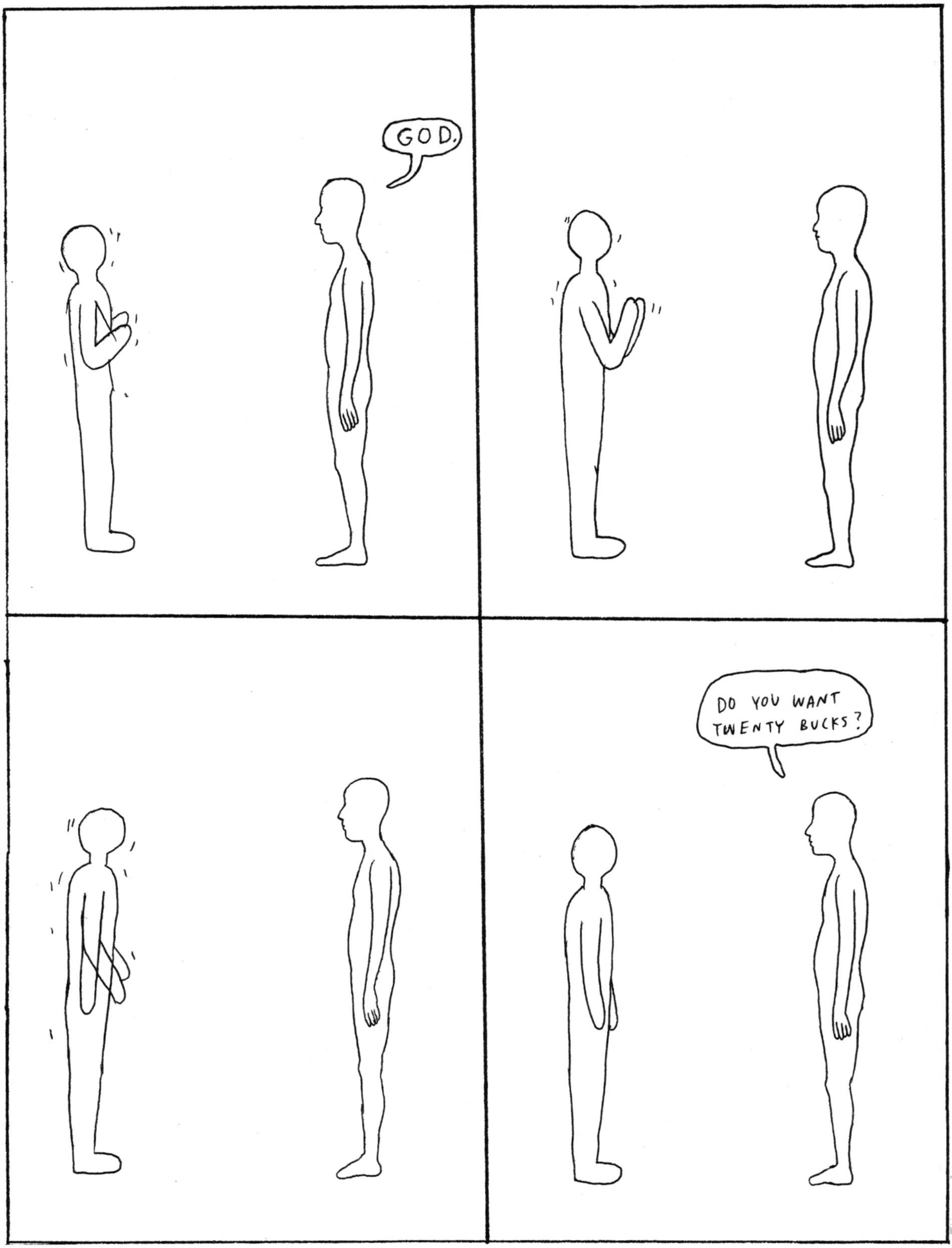
GOD.
DO YOU WANT TWENTY BUCKS?

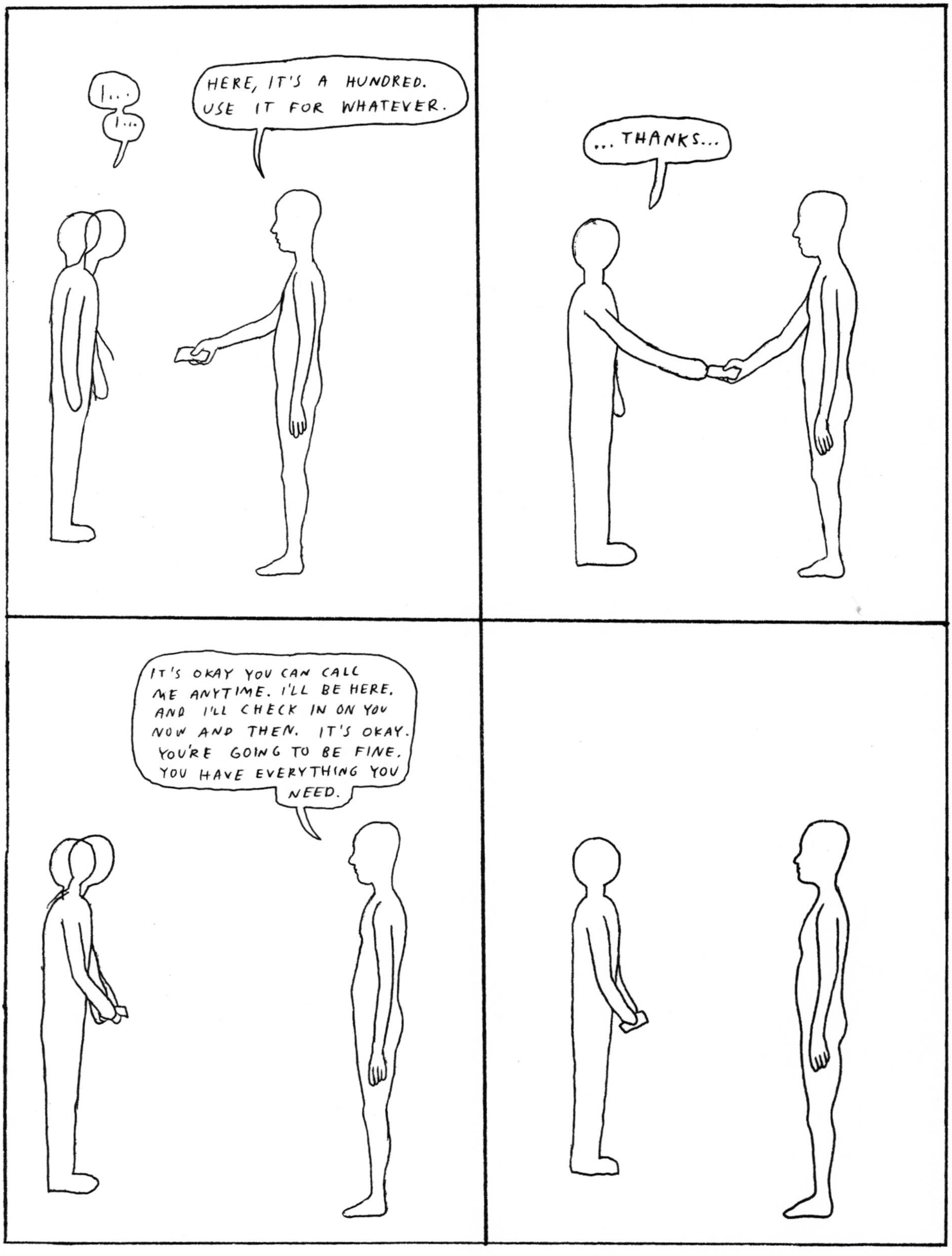
I...
I...
HERE, IT'S A HUNDRED. USE IT FOR WHATEVER.
...THANKS...
IT'S OKAY YOU CAN CALL ME ANYTIME. I'LL BE HERE. AND I'LL CHECK IN ON YOU NOW AND THEN. IT'S OKAY. YOU'RE GOING TO BE FINE. YOU HAVE EVERYTHING YOU NEED.

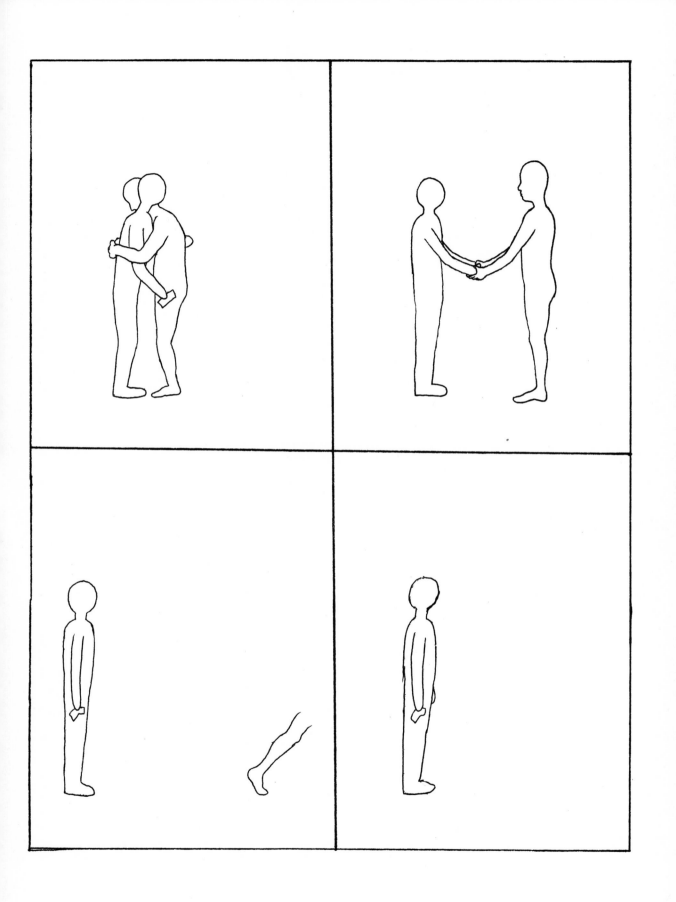

OR MAYBE YOU'RE JUST LOOKING AT THIS THE WRONG WAY ROUND.

LIKE, WHAT IF YOU GREW UP KNOWING THAT ONE DAY OUT OF YOUR WHOLE LIFE, JUST ONCE FOR FIVE MINUTES, YOU WOULD BE SUDDENLY ABLE TO FLY – BUT YOU NEVER KNEW WHEN? WHEN THAT MOMENT CAME, YOU WOULD DO IT, RIGHT? NO MATTER WHAT. YOU WOULDN'T STAY AT YOUR CUBICLE BECAUSE OF YOUR OBLIGATIONS. YOU'D GO. EVEN IF YOU WERE STANDING AT THE ALTAR. EVEN IF YOU WERE AT A FUNERAL.

YOU'D WALK AWAY, AND GO FLYING.

it's AN eternity of this

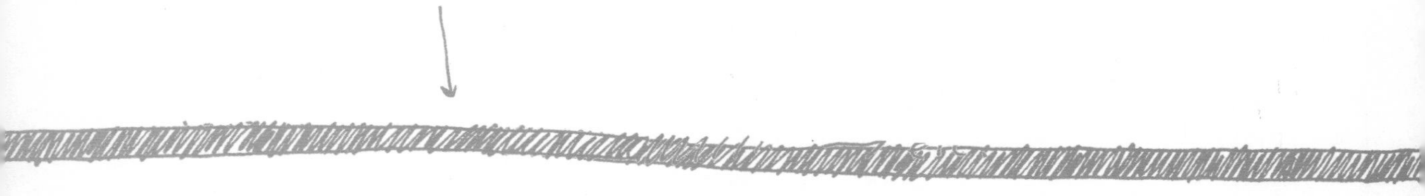

WE EXPERIENCE ETERNITY IN THAT MOMENT, THAT LIFETIME. BUT THE EMPHASIS IN THAT PROPOSITION IS THE WORD *EXPERIENCE* NOT THE WORD *ETERNITY*. ETERNITY IS... ETERNAL. IT'S CONSTANT. WE POKE OUR HEADS THROUGH THE CURTAINS ONCE FOR A MOMENT AND EXPERIENCE IT. THEN WE'RE DONE AND WE DIE. AND WE STOP EXPERIENCING IT. SO ETERNITY, FOR *US* IS AND CAN BE ONLY RIGHT NOW.

SO DO YOUR BEST TO PAY ATTENTION.

WHATEVER *THIS* IS, THERE IS SOMETHING YOU CAN DO WITH IT, THERE IS SOME OPTION.

TAKE IT. GO FLYING.

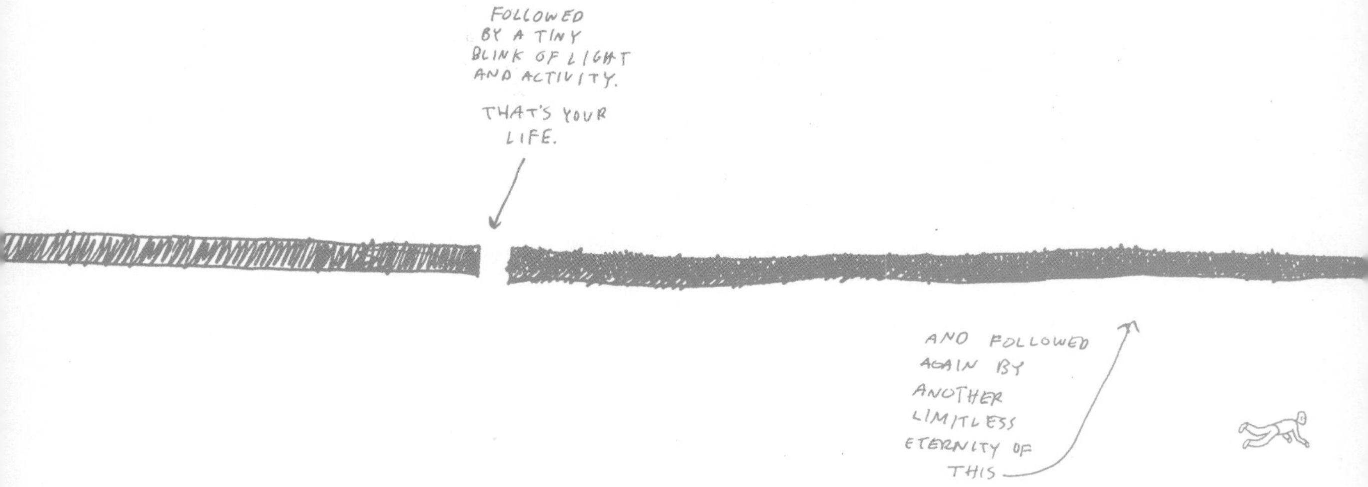
FOLLOWED BY A TINY BLINK OF LIGHT AND ACTIVITY.
THAT'S YOUR LIFE.
AND FOLLOWED AGAIN BY ANOTHER LIMITLESS ETERNITY OF THIS

ESSENTIAL PERSONALITY TEST
SCHEMATIC:

IF SOMEONE RIPS YOUR HEART
OUT OF YOUR CHEST WHAT
DO YOU DO?

A) MAKE SOUP WITH IT, SERVE TO ALL YOUR FRIENDS,
   IF THEY ENJOY IT, START A RESTAURANT.

B) COMPLAIN AND FOLLOW THE PERSON
   AROUND UNTIL THEY RELENT AND
   PUT IT BACK.

C) DIE AND BLEED ALL OVER
   THE PLACE.

I'M SORRY I'M A CARTOONIST INSTEAD OF
A HEAVY METAL DOUBLE BASS DRUMMER
THERE WOULD BE GOOD MATERIAL IN ALL THIS.
LOTS TO SCREAM ABOUT AND BEAT ON THINGS

IT JUST GOES DOWN AND DOWN AND DOWN
INTO THE BLACK TO THE CENTER OF THE EARTH
AND THERE IS NO OTHER SIDE.

I still don't know what to tell people when they ask me how I am

I would like to have another dream about you. I haven't had one in a while. That's not true. I had one the other night. I don't remember it well. something about your legs being swollen. ▓▓ But I'd like one where you're Five. where it's you from a year and a half ago, when you were whole, and we were happy, and the future was spread out before us. complicated but promising.

But I don't even care about the future. That doesn't have to be part of the dream. I just want a few moments in the present with you. Just the warmth of your body, your hair under my fingertips the warmth and weight of you, asleep next to me in bed. your smile your laugh, you saying something funny about one of our friends. you making me feel so lucky.

I want to feel lucky with you again.

I wish I could draw you at will. I wish I could picture you perfectly. Though that might make no difference. You'd still be gone.

I'm exhausted. good night my dear. I wish I thought you were out there really.

I guess I kind of do.

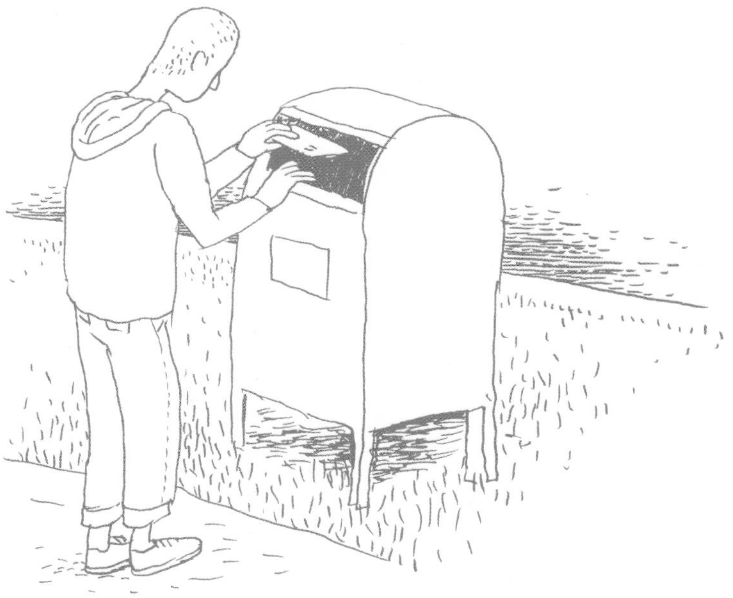

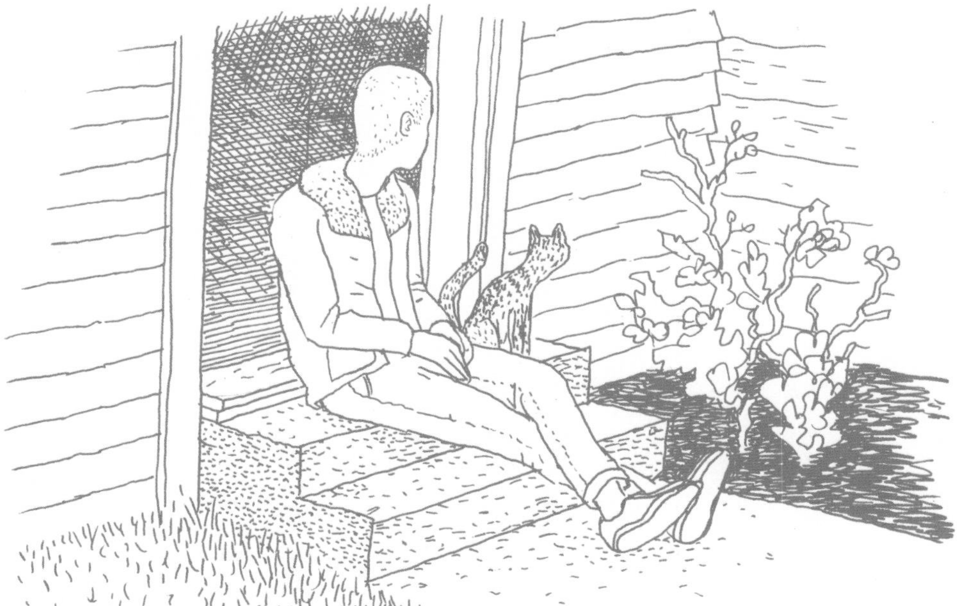

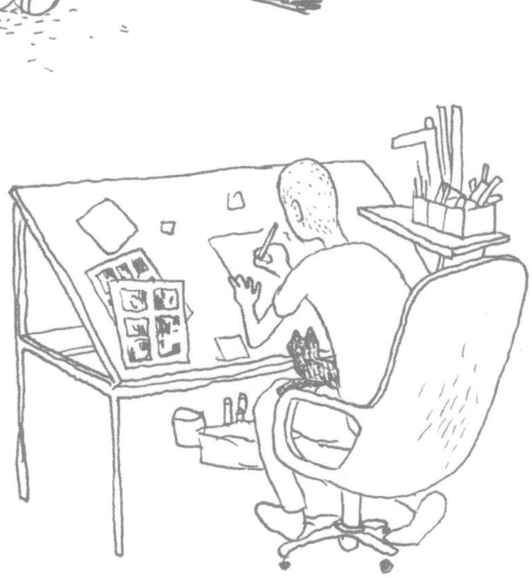

YOU MADE ME BELIEVE LOVE WAS POSSIBLE
AND IN MY GRASP, SOMETHING I COULD HAVE

AND THEN YOU MADE ME THINK NO,
MAYBE I WAS WRONG,

LOVE IS FAKE, A LIE,
AND YOU MADE ME WANT IT EVEN MORE

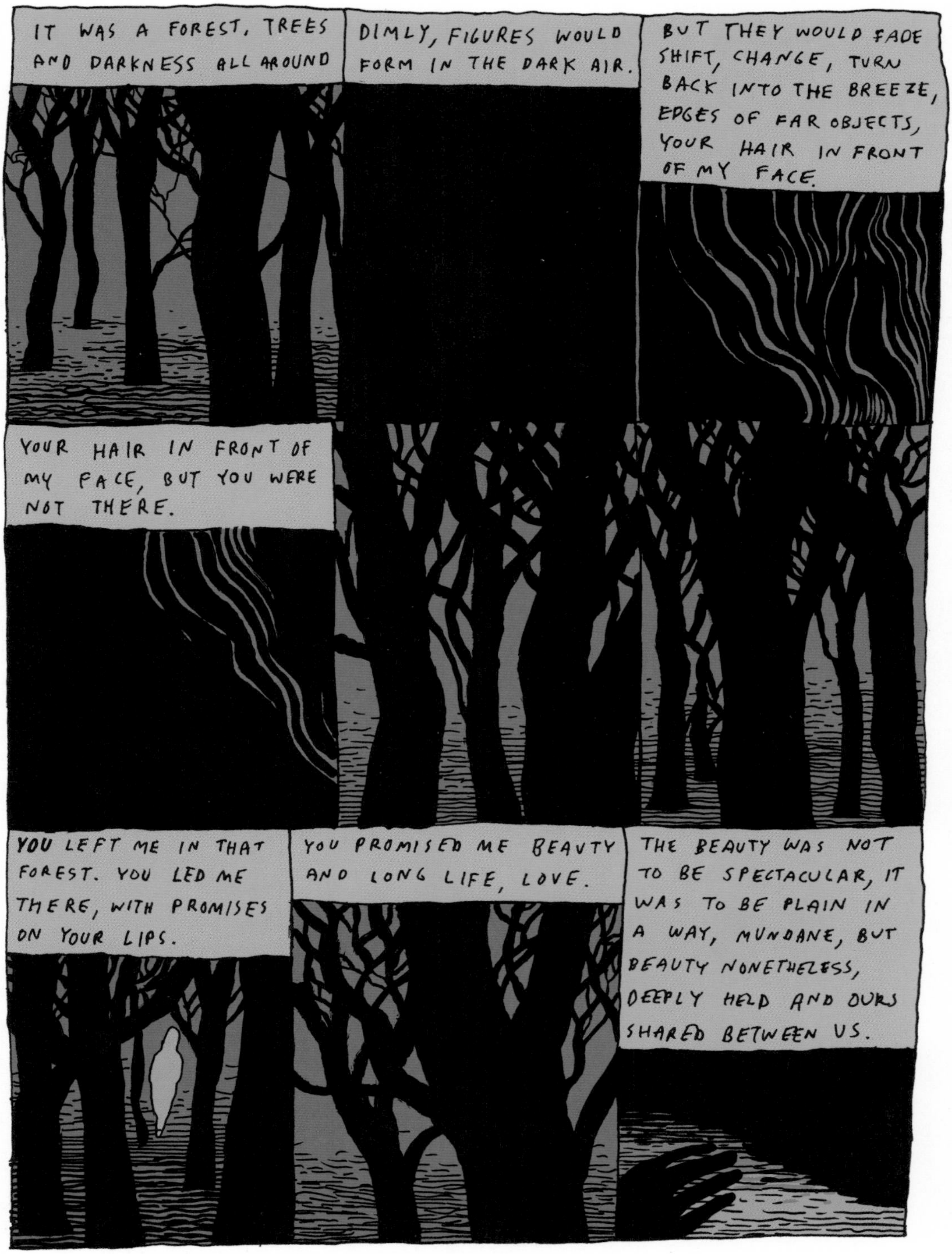
IT WAS A FOREST, TREES AND DARKNESS ALL AROUND
DIMLY, FIGURES WOULD FORM IN THE DARK AIR.
BUT THEY WOULD FADE SHIFT, CHANGE, TURN BACK INTO THE BREEZE, EDGES OF FAR OBJECTS, YOUR HAIR IN FRONT OF MY FACE.
YOUR HAIR IN FRONT OF MY FACE, BUT YOU WERE NOT THERE.
YOU LEFT ME IN THAT FOREST. YOU LED ME THERE, WITH PROMISES ON YOUR LIPS.
YOU PROMISED ME BEAUTY AND LONG LIFE, LOVE.
THE BEAUTY WAS NOT TO BE SPECTACULAR, IT WAS TO BE PLAIN IN A WAY, MUNDANE, BUT BEAUTY NONETHELESS, DEEPLY HELD AND OURS SHARED BETWEEN US.

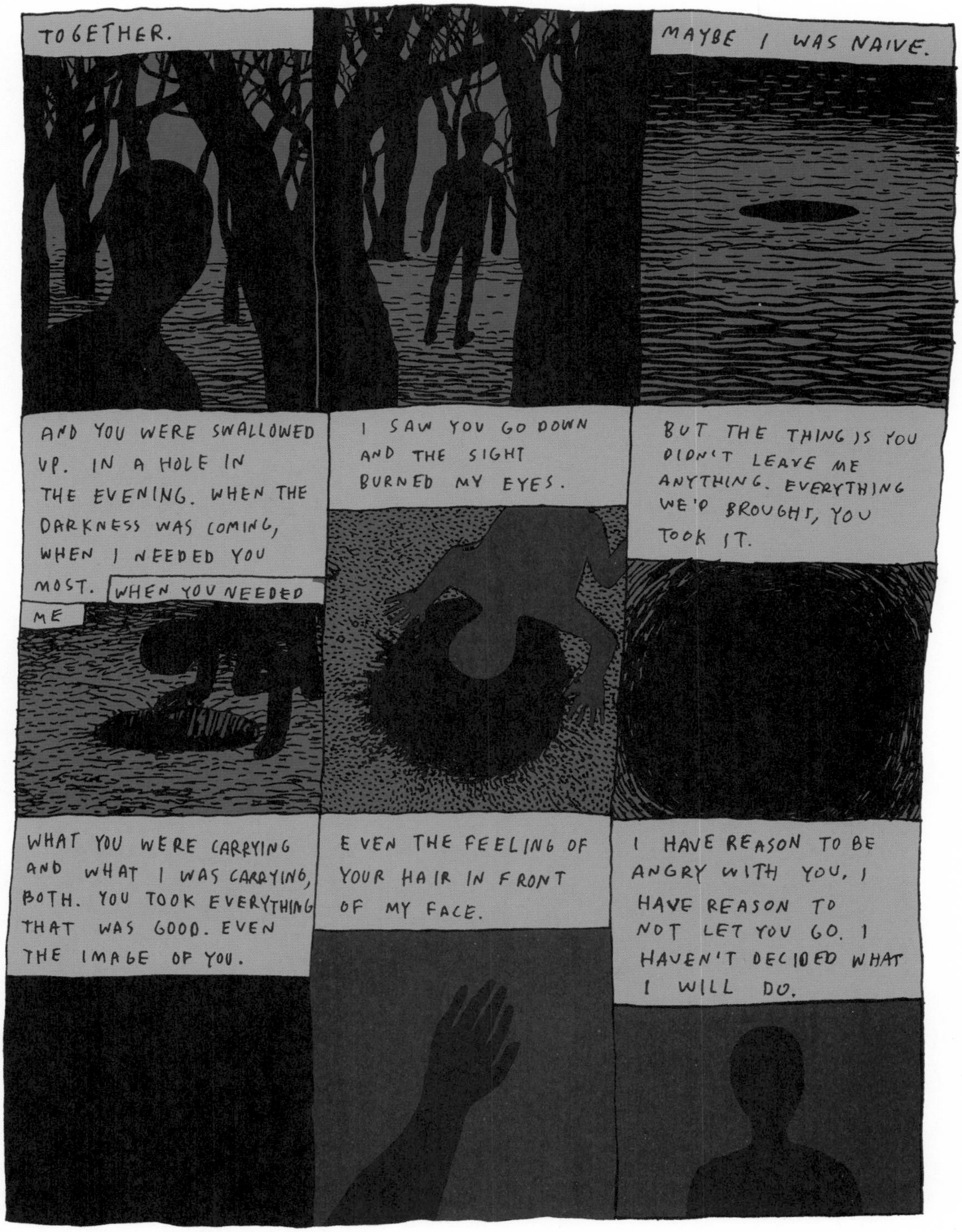
TOGETHER.
MAYBE I WAS NAIVE.
AND YOU WERE SWALLOWED UP. IN A HOLE IN THE EVENING. WHEN THE DARKNESS WAS COMING, WHEN I NEEDED YOU MOST.
WHEN YOU NEEDED ME
I SAW YOU GO DOWN AND THE SIGHT BURNED MY EYES.
BUT THE THING IS YOU DIDN'T LEAVE ME ANYTHING. EVERYTHING WE'D BROUGHT, YOU TOOK IT.
WHAT YOU WERE CARRYING AND WHAT I WAS CARRYING, BOTH. YOU TOOK EVERYTHING THAT WAS GOOD. EVEN THE IMAGE OF YOU.
EVEN THE FEELING OF YOUR HAIR IN FRONT OF MY FACE.
I HAVE REASON TO BE ANGRY WITH YOU, I HAVE REASON TO NOT LET YOU GO. I HAVEN'T DECIDED WHAT I WILL DO.

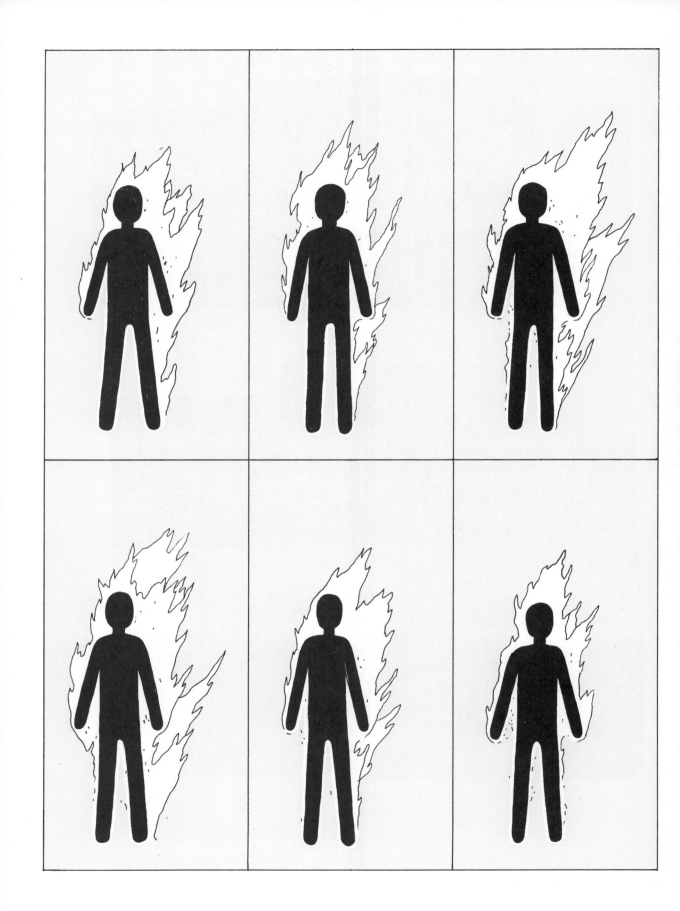

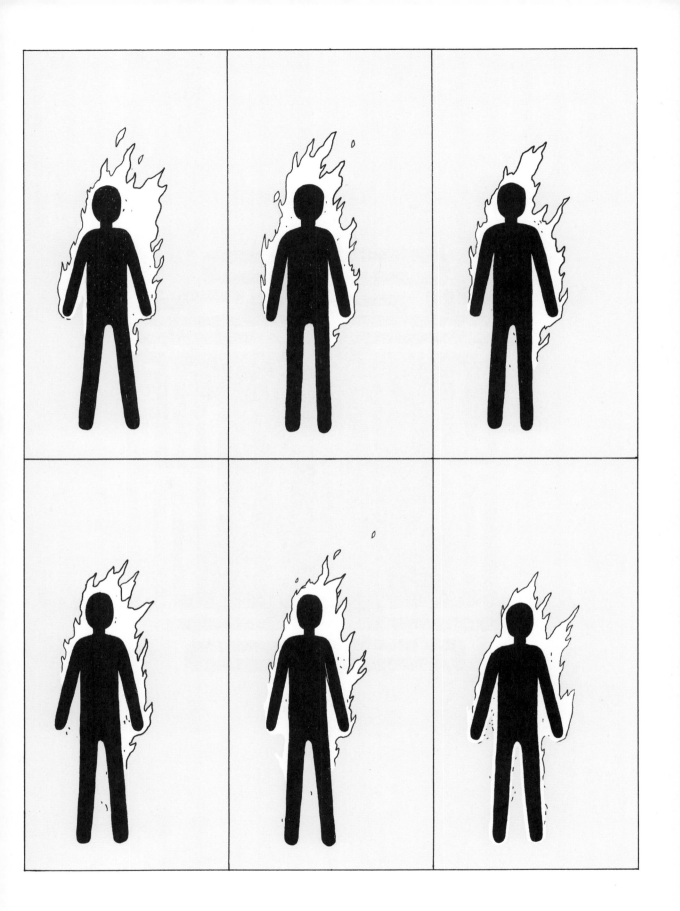

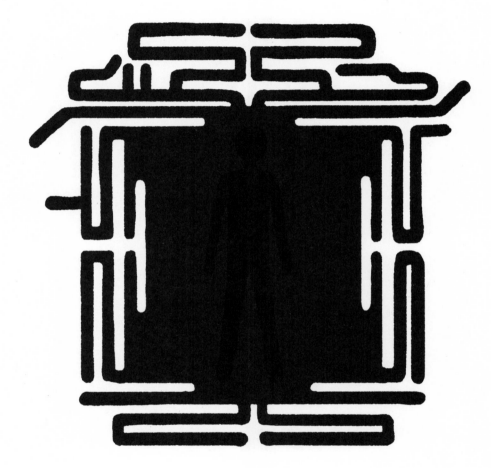

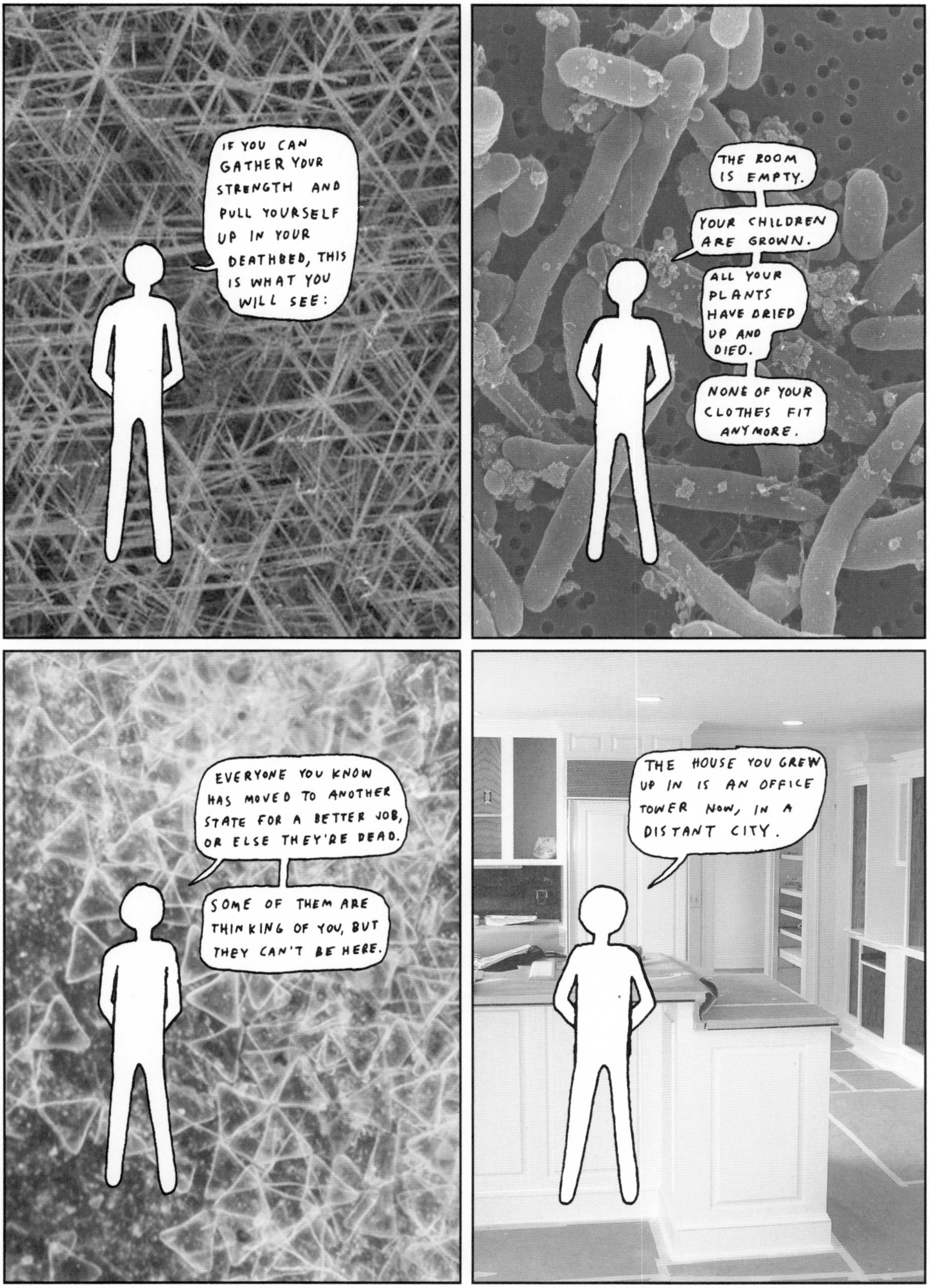
IF YOU CAN GATHER YOUR STRENGTH AND PULL YOURSELF UP IN YOUR DEATHBED, THIS IS WHAT YOU WILL SEE:
THE ROOM IS EMPTY.
YOUR CHILDREN ARE GROWN.
ALL YOUR PLANTS HAVE DRIED UP AND DIED.
NONE OF YOUR CLOTHES FIT ANYMORE.
EVERYONE YOU KNOW HAS MOVED TO ANOTHER STATE FOR A BETTER JOB, OR ELSE THEY'RE DEAD.
SOME OF THEM ARE THINKING OF YOU, BUT THEY CAN'T BE HERE.
THE HOUSE YOU GREW UP IN IS AN OFFICE TOWER NOW, IN A DISTANT CITY.

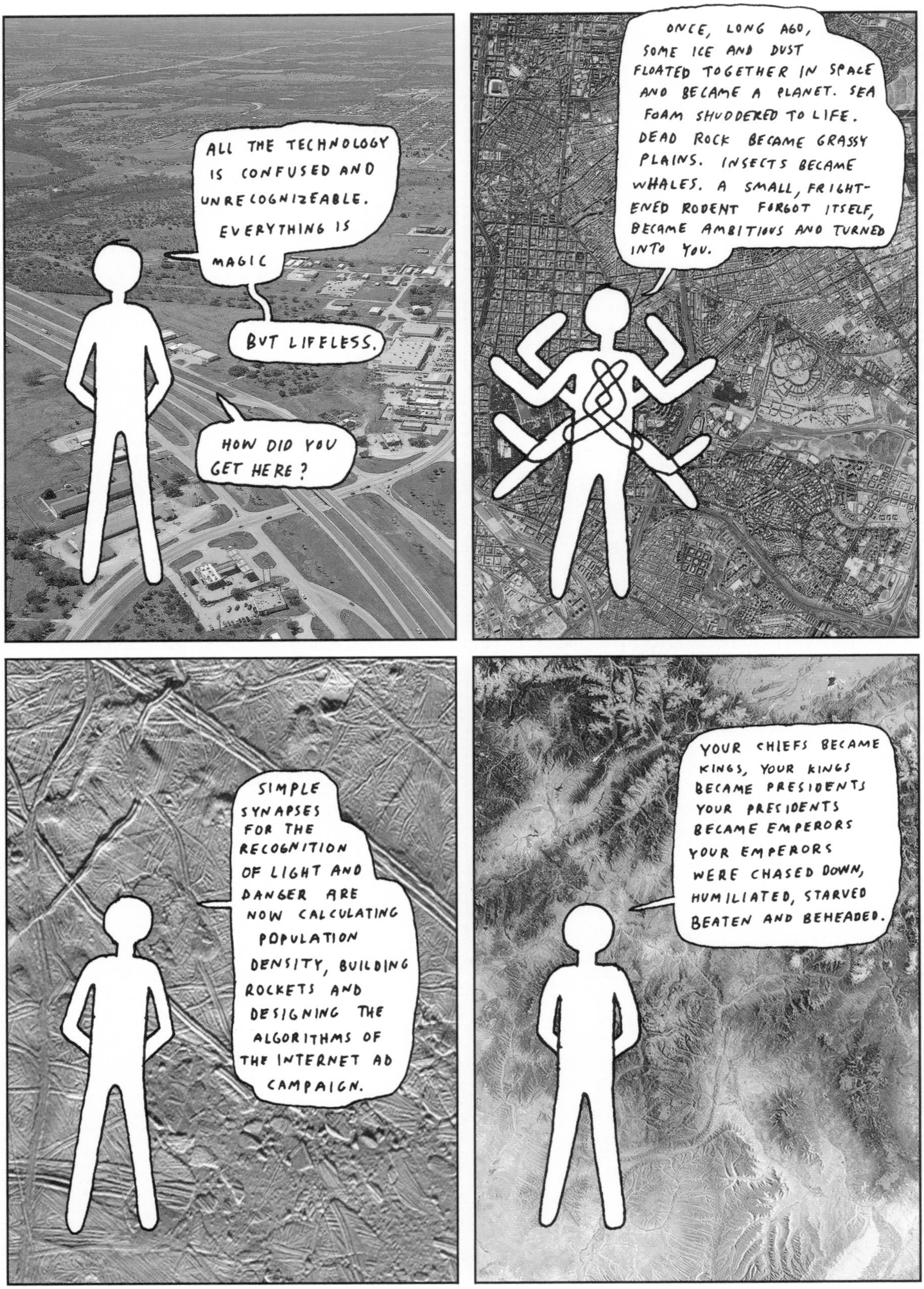
ALL THE TECHNOLOGY IS CONFUSED AND UNRECOGNIZEABLE. EVERYTHING IS MAGIC
BUT LIFELESS.
HOW DID YOU GET HERE?
ONCE, LONG AGO, SOME ICE AND DUST FLOATED TOGETHER IN SPACE AND BECAME A PLANET. SEA FOAM SHUDDERED TO LIFE. DEAD ROCK BECAME GRASSY PLAINS. INSECTS BECAME WHALES. A SMALL, FRIGHT-ENED RODENT FORGOT ITSELF, BECAME AMBITIOUS AND TURNED INTO YOU.
SIMPLE SYNAPSES FOR THE RECOGNITION OF LIGHT AND DANGER ARE NOW CALCULATING POPULATION DENSITY, BUILDING ROCKETS AND DESIGNING THE ALGORITHMS OF THE INTERNET AD CAMPAIGN.
YOUR CHIEFS BECAME KINGS, YOUR KINGS BECAME PRESIDENTS YOUR PRESIDENTS BECAME EMPERORS YOUR EMPERORS WERE CHASED DOWN, HUMILIATED, STARVED BEATEN AND BEHEADED.

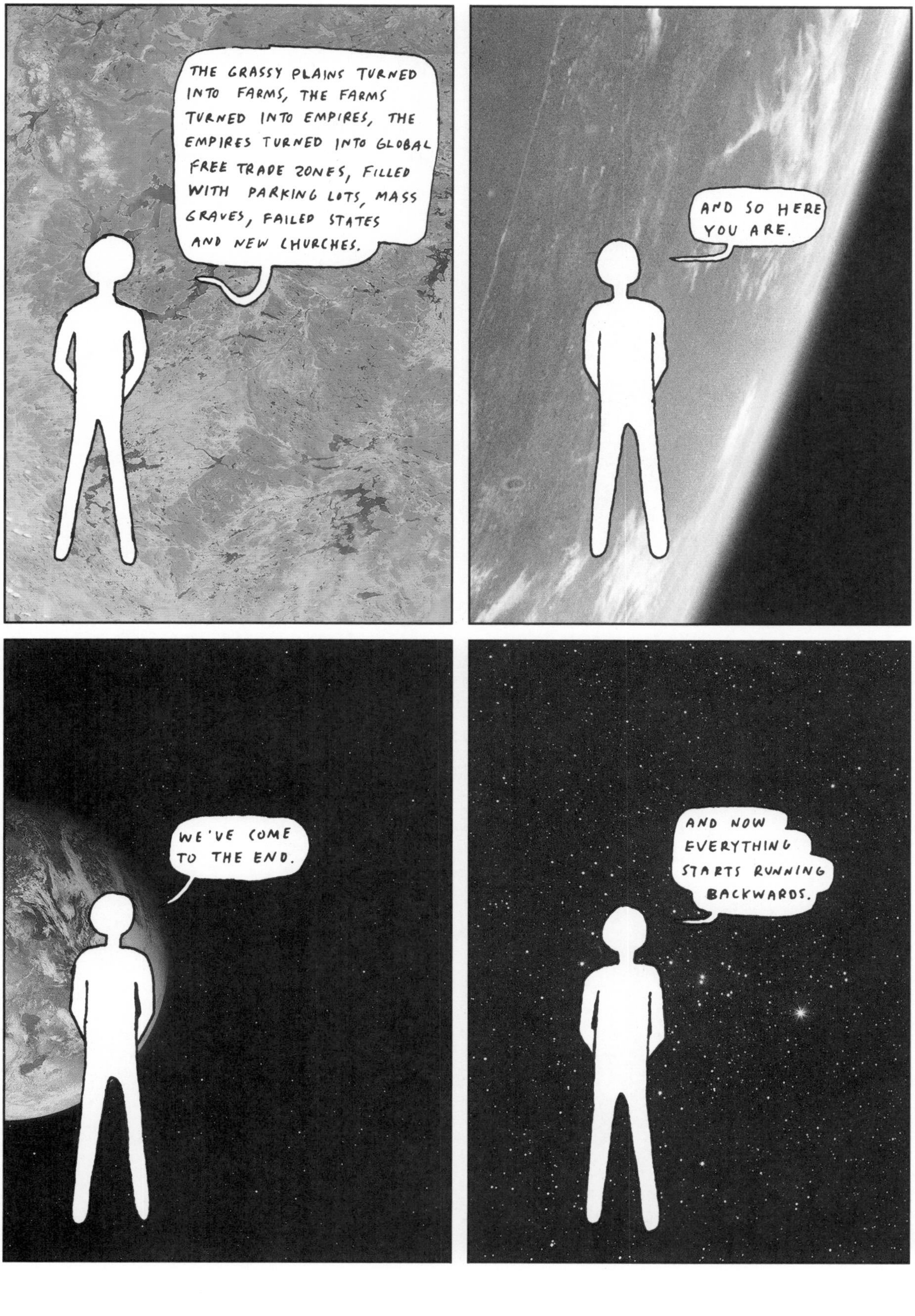
THE GRASSY PLAINS TURNED INTO FARMS, THE FARMS TURNED INTO EMPIRES, THE EMPIRES TURNED INTO GLOBAL FREE TRADE ZONES, FILLED WITH PARKING LOTS, MASS GRAVES, FAILED STATES AND NEW CHURCHES.
AND SO HERE YOU ARE.
WE'VE COME TO THE END.
AND NOW EVERYTHING STARTS RUNNING BACKWARDS.

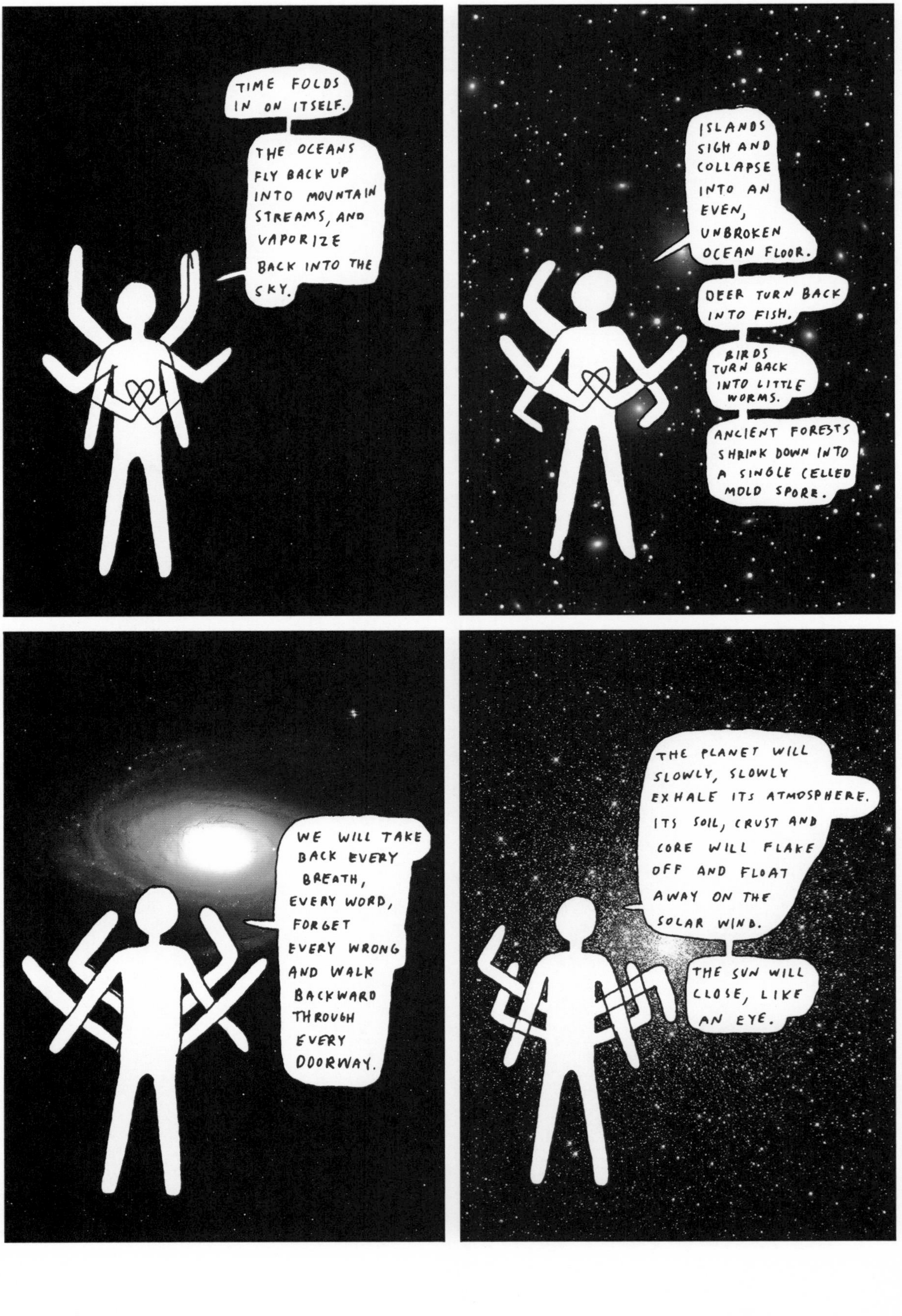
TIME FOLDS IN ON ITSELF.
THE OCEANS FLY BACK UP INTO MOUNTAIN STREAMS, AND VAPORIZE BACK INTO THE SKY.
ISLANDS SIGH AND COLLAPSE INTO AN EVEN, UNBROKEN OCEAN FLOOR.
DEER TURN BACK INTO FISH.
BIRDS TURN BACK INTO LITTLE WORMS.
ANCIENT FORESTS SHRINK DOWN INTO A SINGLE CELLED MOLD SPORE.
WE WILL TAKE BACK EVERY BREATH, EVERY WORD, FORGET EVERY WRONG AND WALK BACKWARD THROUGH EVERY DOORWAY.
THE PLANET WILL SLOWLY, SLOWLY EXHALE ITS ATMOSPHERE. ITS SOIL, CRUST AND CORE WILL FLAKE OFF AND FLOAT AWAY ON THE SOLAR WIND.
THE SUN WILL CLOSE, LIKE AN EYE.

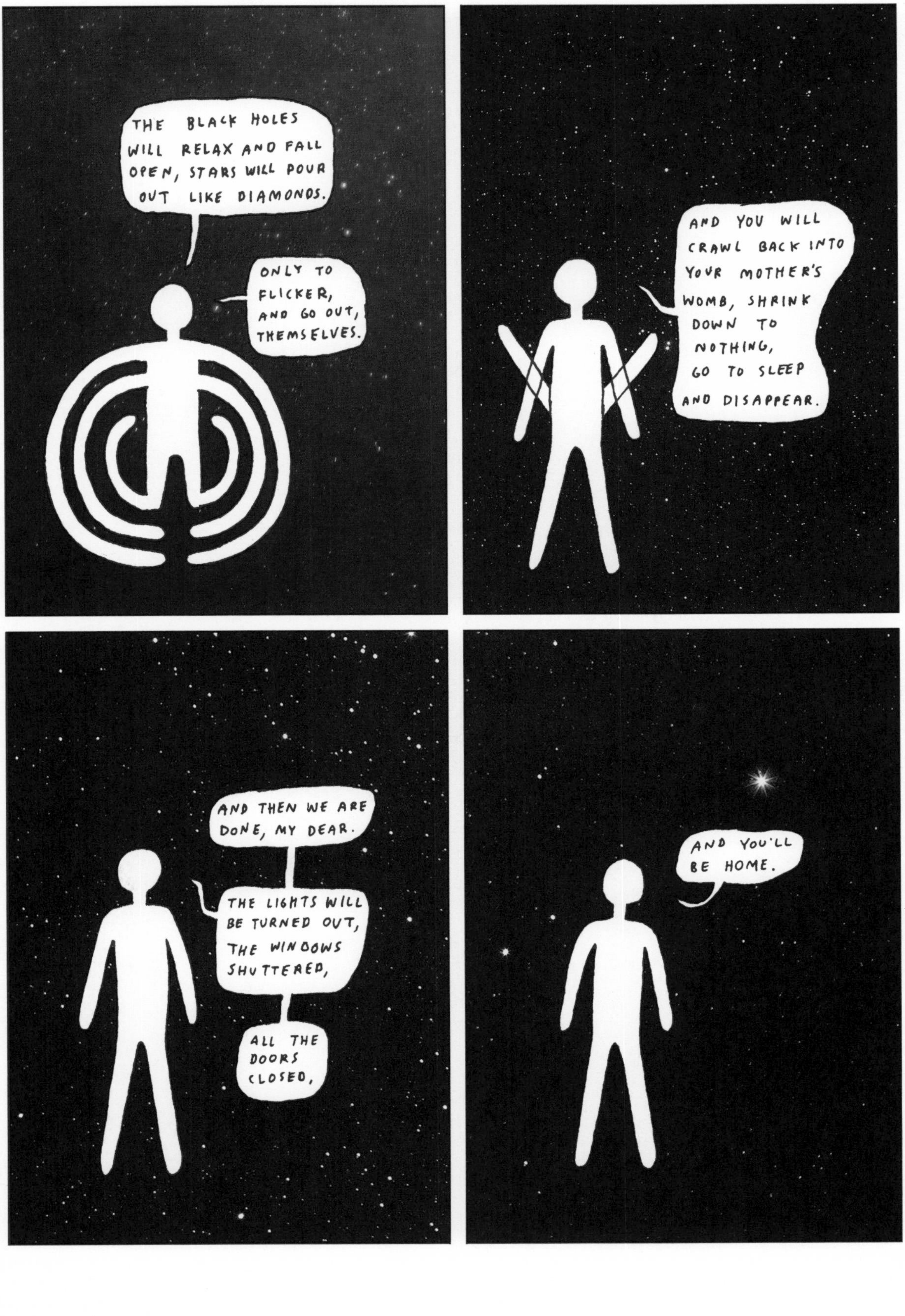
THE BLACK HOLES WILL RELAX AND FALL OPEN, STARS WILL POUR OUT LIKE DIAMONDS.
ONLY TO FLICKER, AND GO OUT, THEMSELVES.
AND YOU WILL CRAWL BACK INTO YOUR MOTHER'S WOMB, SHRINK DOWN TO NOTHING, GO TO SLEEP AND DISAPPEAR.
AND THEN WE ARE DONE, MY DEAR.
THE LIGHTS WILL BE TURNED OUT, THE WINDOWS SHUTTERED,
ALL THE DOORS CLOSED,
AND YOU'LL BE HOME.

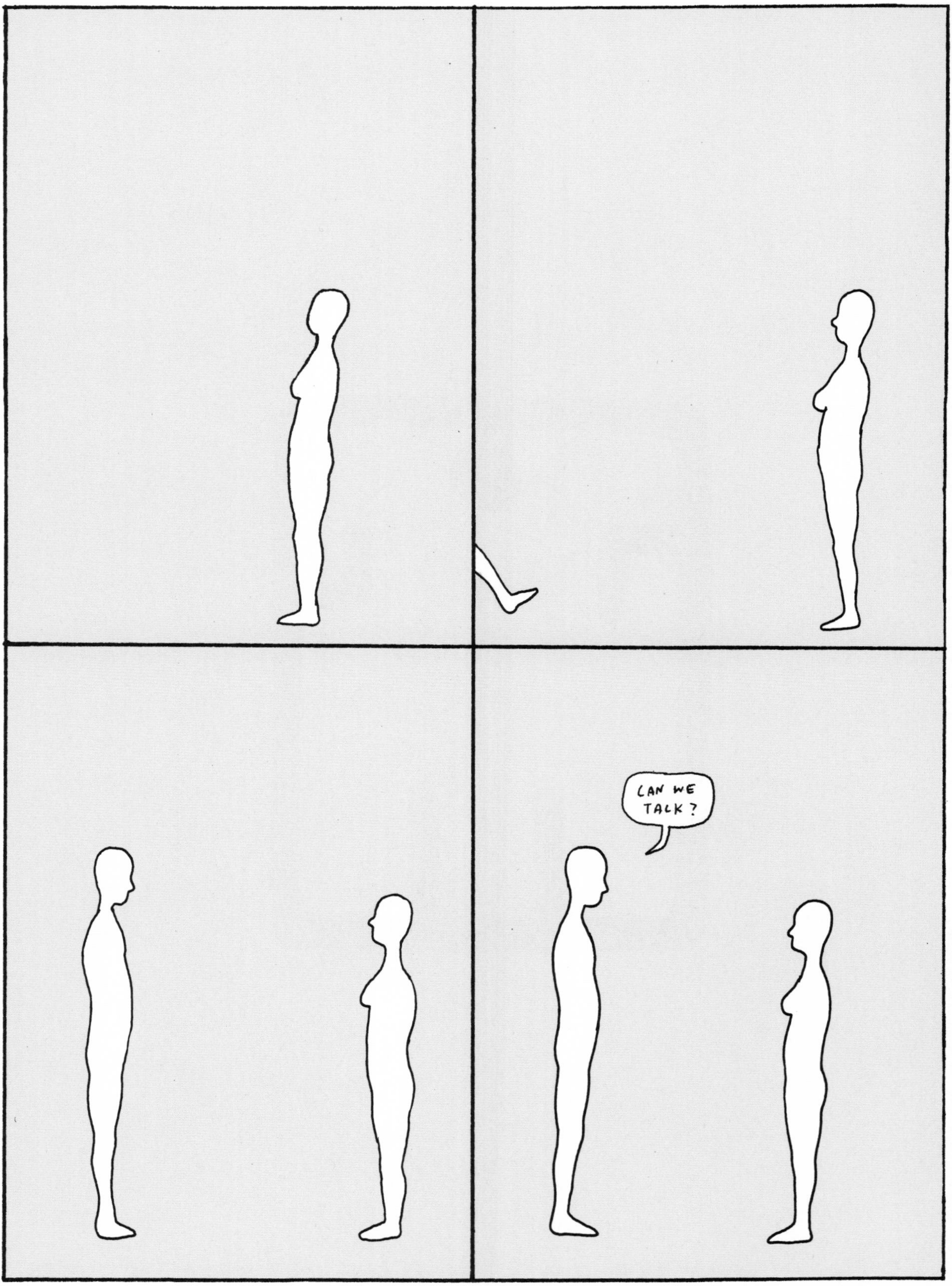
CAN WE TALK?

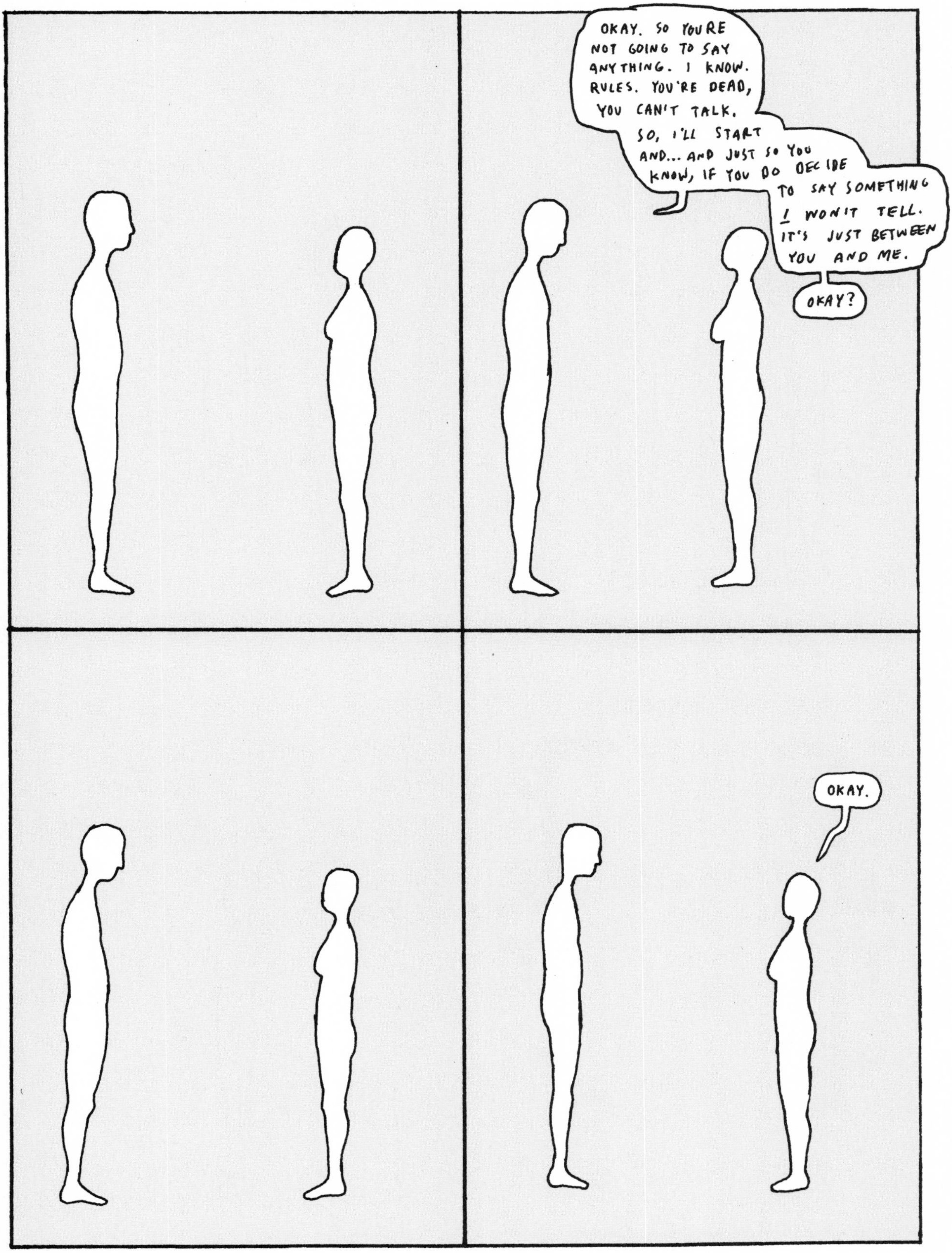
OKAY. SO YOU'RE NOT GOING TO SAY ANYTHING. I KNOW. RULES. YOU'RE DEAD, YOU CAN'T TALK.
SO, I'LL START AND... AND JUST SO YOU KNOW, IF YOU DO DECIDE TO SAY SOMETHING I WON'T TELL. IT'S JUST BETWEEN YOU AND ME.
OKAY?
OKAY.

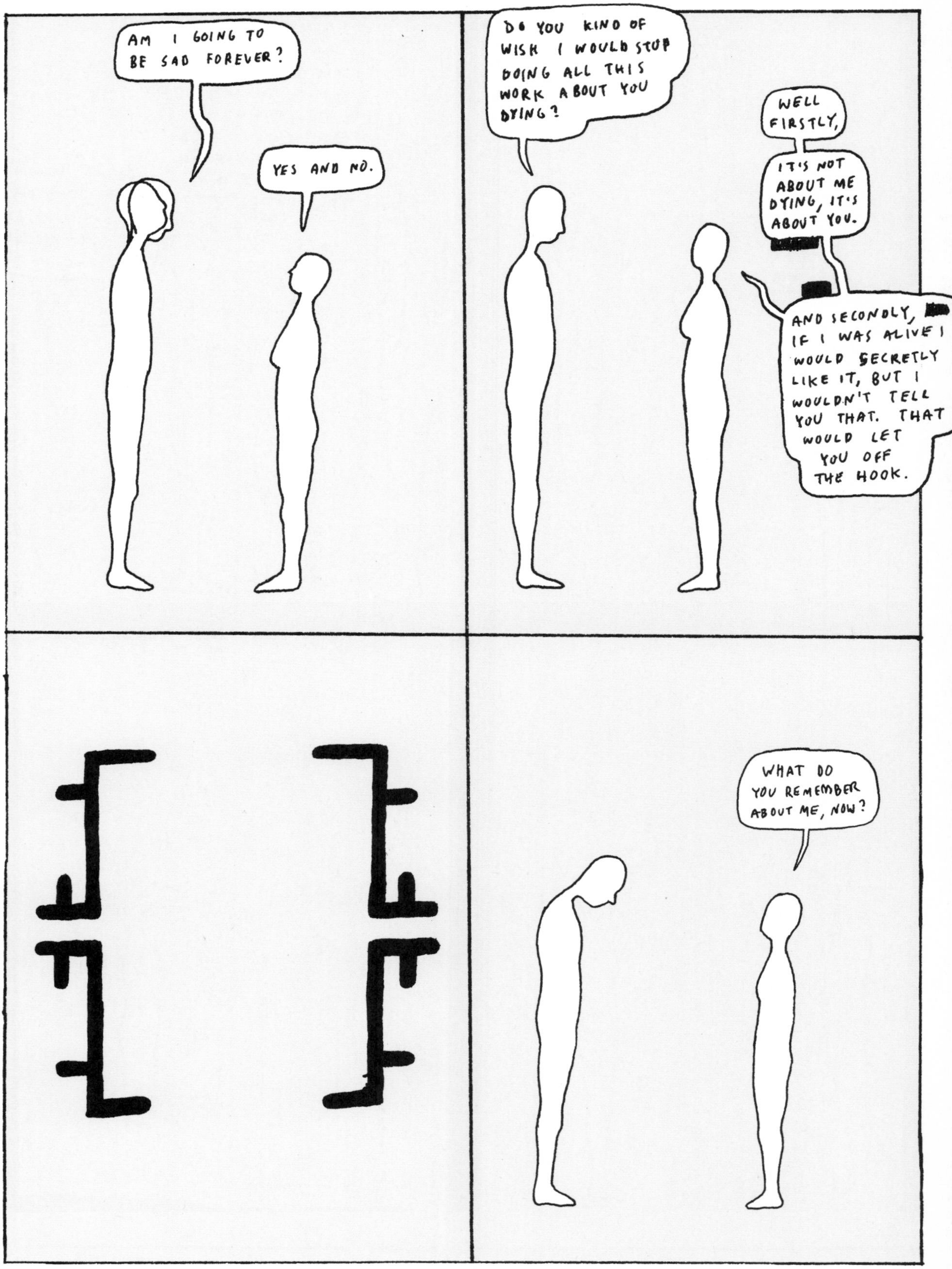
AM I GOING TO BE SAD FOREVER?
YES AND NO.
DO YOU KIND OF WISH I WOULD STOP DOING ALL THIS WORK ABOUT YOU DYING?
WELL FIRSTLY,
IT'S NOT ABOUT ME DYING, IT'S ABOUT YOU.
[redacted]
AND SECONDLY, [redacted] IF I WAS ALIVE I WOULD SECRETLY LIKE IT, BUT I WOULDN'T TELL YOU THAT. THAT WOULD LET YOU OFF THE HOOK.
WHAT DO YOU REMEMBER ABOUT ME, NOW?

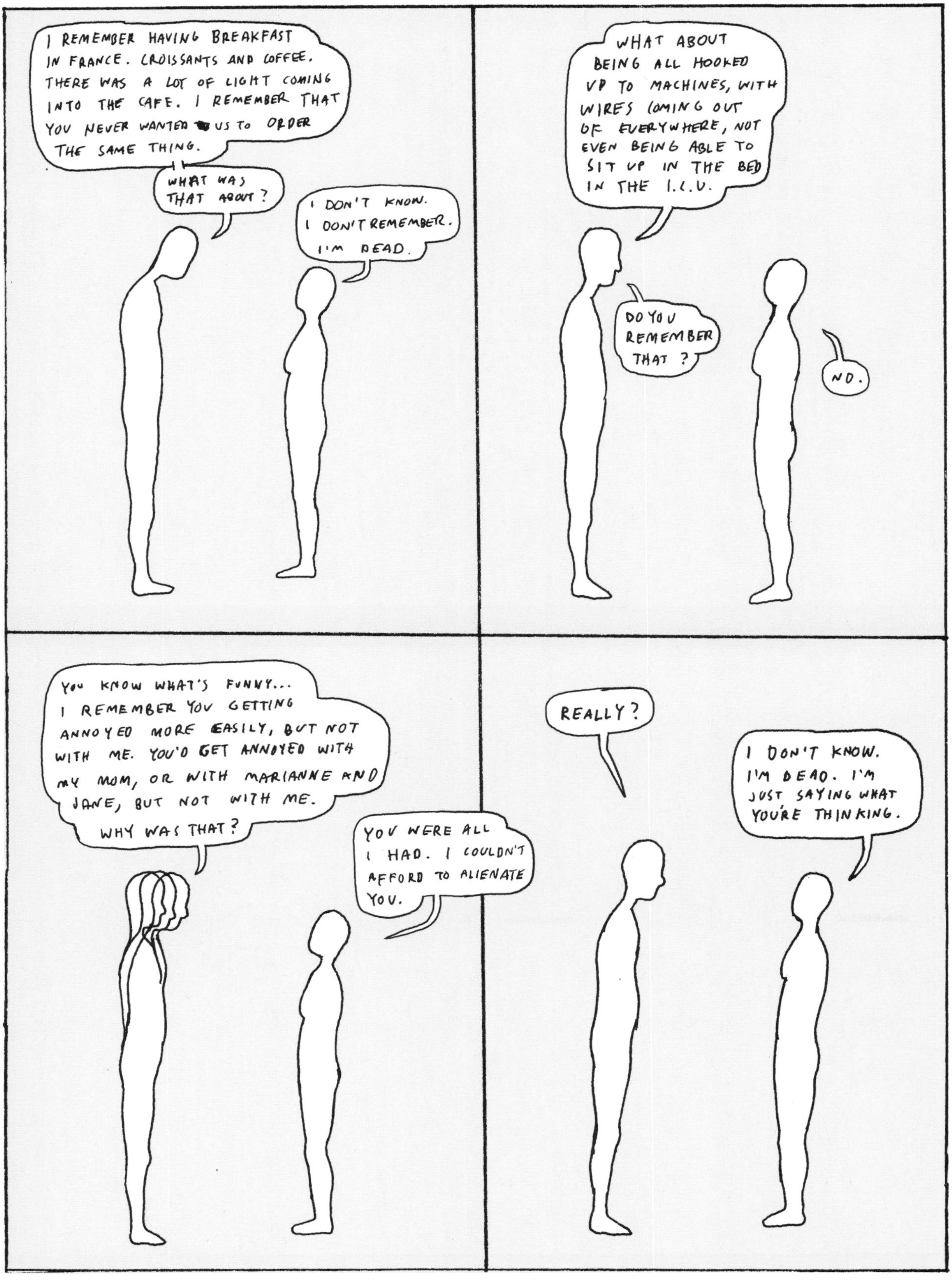
I REMEMBER HAVING BREAKFAST IN FRANCE. CROISSANTS AND COFFEE. THERE WAS A LOT OF LIGHT COMING INTO THE CAFE. I REMEMBER THAT YOU NEVER WANTED US TO ORDER THE SAME THING.
WHAT WAS THAT ABOUT?
I DON'T KNOW. I DON'T REMEMBER. I'M DEAD.
WHAT ABOUT BEING ALL HOOKED UP TO MACHINES, WITH WIRES COMING OUT OF EVERYWHERE, NOT EVEN BEING ABLE TO SIT UP IN THE BED IN THE I.C.U.
DO YOU REMEMBER THAT?
NO.
YOU KNOW WHAT'S FUNNY... I REMEMBER YOU GETTING ANNOYED MORE EASILY, BUT NOT WITH ME. YOU'D GET ANNOYED WITH MY MOM, OR WITH MARIANNE AND JANE, BUT NOT WITH ME. WHY WAS THAT?
YOU WERE ALL I HAD. I COULDN'T AFFORD TO ALIENATE YOU.
REALLY?
I DON'T KNOW. I'M DEAD. I'M JUST SAYING WHAT YOU'RE THINKING.

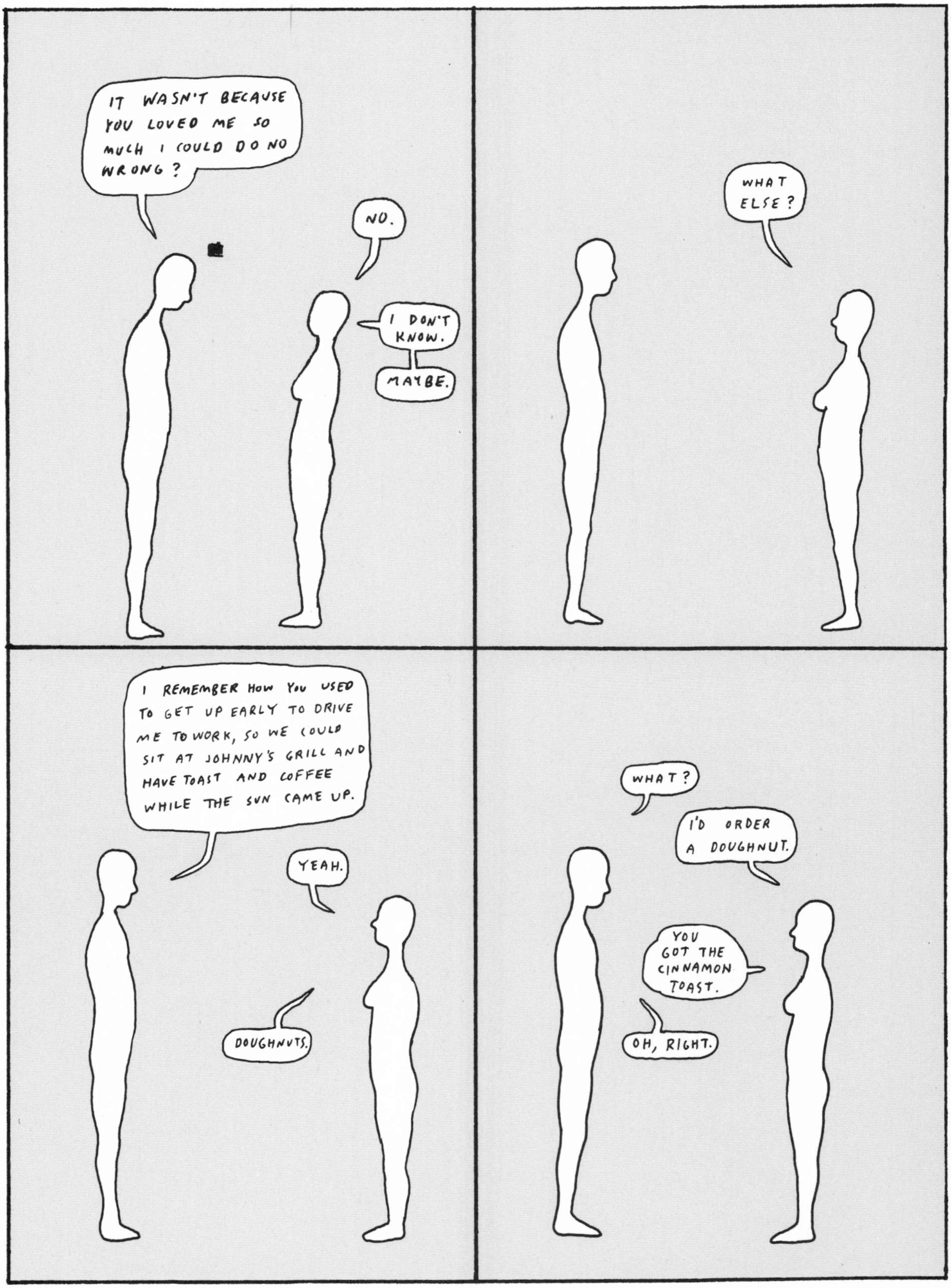
IT WASN'T BECAUSE YOU LOVED ME SO MUCH I COULD DO NO WRONG?
NO.
I DON'T KNOW.
MAYBE.
WHAT ELSE?
I REMEMBER HOW YOU USED TO GET UP EARLY TO DRIVE ME TO WORK, SO WE COULD SIT AT JOHNNY'S GRILL AND HAVE TOAST AND COFFEE WHILE THE SUN CAME UP.
YEAH.
DOUGHNUTS.
WHAT?
I'D ORDER A DOUGHNUT.
YOU GOT THE CINNAMON TOAST.
OH, RIGHT.

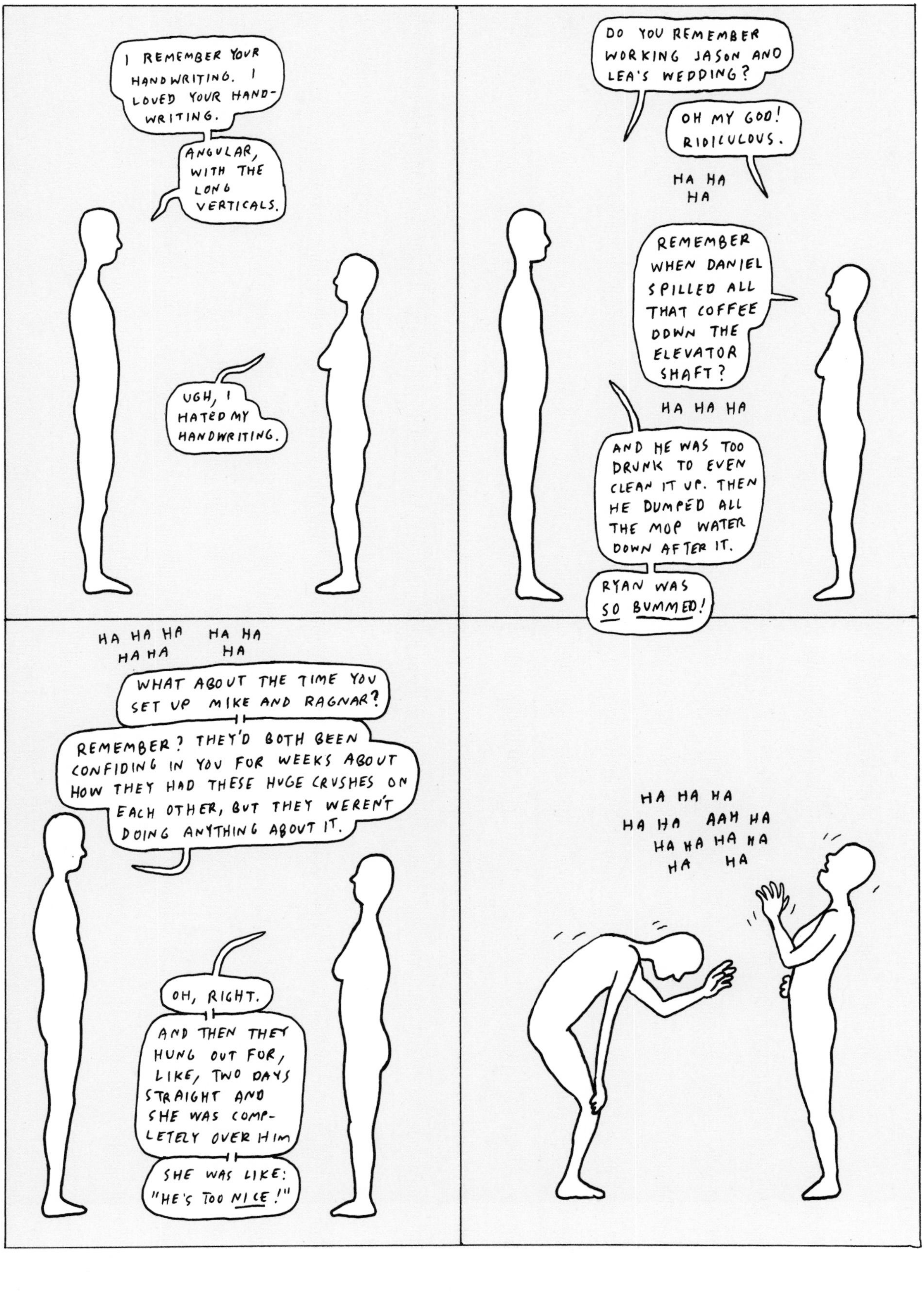
I REMEMBER YOUR HANDWRITING. I LOVED YOUR HANDWRITING.
ANGULAR, WITH THE LONG VERTICALS.
UGH, I HATED MY HANDWRITING.
DO YOU REMEMBER WORKING JASON AND LEA'S WEDDING?
OH MY GOD! RIDICULOUS.
HA HA HA
REMEMBER WHEN DANIEL SPILLED ALL THAT COFFEE DOWN THE ELEVATOR SHAFT?
HA HA HA
AND HE WAS TOO DRUNK TO EVEN CLEAN IT UP. THEN HE DUMPED ALL THE MOP WATER DOWN AFTER IT.
RYAN WAS SO BUMMED!
HA HA HA HA HA HA HA HA
WHAT ABOUT THE TIME YOU SET UP MIKE AND RAGNAR?
REMEMBER? THEY'D BOTH BEEN CONFIDING IN YOU FOR WEEKS ABOUT HOW THEY HAD THESE HUGE CRUSHES ON EACH OTHER, BUT THEY WEREN'T DOING ANYTHING ABOUT IT.
OH, RIGHT.
AND THEN THEY HUNG OUT FOR, LIKE, TWO DAYS STRAIGHT AND SHE WAS COMPLETELY OVER HIM
SHE WAS LIKE: "HE'S TOO NICE!"
HA HA HA HA HA AAH HA HA HA HA HA HA HA

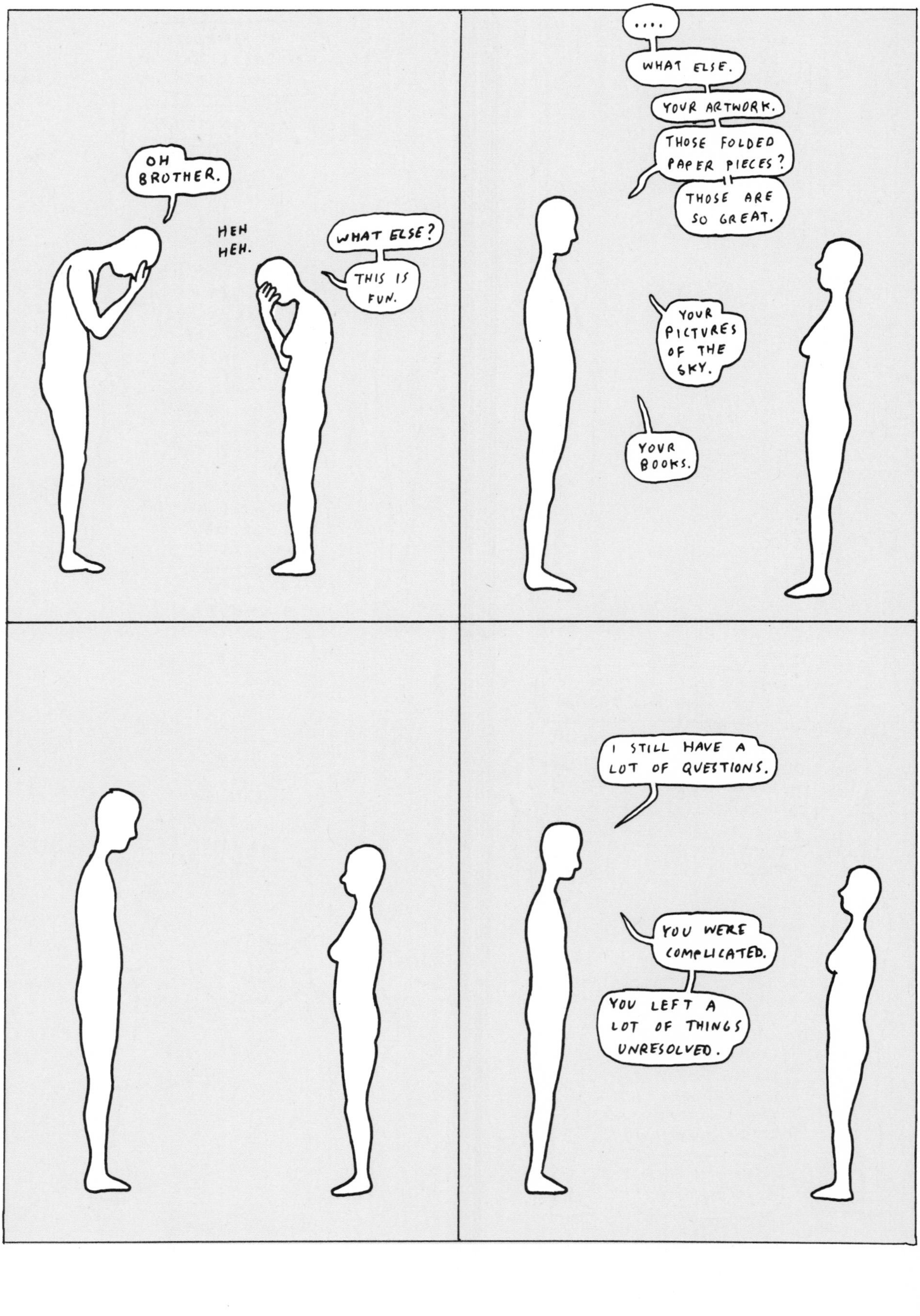
OH BROTHER.
HEH HEH.
WHAT ELSE?
THIS IS FUN.
....
WHAT ELSE.
YOUR ARTWORK.
THOSE FOLDED PAPER PIECES?
THOSE ARE SO GREAT.
YOUR PICTURES OF THE SKY.
YOUR BOOKS.
I STILL HAVE A LOT OF QUESTIONS.
YOU WERE COMPLICATED.
YOU LEFT A LOT OF THINGS UNRESOLVED.

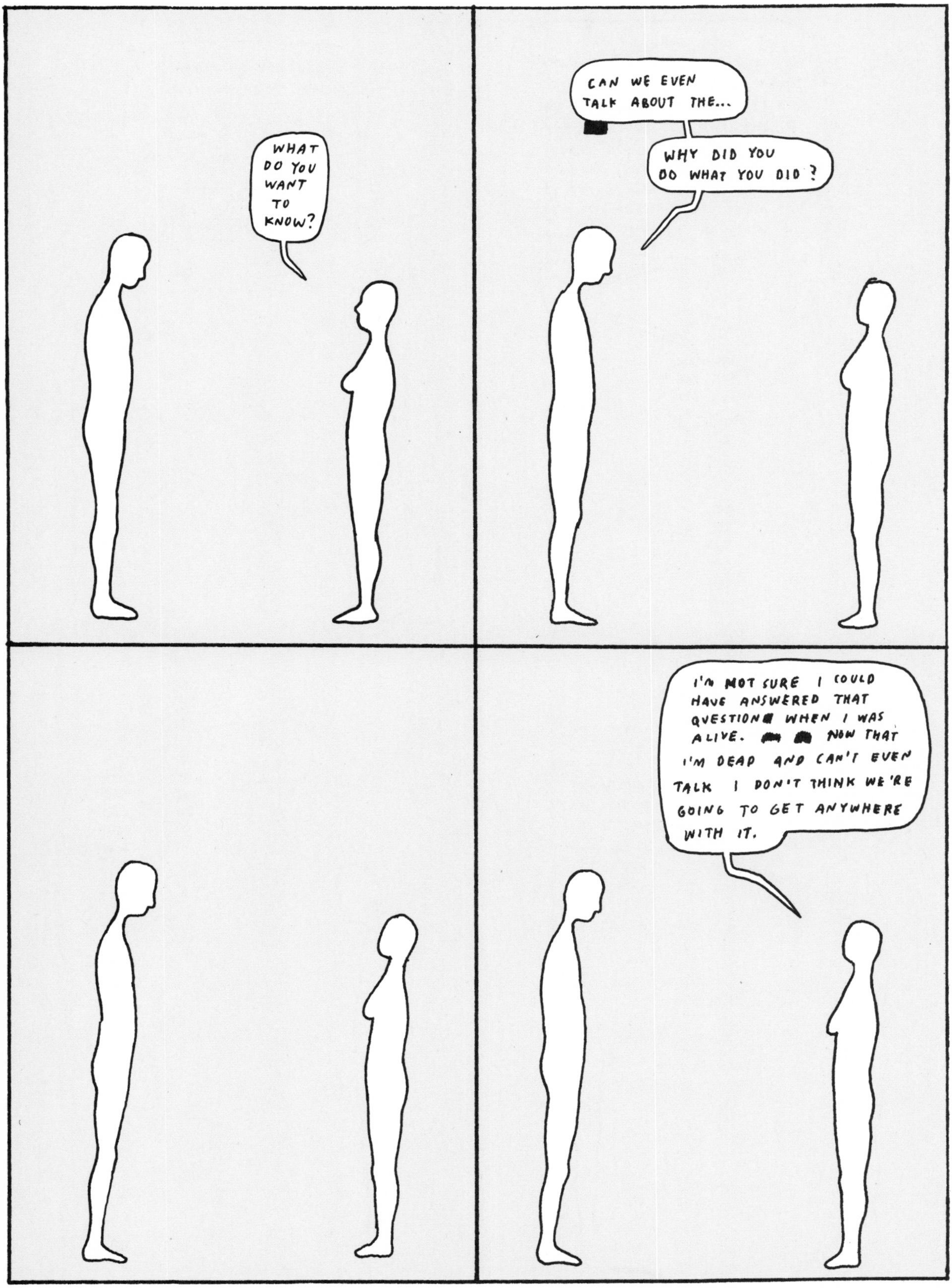
WHAT DO YOU WANT TO KNOW?
CAN WE EVEN TALK ABOUT THE...
[redacted]
WHY DID YOU DO WHAT YOU DID?
I'M NOT SURE I COULD HAVE ANSWERED THAT QUESTION[redacted] WHEN I WAS ALIVE. [redacted] NOW THAT I'M DEAD AND CAN'T EVEN TALK I DON'T THINK WE'RE GOING TO GET ANYWHERE WITH IT.

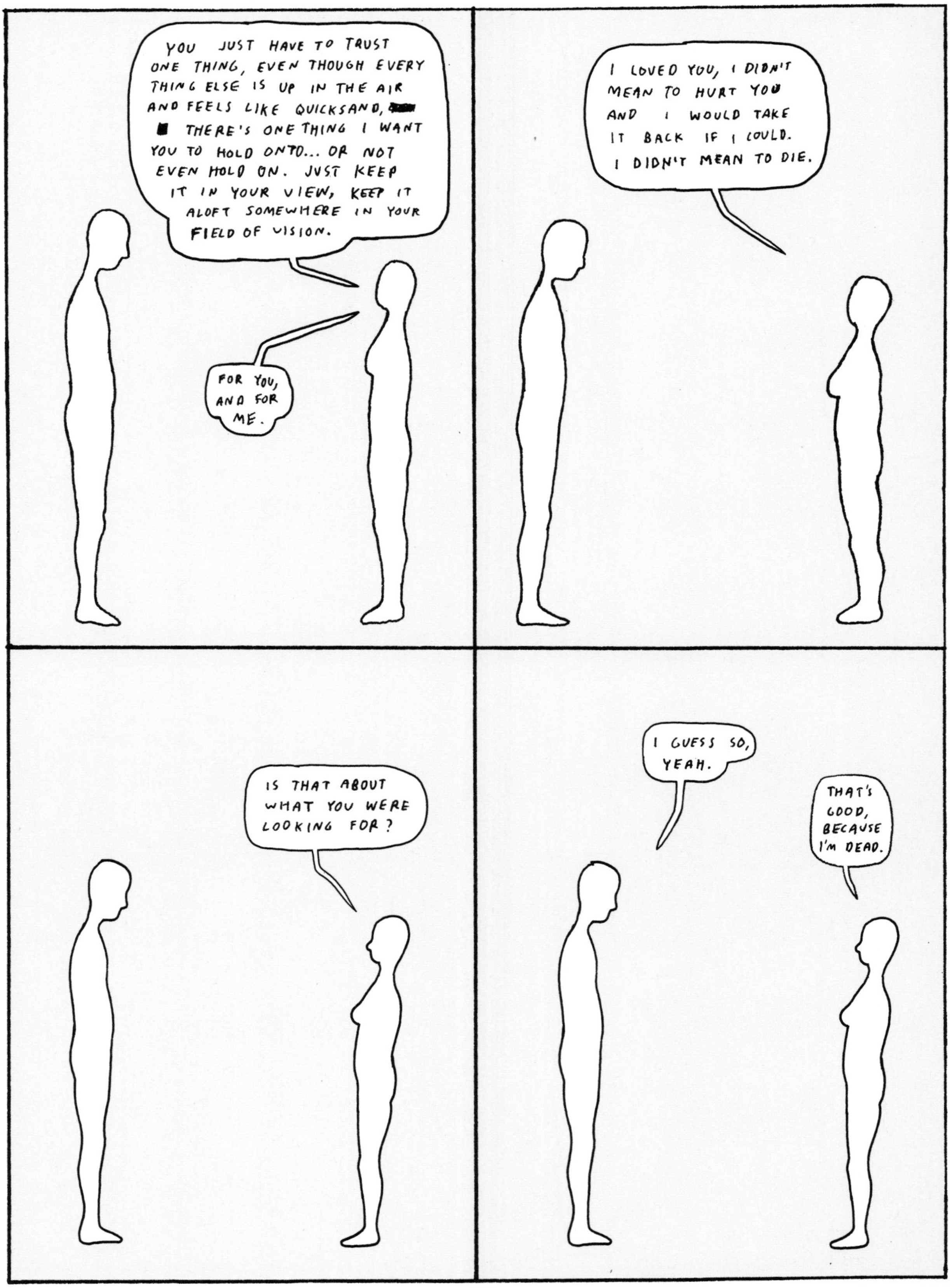

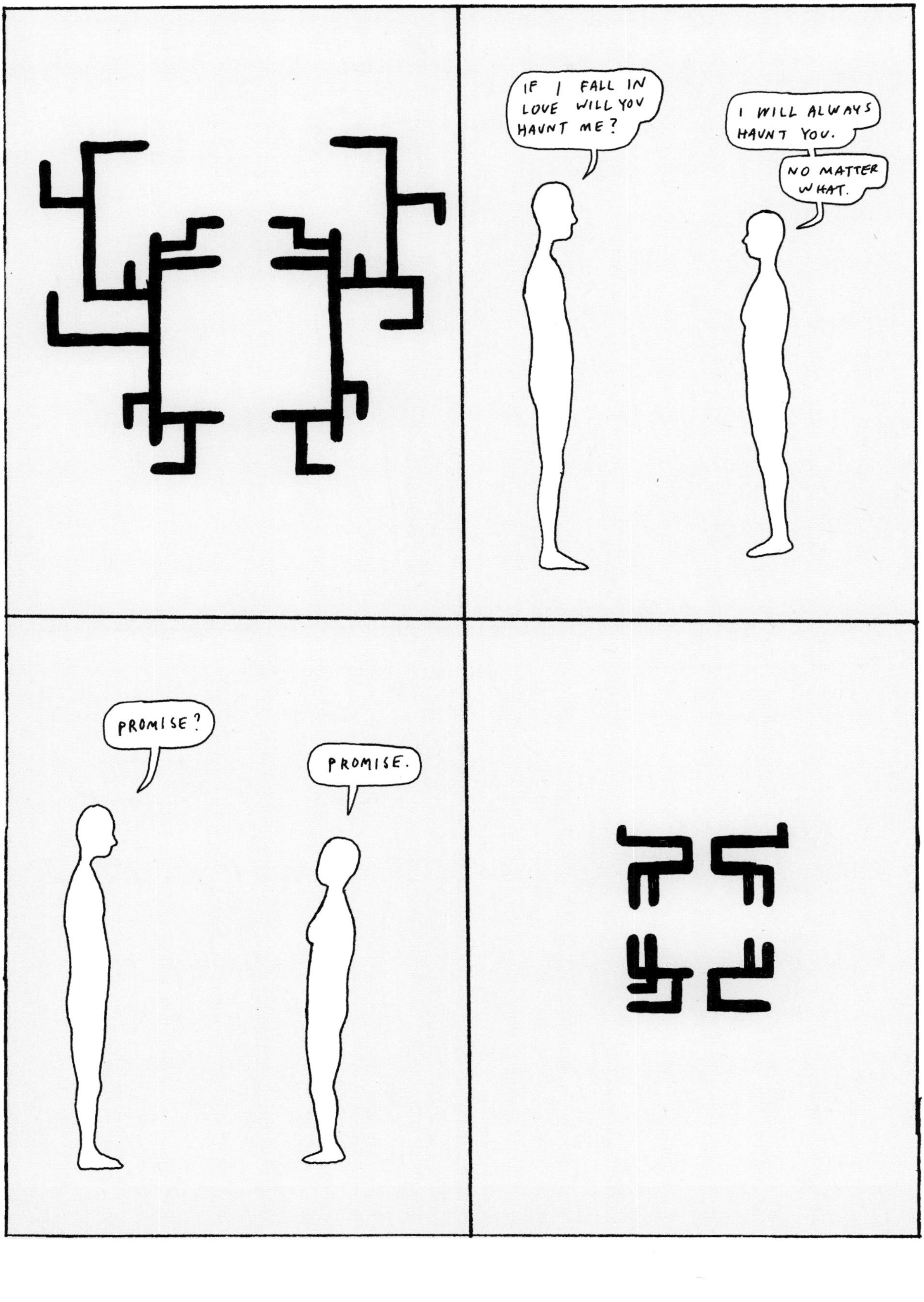
IF I FALL IN LOVE WILL YOU HAUNT ME?
I WILL ALWAYS HAUNT YOU.
NO MATTER WHAT.
PROMISE?
PROMISE.

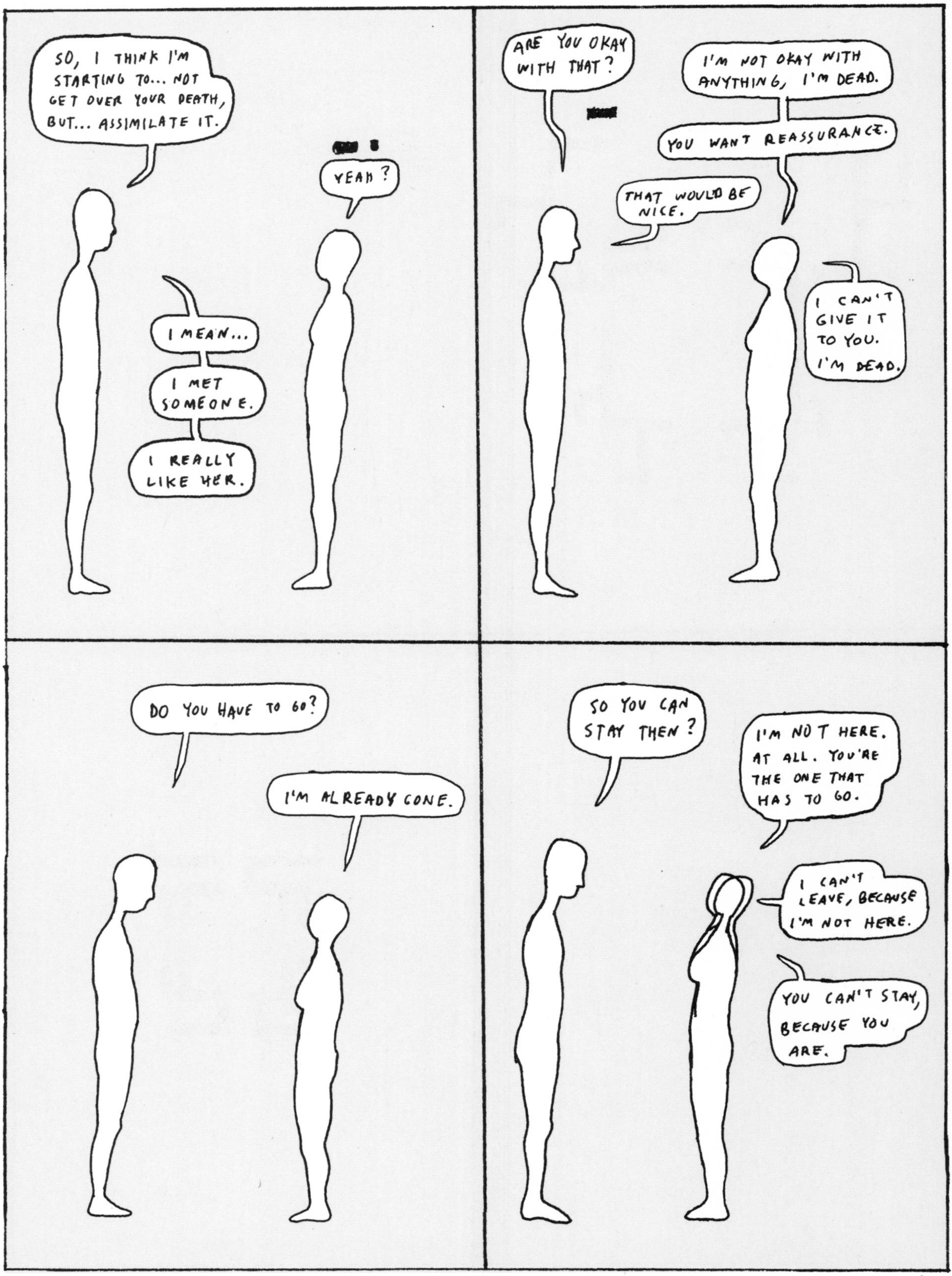
SO, I THINK I'M STARTING TO... NOT GET OVER YOUR DEATH, BUT... ASSIMILATE IT.
YEAH?
I MEAN...
I MET SOMEONE.
I REALLY LIKE HER.
ARE YOU OKAY WITH THAT?
I'M NOT OKAY WITH ANYTHING, I'M DEAD.
YOU WANT REASSURANCE.
THAT WOULD BE NICE.
I CAN'T GIVE IT TO YOU. I'M DEAD.
DO YOU HAVE TO GO?
I'M ALREADY GONE.
SO YOU CAN STAY THEN?
I'M NOT HERE. AT ALL. YOU'RE THE ONE THAT HAS TO GO.
I CAN'T LEAVE, BECAUSE I'M NOT HERE.
YOU CAN'T STAY, BECAUSE YOU ARE.

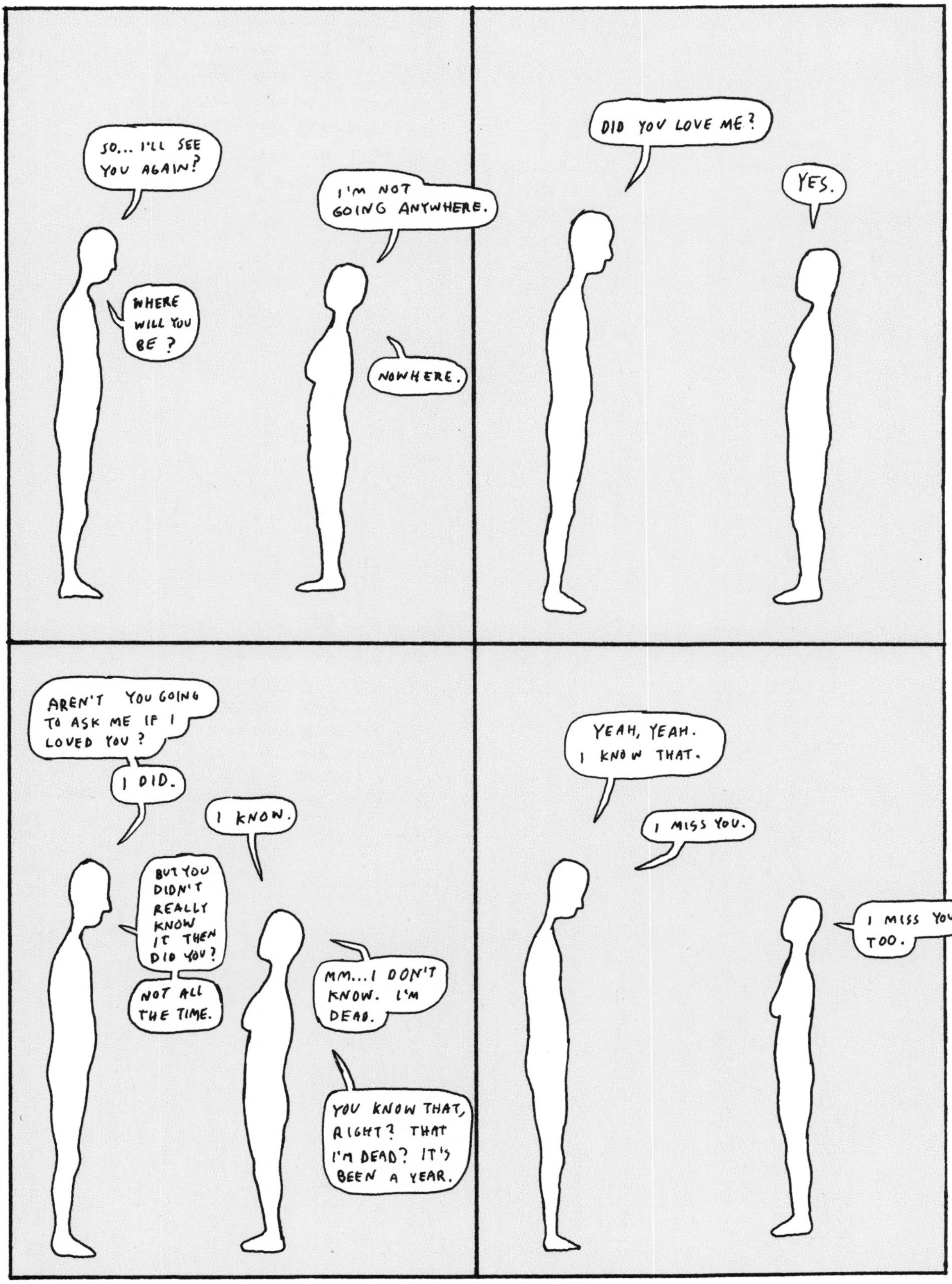
SO... I'LL SEE YOU AGAIN?
I'M NOT GOING ANYWHERE.
WHERE WILL YOU BE?
NOWHERE.
DID YOU LOVE ME?
YES.
AREN'T YOU GOING TO ASK ME IF I LOVED YOU?
I DID.
I KNOW.
BUT YOU DIDN'T REALLY KNOW IT THEN DID YOU?
NOT ALL THE TIME.
MM...I DON'T KNOW. I'M DEAD.
YOU KNOW THAT, RIGHT? THAT I'M DEAD? IT'S BEEN A YEAR.
YEAH, YEAH. I KNOW THAT.
I MISS YOU.
I MISS YOU, TOO.

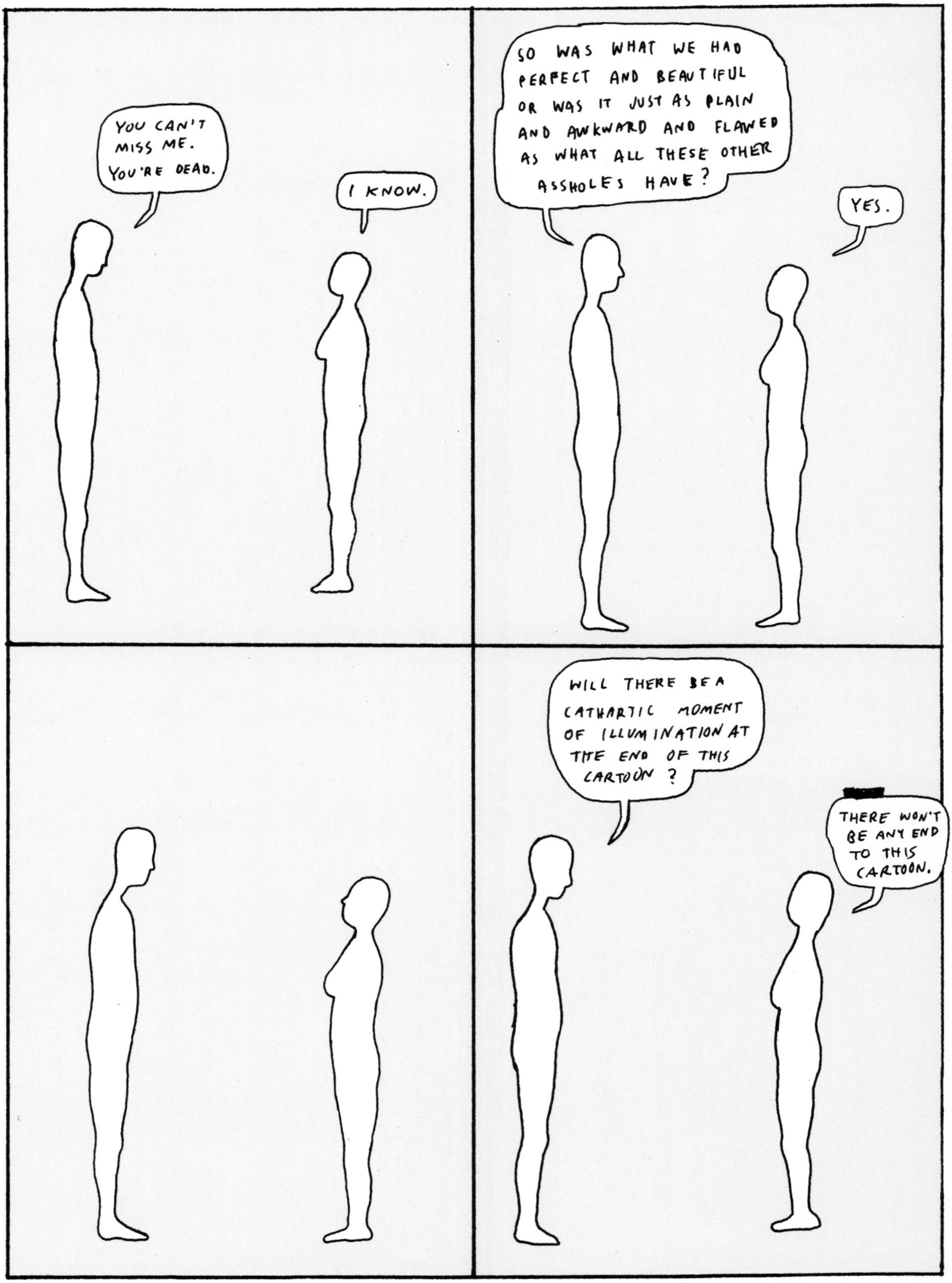
YOU CAN'T MISS ME. YOU'RE DEAD.
I KNOW.
SO WAS WHAT WE HAD PERFECT AND BEAUTIFUL OR WAS IT JUST AS PLAIN AND AWKWARD AND FLAWED AS WHAT ALL THESE OTHER ASSHOLES HAVE?
YES.
WILL THERE BE A CATHARTIC MOMENT OF ILLUMINATION AT THE END OF THIS CARTOON?
THERE WON'T BE ANY END TO THIS CARTOON.

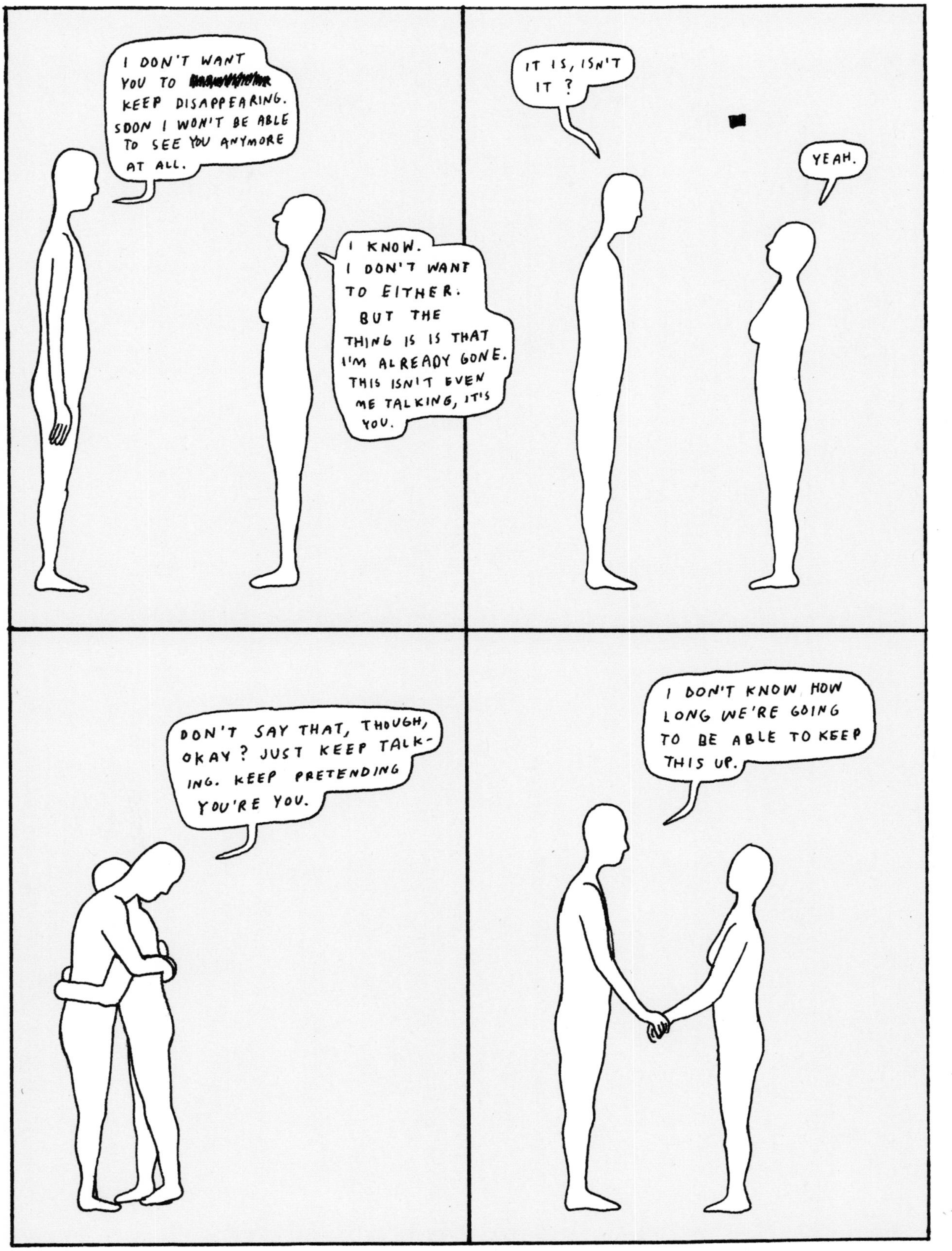
I DON'T WANT YOU TO KEEP DISAPPEARING. SOON I WON'T BE ABLE TO SEE YOU ANYMORE AT ALL.
I KNOW. I DON'T WANT TO EITHER. BUT THE THING IS IS THAT I'M ALREADY GONE. THIS ISN'T EVEN ME TALKING, IT'S YOU.
IT IS, ISN'T IT ?
YEAH.
DON'T SAY THAT, THOUGH, OKAY ? JUST KEEP TALK-ING. KEEP PRETENDING YOU'RE YOU.
I DON'T KNOW HOW LONG WE'RE GOING TO BE ABLE TO KEEP THIS UP.

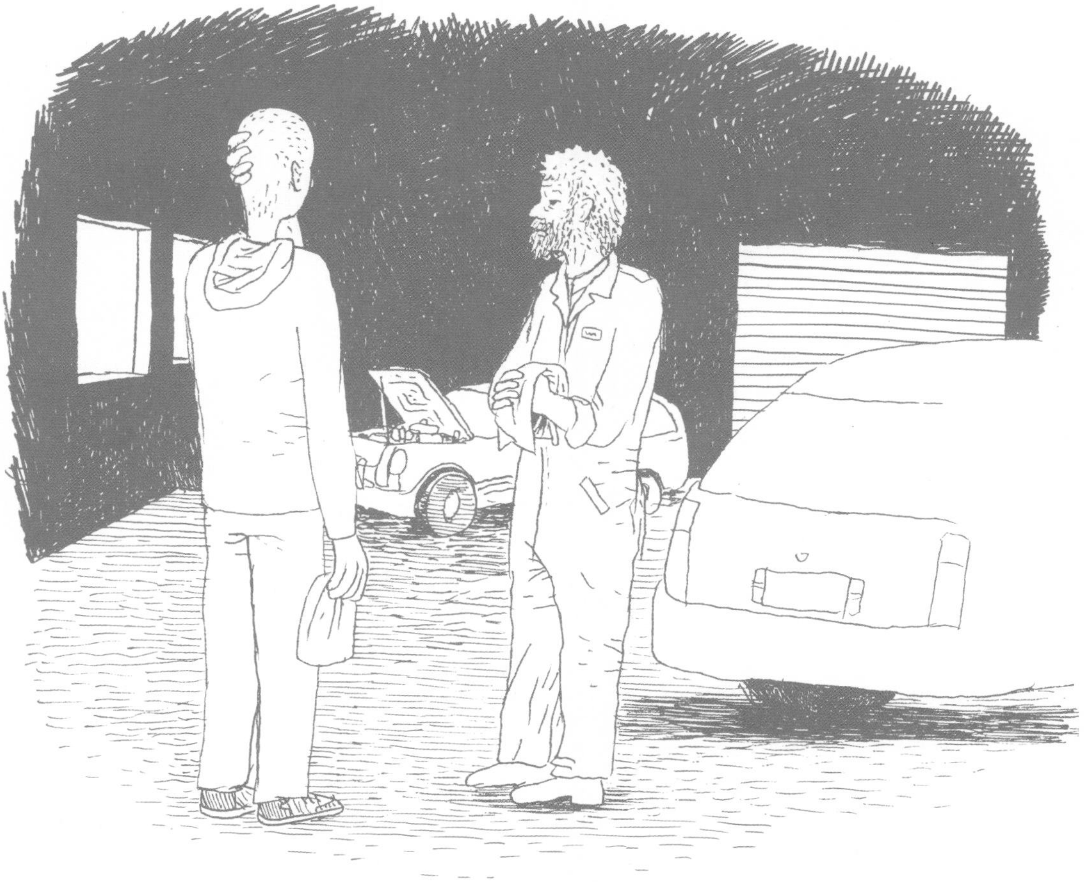

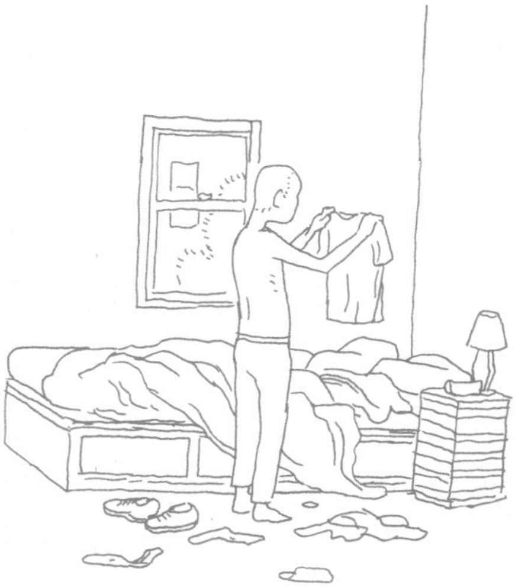

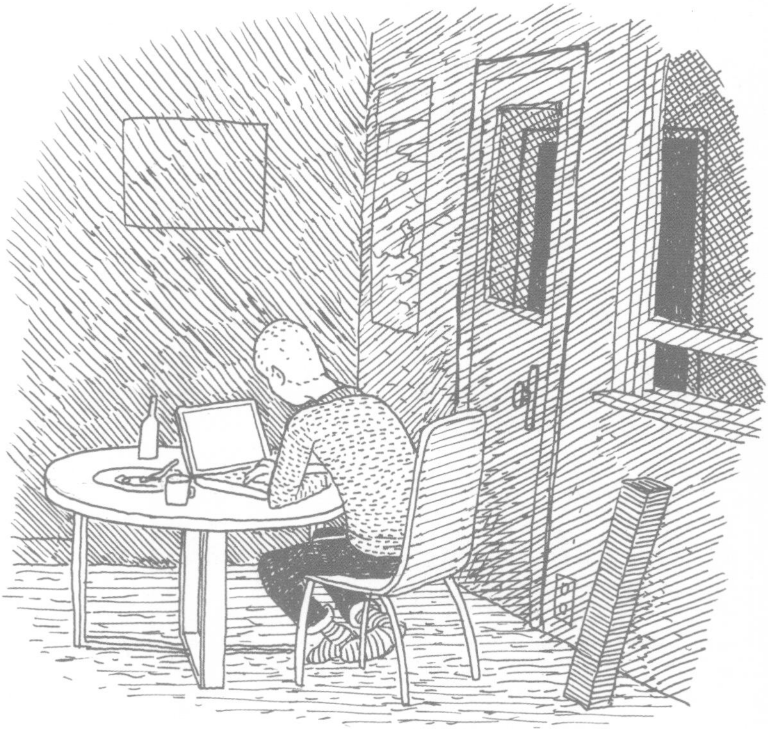

HOW TO DESPAIR:

THROW UP HANDS
TEAR HAIR
CRY
STARE BLANKLY UNMOVING FOR A LONG TIME
THROW SELF IN RIVER
RIDE BICYCLE AROUND AIMLESSLY
GO ABOUT BUSINESS AS NORMAL

HOW IS THIS SUPPOSED TO WORK?
IS THIS FREE-FALL OR JUST ME
SITTING ON THE PIER STARING OUT INTO
THE DARK WATER AND THE NIGHT?

MY MIND IS EMPTY
AND FILLED WITH LONGING.

MY HEART IS EMPTY
AND FILLED WITH LONGING.

MY MIND IS EMPTY

THE WATER IS DARK

BEEN feeling shitty and lethargic all day, not sure at all why. putting off going through/editing down THE END #2. finally got to it a couple of hours ago. culled it down to 29-ish pages plus a couple of ideas to fill it out.

and then I am cried for an hour. just cried and cried. now I'm exhausted again. It made me... I don't know. I still don't know what to do with this. THE END #2. I don't know if I can WORK ON IT. I don't know what it means, this bubbling up of emotion that I'd sort of thought I'd grown away from or detached from or something. I thought I was in the future. But I'm still in the present. In the present in the past in the present. Just imagining, FEELING, REMEMBERING cheryl's presence in the house. The feeling of her being nearby. of knowing she was there. what my life felt like. It's been almost two years. 21 months this month. I can remember her. The feeling of her presence in my life, in this house. I really do miss it. I'm so so sorry for all of this. for her absence. for this growing distance.

And still I don't know what it means. I don't know what I should do.

MY DEAR CHERYL,

    I STILL DON'T WANT TO GET USED TO THIS
LIFE I HAVE WITHOUT YOU.
BUT IT'S HAPPENING ANYWAY.
IF I CAN'T HAVE YOU, I WANT AT LEAST
MY SORROW. MY SORROW IS MY ONLY COMFORT

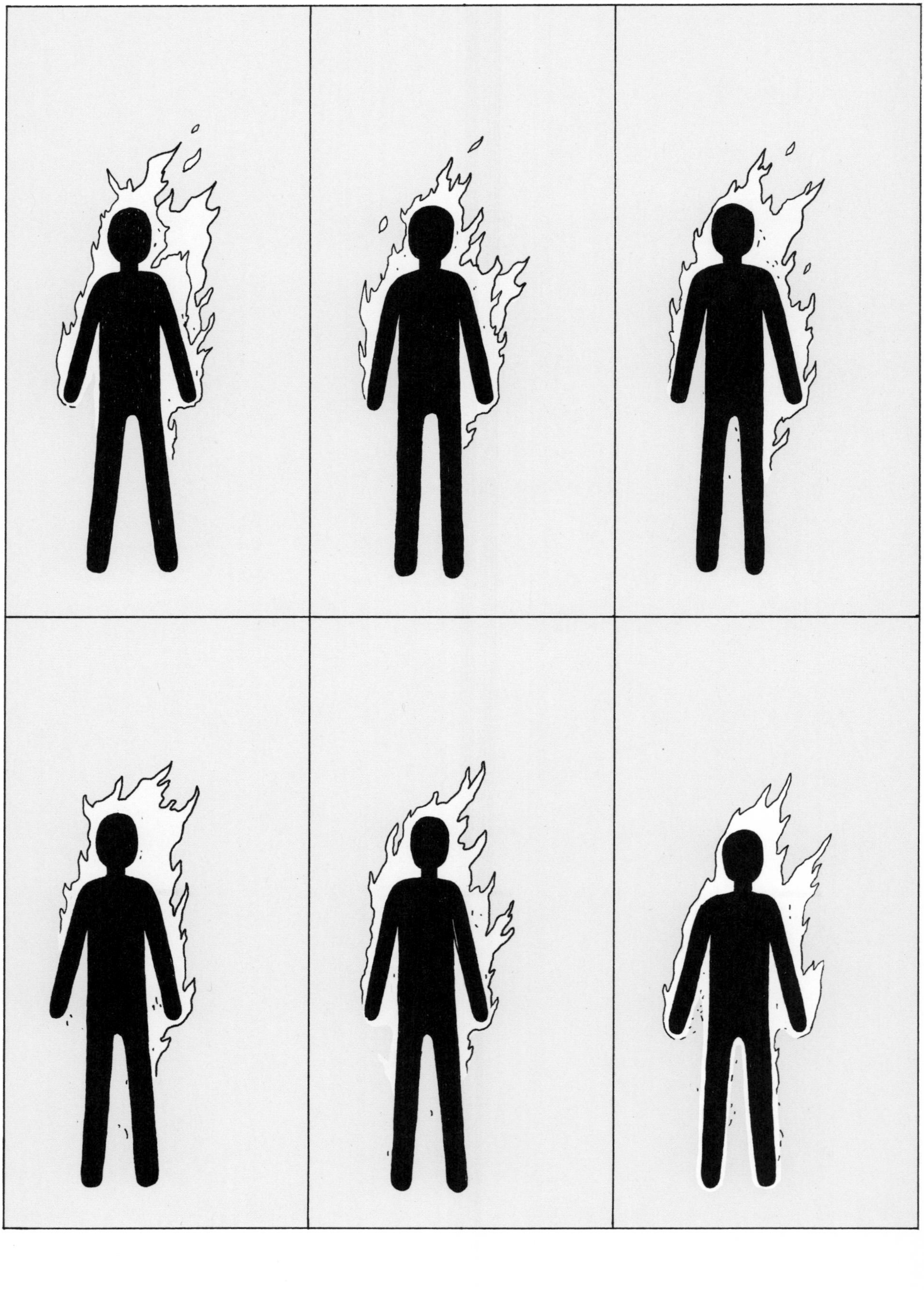

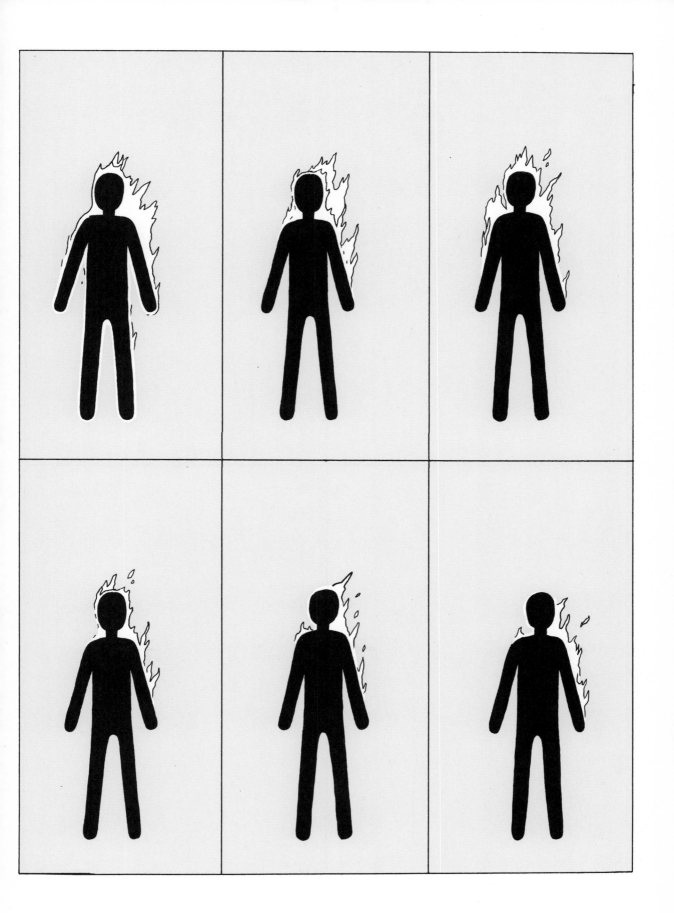

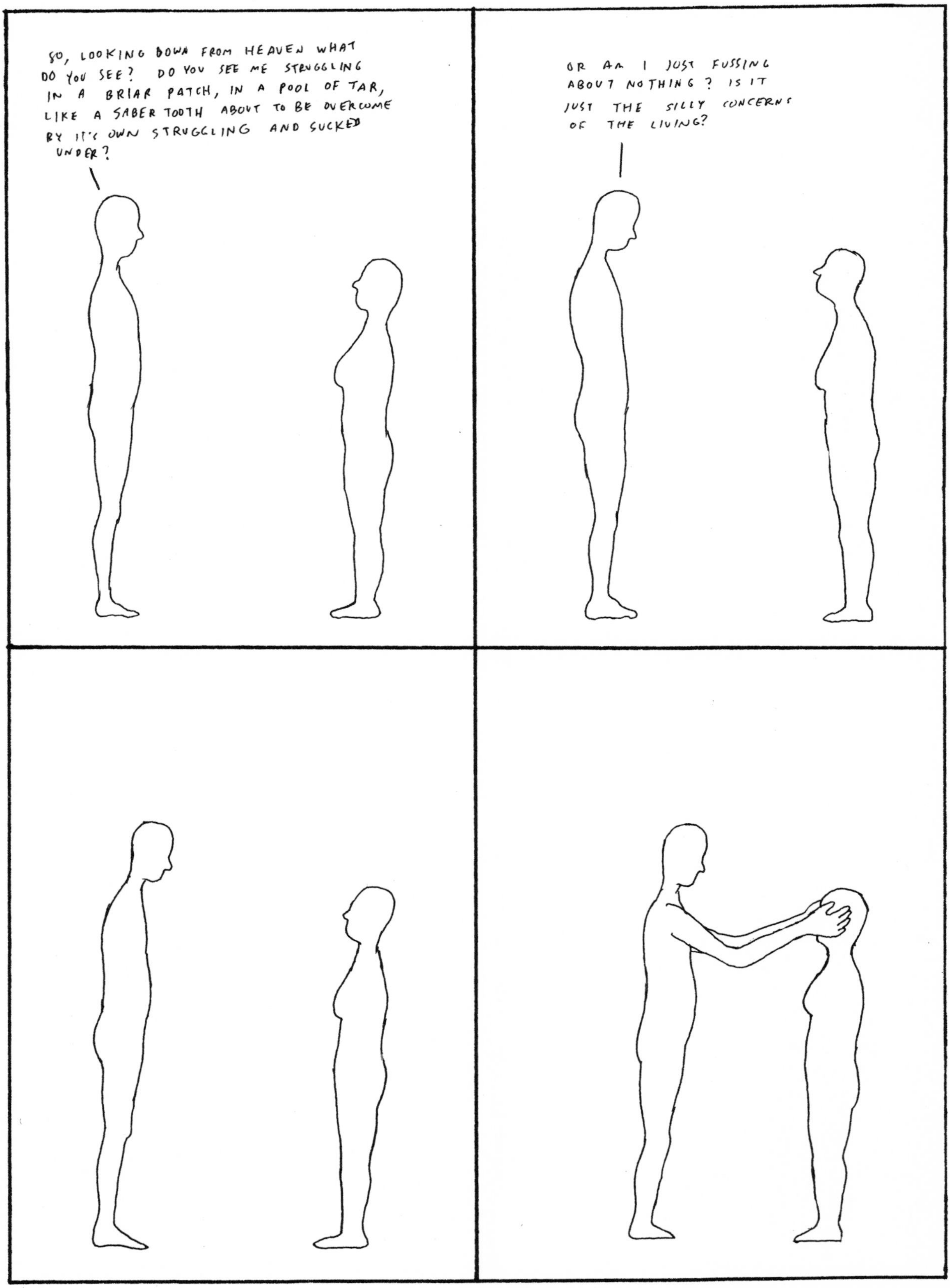
SO, LOOKING DOWN FROM HEAVEN WHAT DO YOU SEE? DO YOU SEE ME STRUGGLING IN A BRIAR PATCH, IN A POOL OF TAR, LIKE A SABER TOOTH ABOUT TO BE OVERCOME BY IT'S OWN STRUGGLING AND SUCKED UNDER?
OR AM I JUST FUSSING ABOUT NOTHING? IS IT JUST THE SILLY CONCERNS OF THE LIVING?

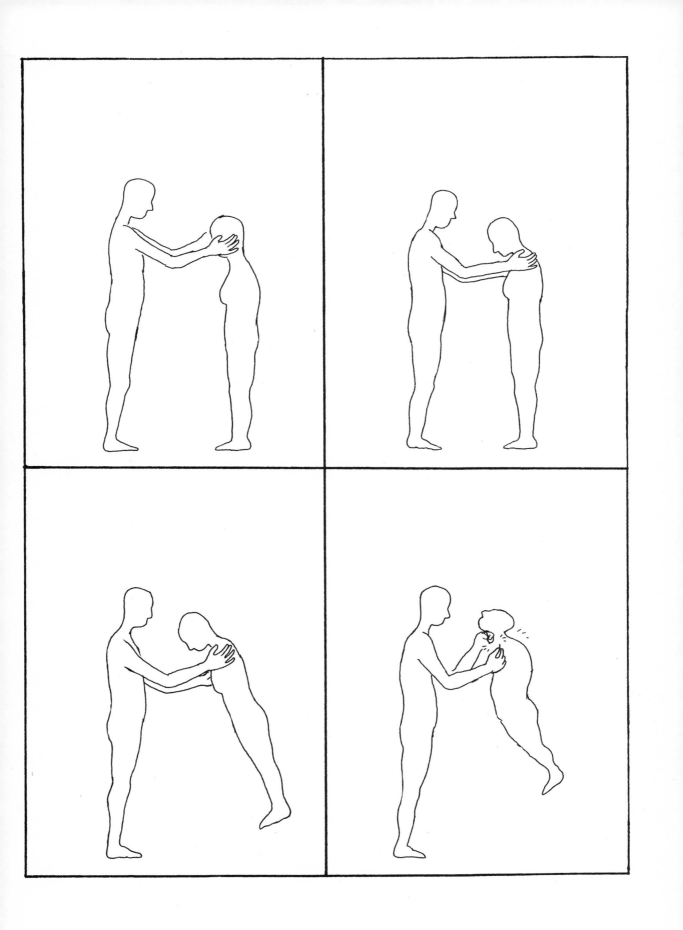

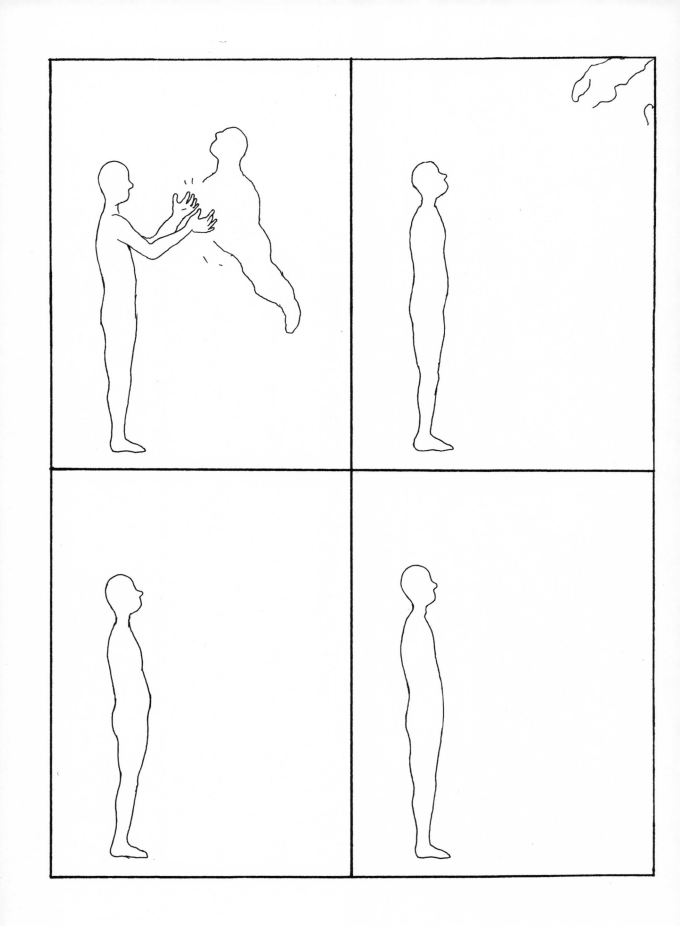

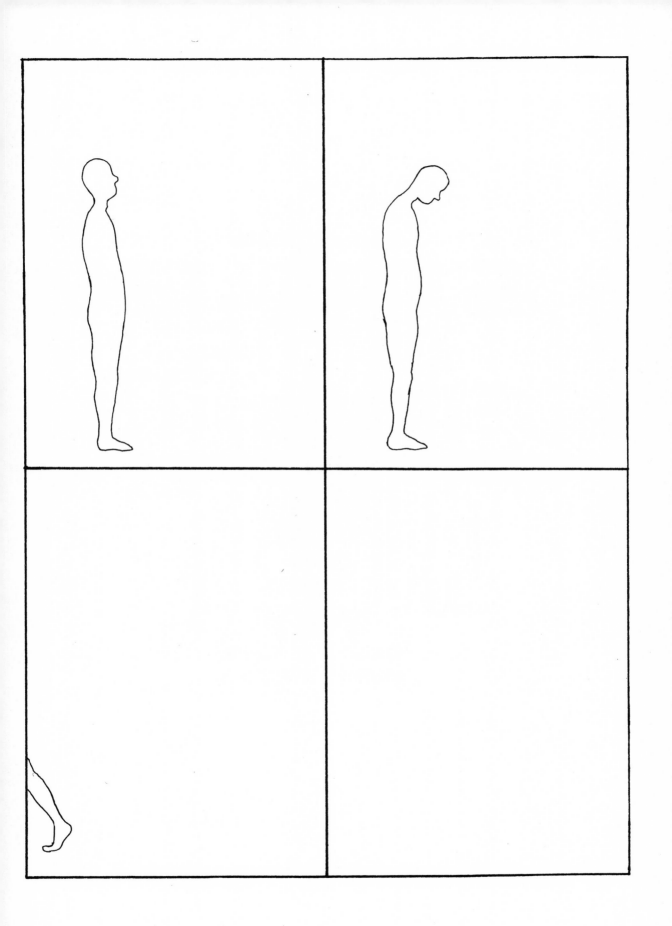

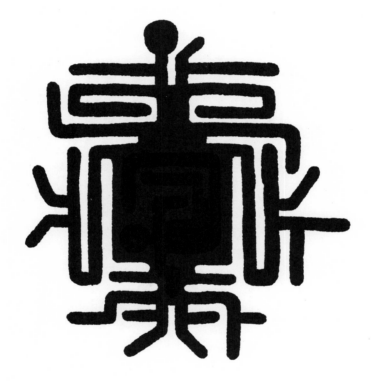

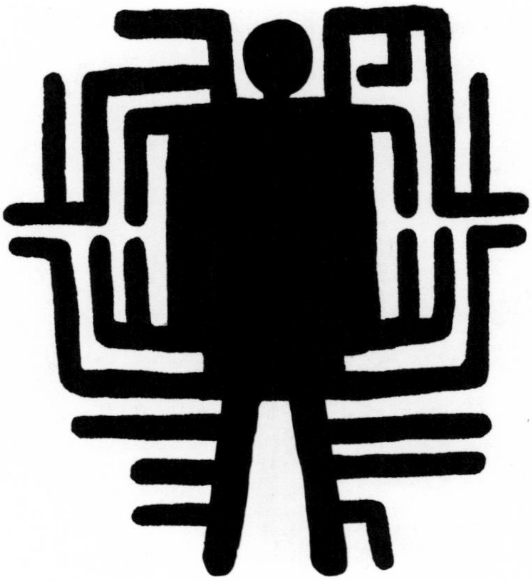

SOMETIMES
IT'S LIKE.

WELL, I AM OUT
OF METAPHORS FOR
UNDERSTANDING MY
PREDICAMENT.

I WILL JUST SIT HERE
NOW. I WILL WAIT UNTIL
SOMETHING HAPPENS.

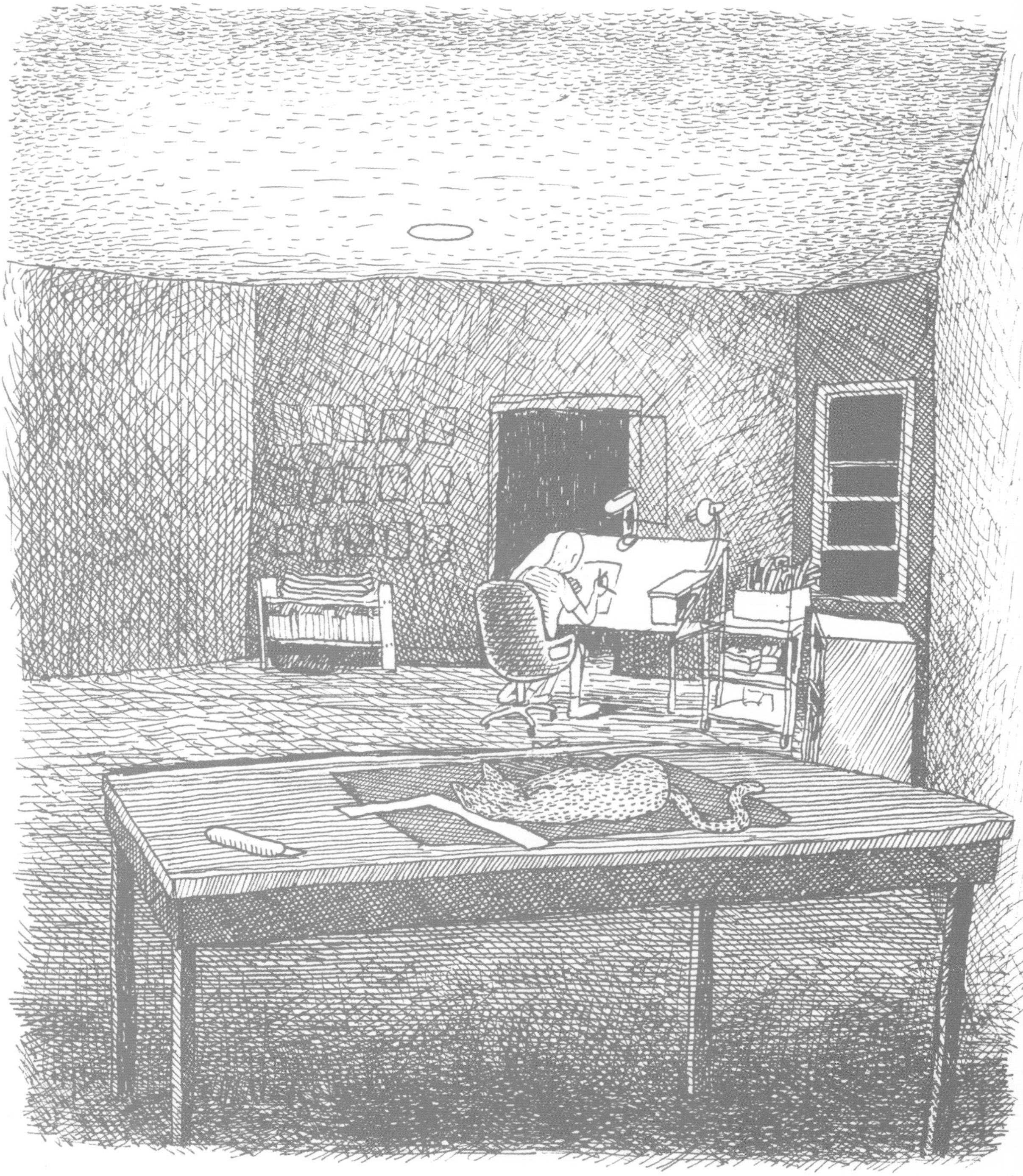

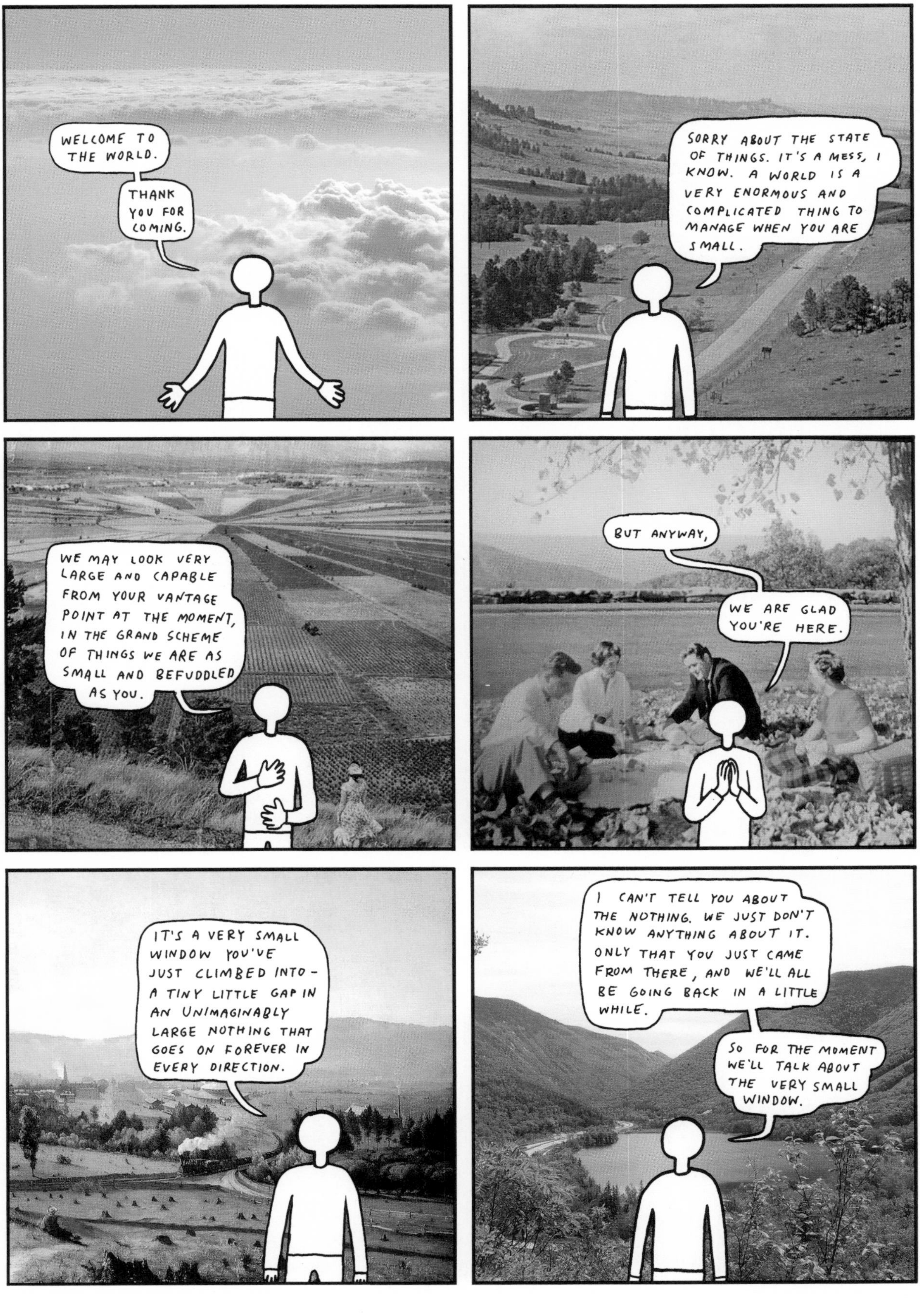
WELCOME TO THE WORLD.
THANK YOU FOR COMING.
SORRY ABOUT THE STATE OF THINGS. IT'S A MESS, I KNOW. A WORLD IS A VERY ENORMOUS AND COMPLICATED THING TO MANAGE WHEN YOU ARE SMALL.
WE MAY LOOK VERY LARGE AND CAPABLE FROM YOUR VANTAGE POINT AT THE MOMENT, IN THE GRAND SCHEME OF THINGS WE ARE AS SMALL AND BEFUDDLED AS YOU.
BUT ANYWAY,
WE ARE GLAD YOU'RE HERE.
IT'S A VERY SMALL WINDOW YOU'VE JUST CLIMBED INTO - A TINY LITTLE GAP IN AN UNIMAGINABLY LARGE NOTHING THAT GOES ON FOREVER IN EVERY DIRECTION.
I CAN'T TELL YOU ABOUT THE NOTHING. WE JUST DON'T KNOW ANYTHING ABOUT IT. ONLY THAT YOU JUST CAME FROM THERE, AND WE'LL ALL BE GOING BACK IN A LITTLE WHILE.
SO FOR THE MOMENT WE'LL TALK ABOUT THE VERY SMALL WINDOW.

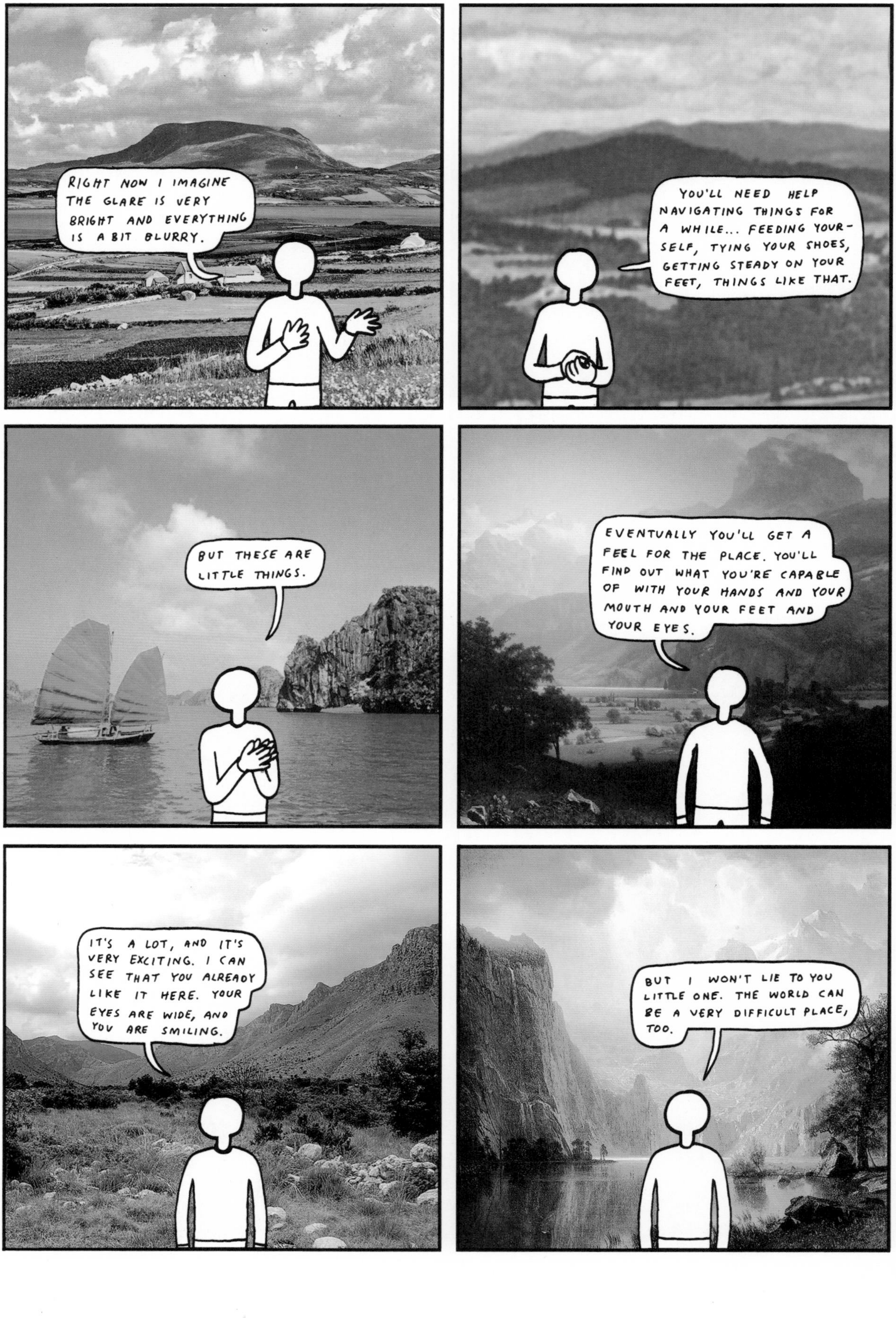
RIGHT NOW I IMAGINE THE GLARE IS VERY BRIGHT AND EVERYTHING IS A BIT BLURRY.
YOU'LL NEED HELP NAVIGATING THINGS FOR A WHILE... FEEDING YOUR-SELF, TYING YOUR SHOES, GETTING STEADY ON YOUR FEET, THINGS LIKE THAT.
BUT THESE ARE LITTLE THINGS.
EVENTUALLY YOU'LL GET A FEEL FOR THE PLACE. YOU'LL FIND OUT WHAT YOU'RE CAPABLE OF WITH YOUR HANDS AND YOUR MOUTH AND YOUR FEET AND YOUR EYES.
IT'S A LOT, AND IT'S VERY EXCITING. I CAN SEE THAT YOU ALREADY LIKE IT HERE. YOUR EYES ARE WIDE, AND YOU ARE SMILING.
BUT I WON'T LIE TO YOU LITTLE ONE. THE WORLD CAN BE A VERY DIFFICULT PLACE, TOO.

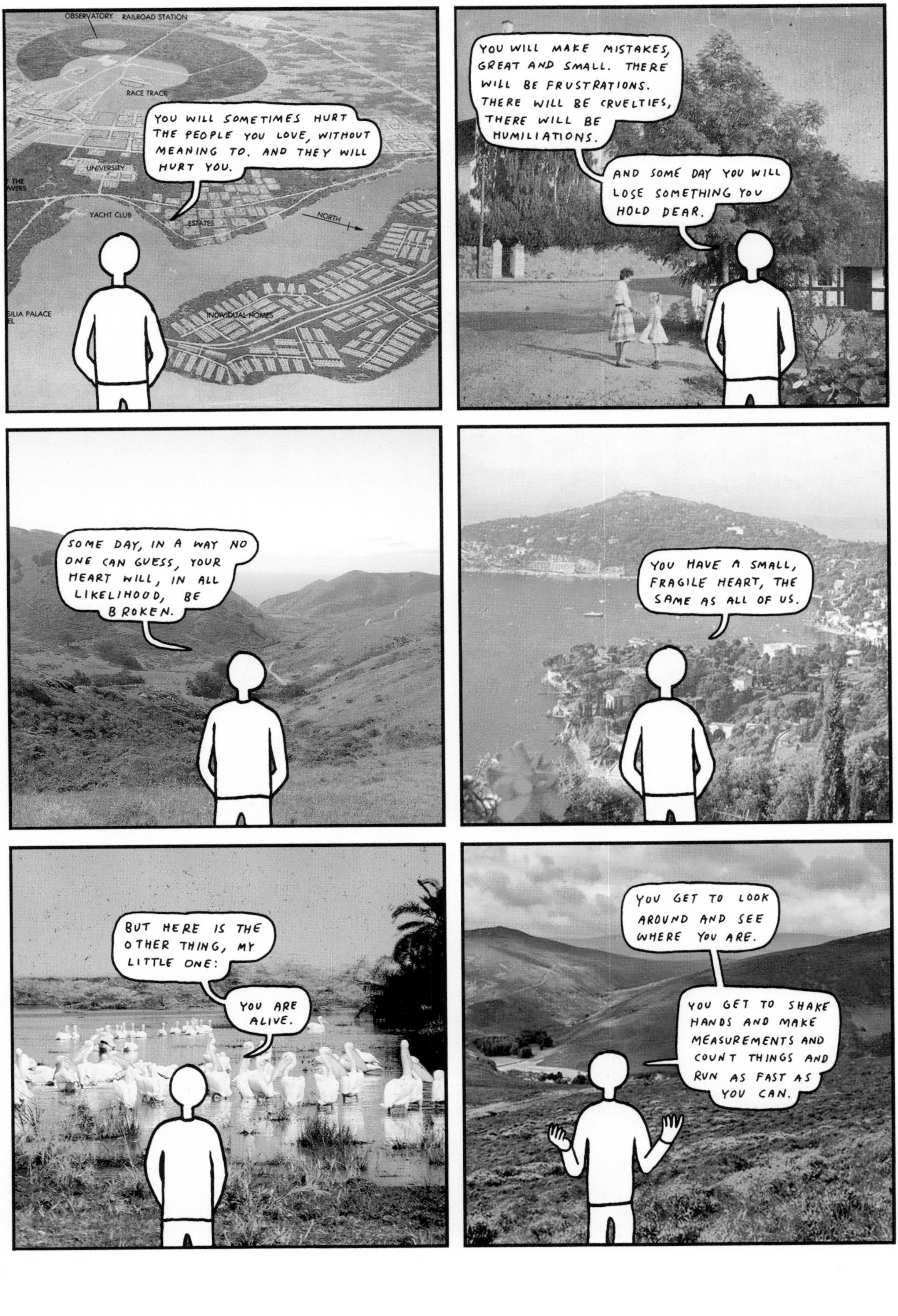
OBSERVATORY
RAILROAD STATION
RACE TRACK
UNIVERSITY
YACHT CLUB
ESTATES
NORTH
INDIVIDUAL HOMES
YOU WILL SOMETIMES HURT THE PEOPLE YOU LOVE, WITHOUT MEANING TO. AND THEY WILL HURT YOU.
YOU WILL MAKE MISTAKES, GREAT AND SMALL. THERE WILL BE FRUSTRATIONS. THERE WILL BE CRUELTIES, THERE WILL BE HUMILIATIONS.
AND SOME DAY YOU WILL LOSE SOMETHING YOU HOLD DEAR.
SOME DAY, IN A WAY NO ONE CAN GUESS, YOUR HEART WILL, IN ALL LIKELIHOOD, BE BROKEN.
YOU HAVE A SMALL, FRAGILE HEART, THE SAME AS ALL OF US.
BUT HERE IS THE OTHER THING, MY LITTLE ONE:
YOU ARE ALIVE.
YOU GET TO LOOK AROUND AND SEE WHERE YOU ARE.
YOU GET TO SHAKE HANDS AND MAKE MEASUREMENTS AND COUNT THINGS AND RUN AS FAST AS YOU CAN.

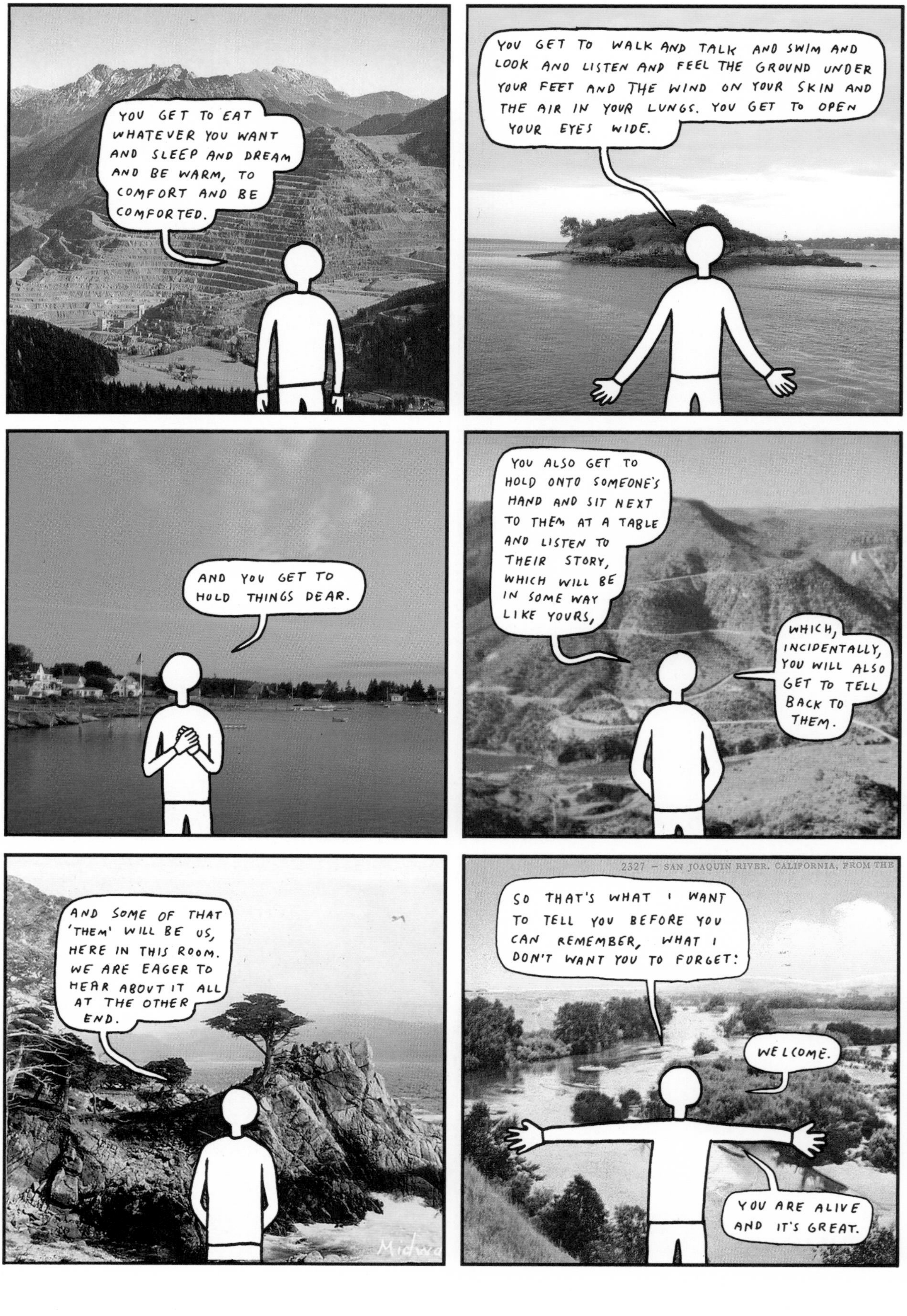
YOU GET TO EAT WHATEVER YOU WANT AND SLEEP AND DREAM AND BE WARM, TO COMFORT AND BE COMFORTED.
YOU GET TO WALK AND TALK AND SWIM AND LOOK AND LISTEN AND FEEL THE GROUND UNDER YOUR FEET AND THE WIND ON YOUR SKIN AND THE AIR IN YOUR LUNGS. YOU GET TO OPEN YOUR EYES WIDE.
AND YOU GET TO HOLD THINGS DEAR.
YOU ALSO GET TO HOLD ONTO SOMEONE'S HAND AND SIT NEXT TO THEM AT A TABLE AND LISTEN TO THEIR STORY, WHICH WILL BE IN SOME WAY LIKE YOURS,
WHICH, INCIDENTALLY, YOU WILL ALSO GET TO TELL BACK TO THEM.
AND SOME OF THAT 'THEM' WILL BE US, HERE IN THIS ROOM. WE ARE EAGER TO HEAR ABOUT IT ALL AT THE OTHER END.
Midwa
2327 – SAN JOAQUIN RIVER, CALIFORNIA, FROM THE
SO THAT'S WHAT I WANT TO TELL YOU BEFORE YOU CAN REMEMBER, WHAT I DON'T WANT YOU TO FORGET:
WELCOME.
YOU ARE ALIVE AND IT'S GREAT.

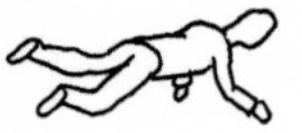

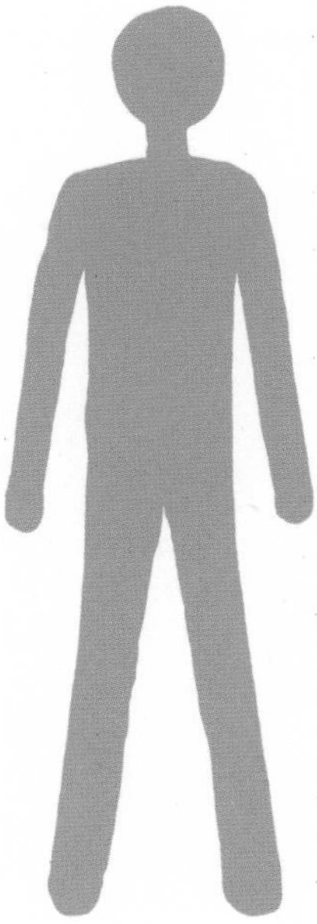

LOOK AT THE SKY
IT'S BLUE. A FEW CLOUDS.
THAT IS THE SKY IN YOUR OLD LIFE

THOSE CARS OUTSIDE,
GOING WHEREVER THEY'RE GOING

THOSE ARE THE CARS IN YOUR OLD LIFE.

THE AIR YOU'RE BREATHING
IS THE AIR OF YOUR OLD LIFE

IT SMELLS LIKE THE SWEATERS SHE WORE USED TO SMELL
BUT THEY WON'T SMELL LIKE THAT ANYMORE
THEY'LL JUST BE SWEATERS

AND YOU CAN'T HOLD THAT AIR IN ANYMORE
THAT AIR, THAT SMELL, YOUR BREATH.

THAT KID IN THE YELLOW AND BLACK SHIRT
RUNNING FASTER THAN HIS GRANDFATHER
AND THE MAILWOMAN AND THE GIRL ON THE BIKE
THEY ARE MOVING THROUGH THE AIR, UNDER THE SKY
ACROSS THE SURFACE OF THE EARTH IN YOUR OLD LIFE

WATCH THAT OLD MAN WALKING
THE SUN IS OUT
IT'S A BEAUTIFUL DAY
THE LEAVES AND GRASS ARE GREEN
THE AIR IS COOL
HE'S WALKING SLOWLY
BUT HE'S GOING TO GET WHERE HE'S GOING.

AND WHEN HE GETS THERE

IN A WEEK OR A DAY OR A YEAR

HE'LL BE WHEREVER HE IS

AND YOU'LL BE IN YOUR NEW LIFE

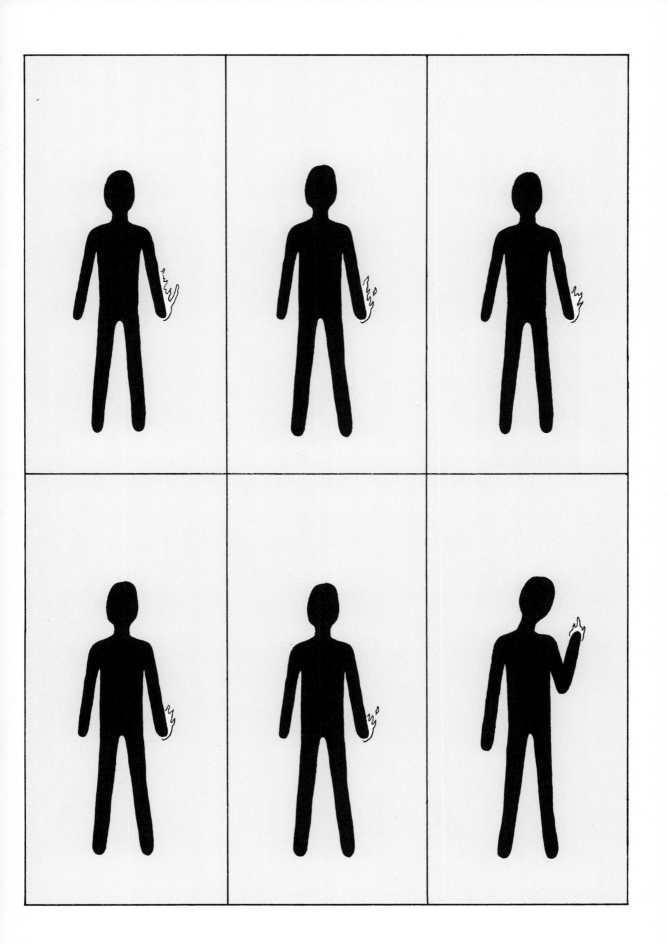

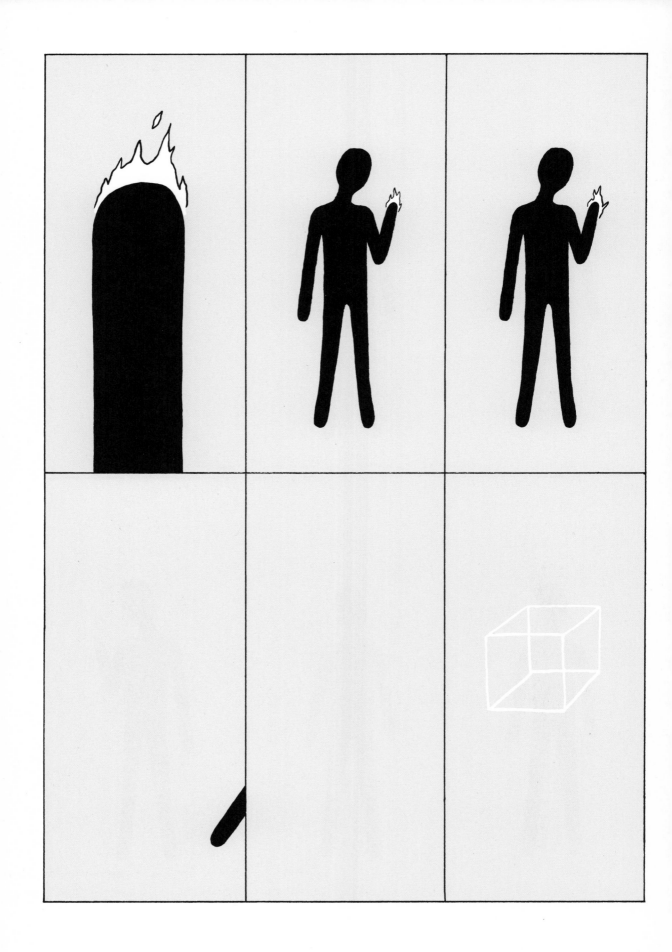

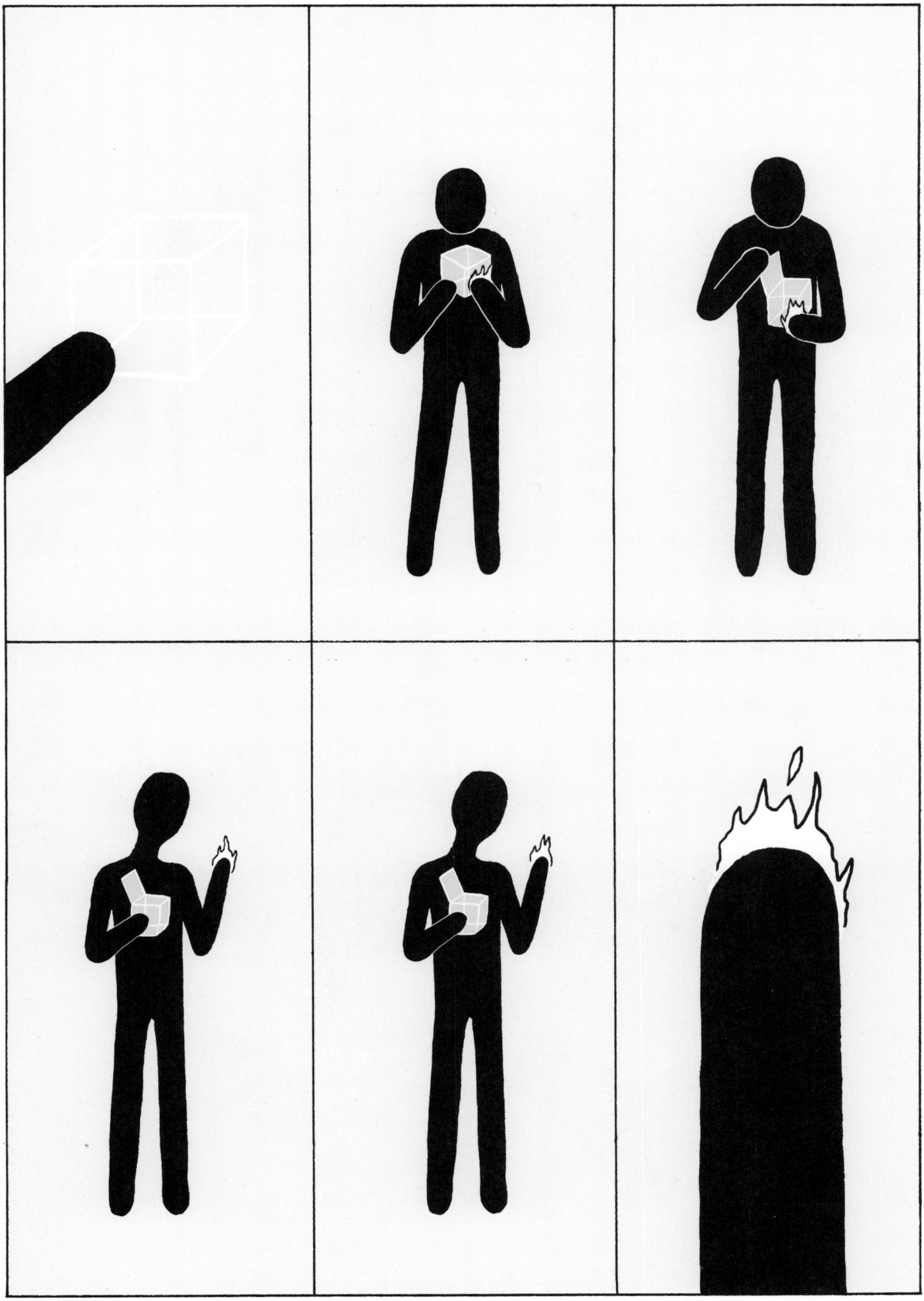

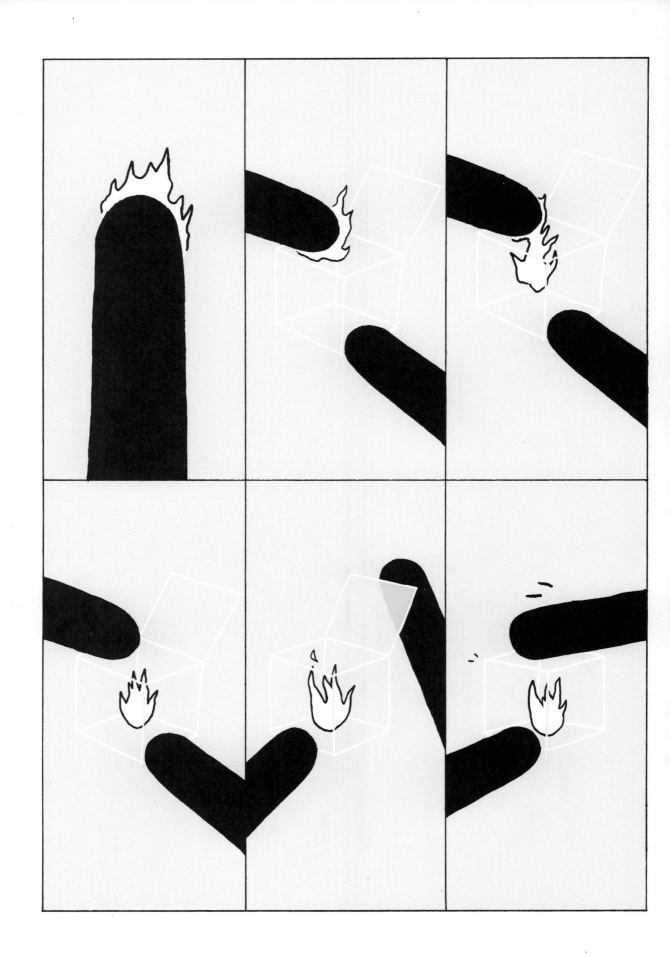

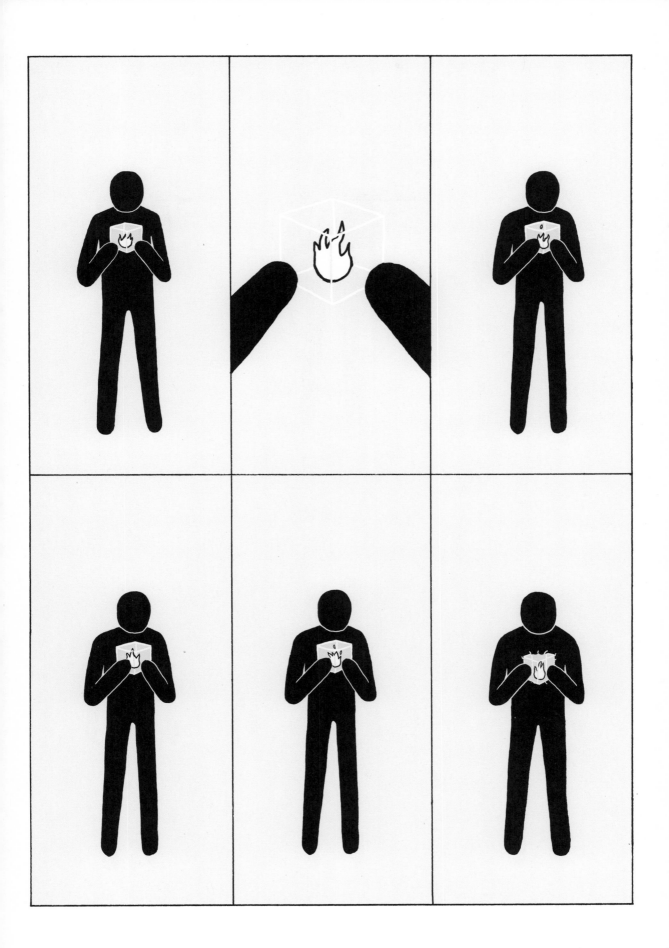

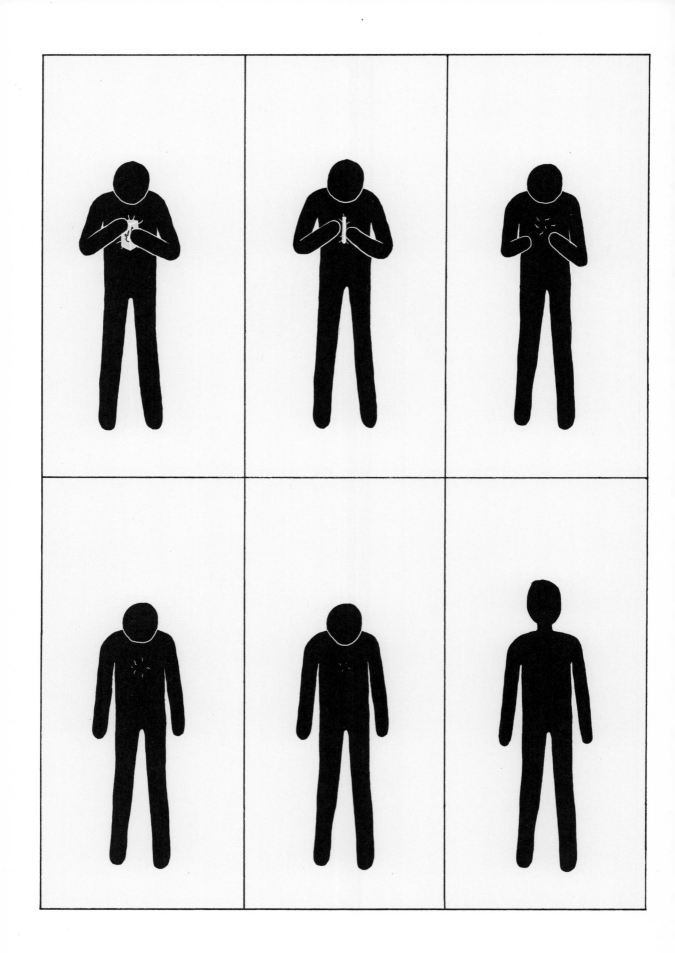

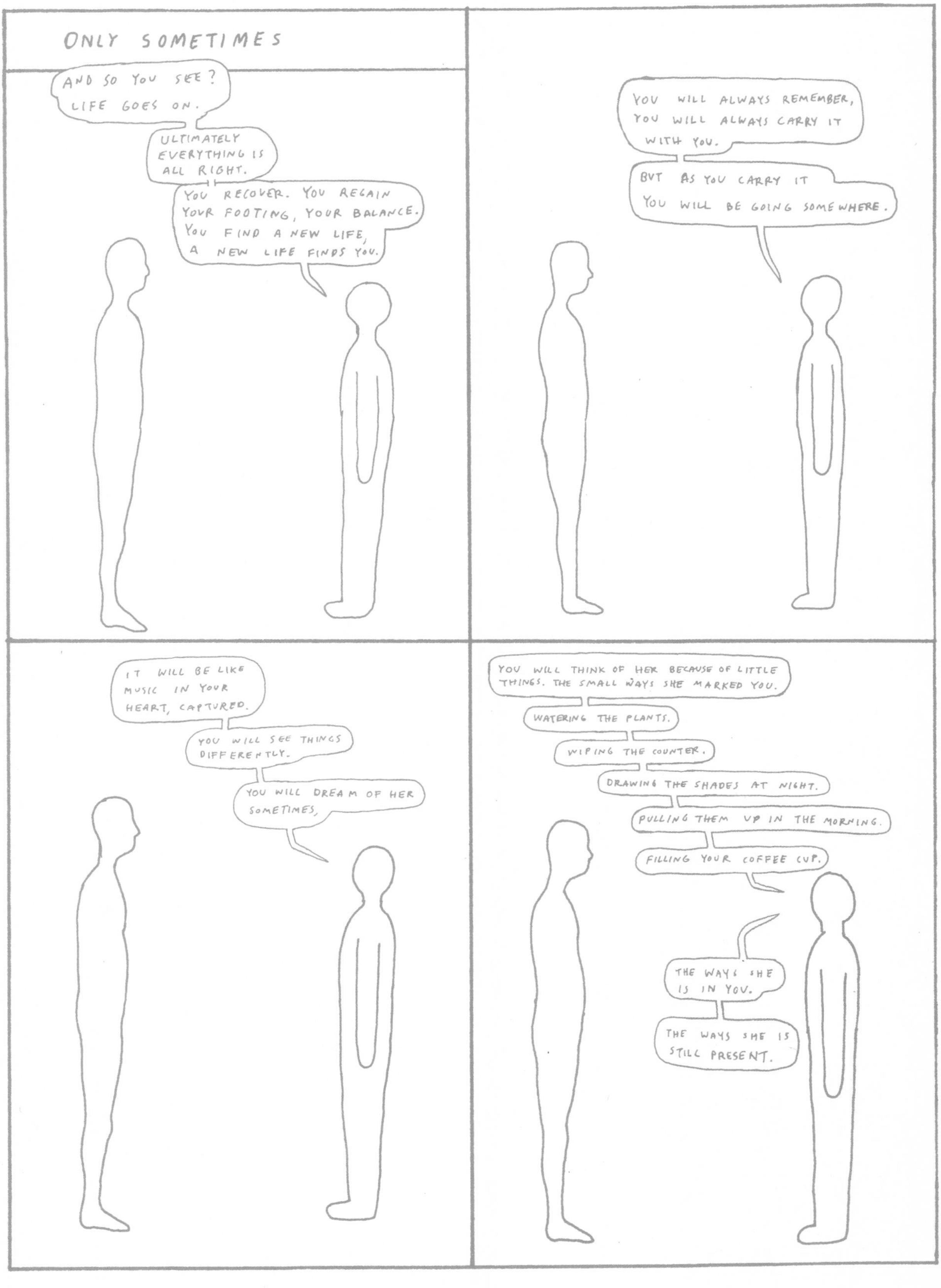

ONLY SOMETIMES
AND SO YOU SEE? LIFE GOES ON.
ULTIMATELY EVERYTHING IS ALL RIGHT.
YOU RECOVER. YOU REGAIN YOUR FOOTING, YOUR BALANCE. YOU FIND A NEW LIFE, A NEW LIFE FINDS YOU.
YOU WILL ALWAYS REMEMBER, YOU WILL ALWAYS CARRY IT WITH YOU.
BUT AS YOU CARRY IT YOU WILL BE GOING SOMEWHERE.
IT WILL BE LIKE MUSIC IN YOUR HEART, CAPTURED.
YOU WILL SEE THINGS DIFFERENTLY.
YOU WILL DREAM OF HER SOMETIMES,
YOU WILL THINK OF HER BECAUSE OF LITTLE THINGS. THE SMALL WAYS SHE MARKED YOU.
WATERING THE PLANTS.
WIPING THE COUNTER.
DRAWING THE SHADES AT NIGHT.
PULLING THEM UP IN THE MORNING.
FILLING YOUR COFFEE CUP.
THE WAYS SHE IS IN YOU.
THE WAYS SHE IS STILL PRESENT.

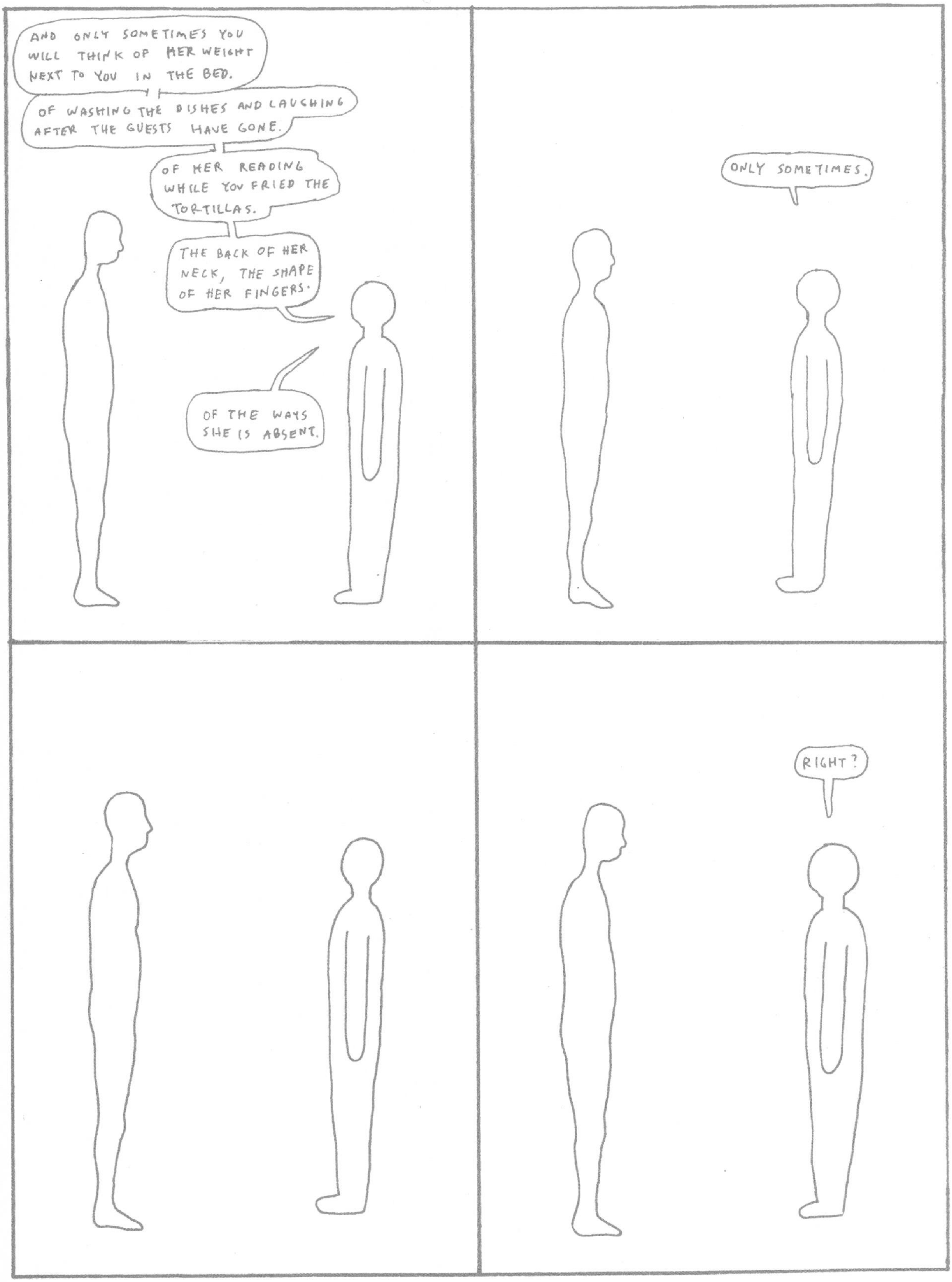
AND ONLY SOMETIMES YOU WILL THINK OF HER WEIGHT NEXT TO YOU IN THE BED.
OF WASHING THE DISHES AND LAUGHING AFTER THE GUESTS HAVE GONE.
OF HER READING WHILE YOU FRIED THE TORTILLAS.
THE BACK OF HER NECK, THE SHAPE OF HER FINGERS.
OF THE WAYS SHE IS ABSENT.
ONLY SOMETIMES.
RIGHT?

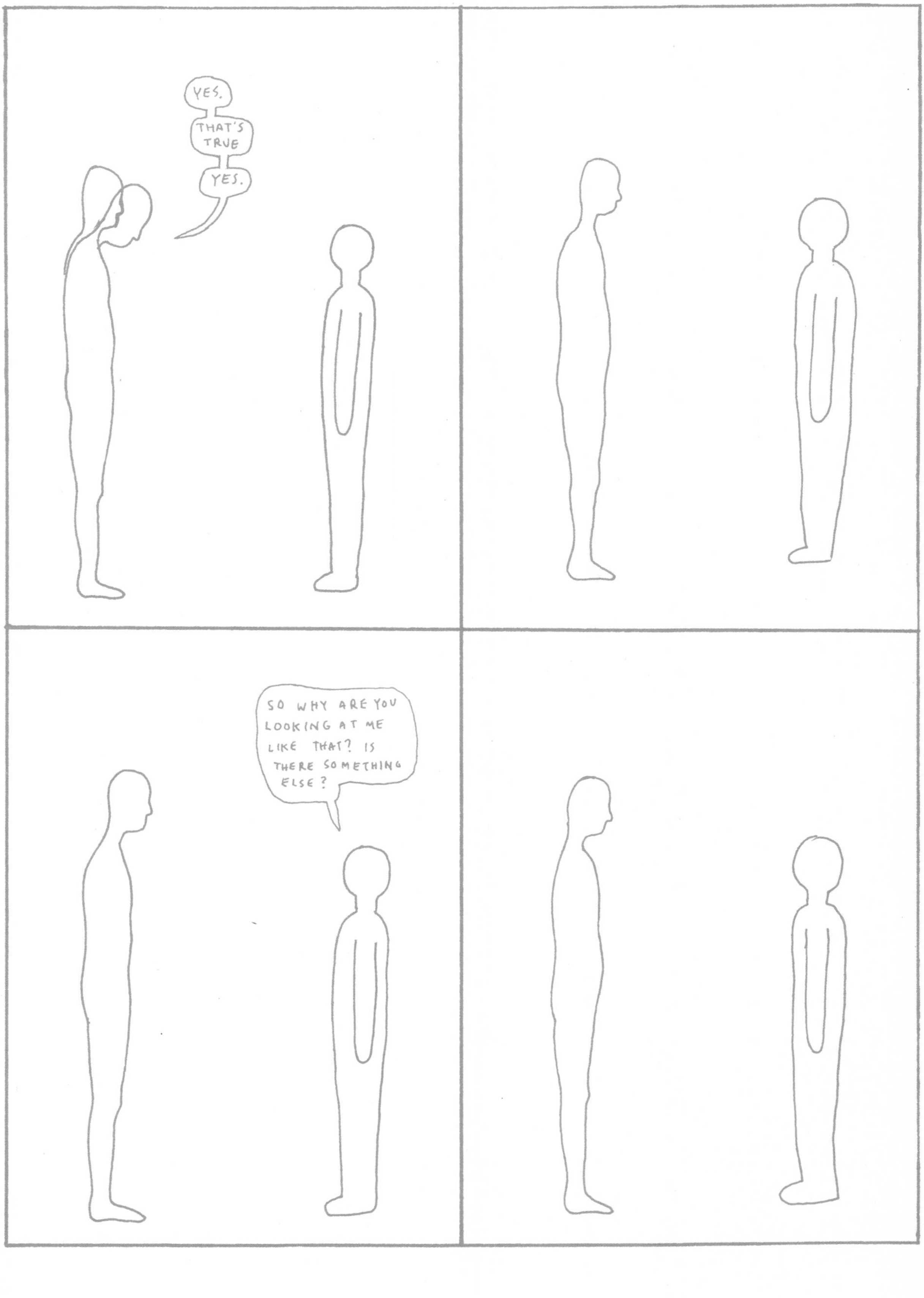
YES.
THAT'S TRUE
YES.
SO WHY ARE YOU LOOKING AT ME LIKE THAT? IS THERE SOMETHING ELSE?

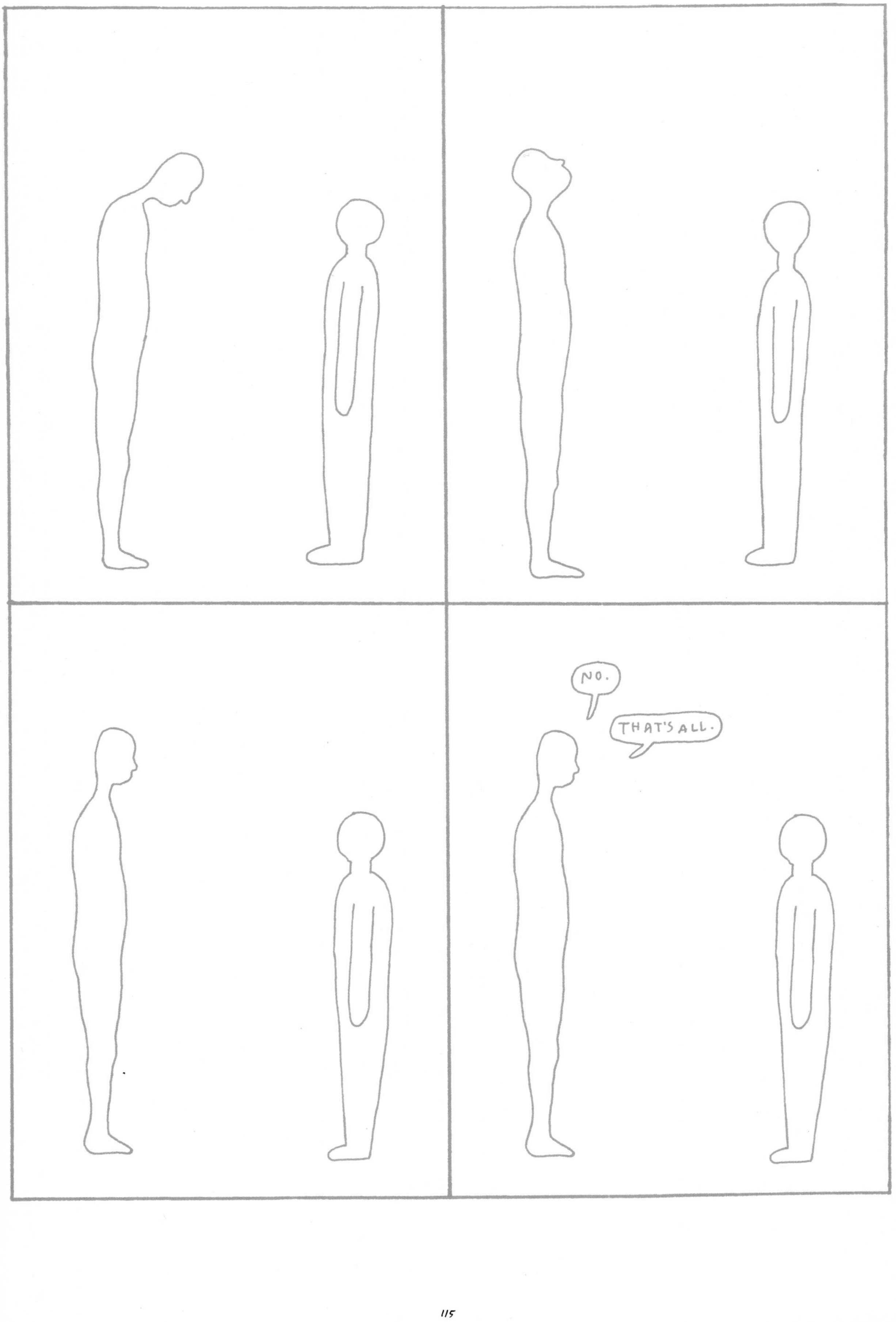
NO.
THAT'S ALL.

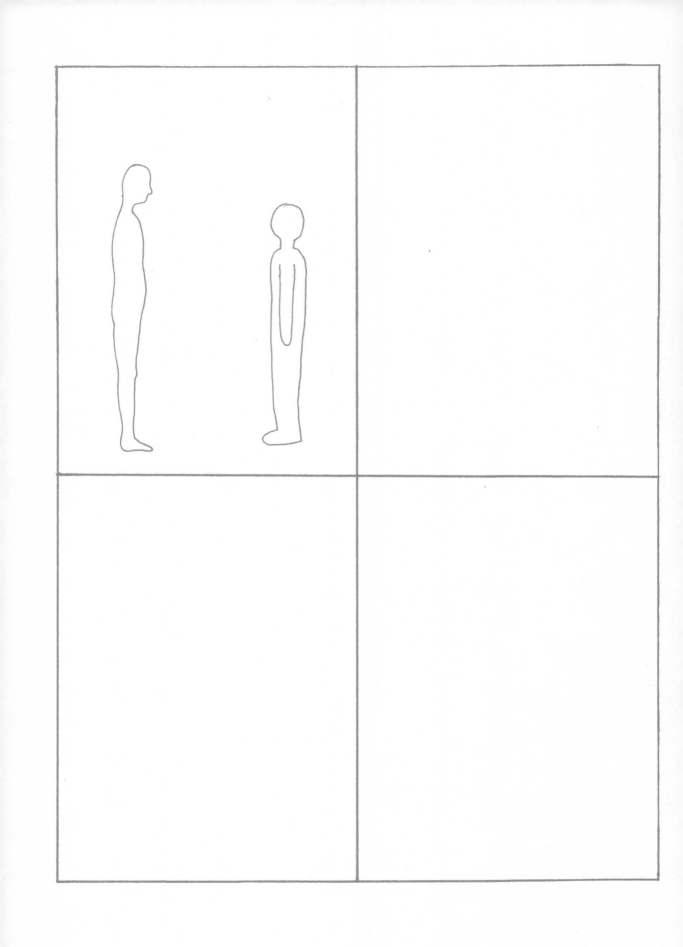

AFTERWORD

I. What This Book Is

Every book has two stories. There is, on the one hand, the story the book tells (if it's that sort of book), and there is the story of its coming to be. They illuminate one another and hold each other up. They revolve about one another like two planetesimals in space. Sometimes, depending on your point of view – say from the surface of one or the other of the two bodies, one of the stories might become eclipsed by its twin and be lost from view. But with time vantage points change.

As you'll have gathered if you have read to this point, this book concerns a death and its aftermath. In late 2004 my then-fiancée, Cheryl Weaver, began experiencing a constellation of apparently unrelated, small maladies. We brushed them off for a while, in part because we didn't have health insurance and couldn't afford unnecessary doctor's visits. When the symptoms got worse, she did finally go, under strict instructions from a worried acupuncturist, and she was diagnosed with Hodgkins Lymphoma. That was in March of 2005. Despite an initially promising prognosis, treatment didn't seem to help. On November 13th the disease killed her. Soon after that my sketchbooks began filling up with writing and drawing and comics about her loss. This book is drawn from a selection of that accumulated material.

But what you are holding is not its original arrangement. You are reading the third version of this book, depending on how you count. The first version came out in 2007 and was comprised of what is roughly the initial third of the present volume. Titled *The End #1*, it was released as a large-format, 32-page comic as part of Fantagraphics Books' Ignatz series. I hadn't actually meant to publish a book about my experience of Cheryl's death, but as it happened I was under contract. I had agreed to do a book for the Ignatz line a few years before, long before Cheryl had become ill.

I had even chosen a title – *The End* – figuring I had a few years to finish other projects and figure out what it would be about. But time always passes more quickly than one expects. Events transpire. The due date for my first issue was approaching and I was still very much occupied with those other projects. I could have begged off, certainly. And yet... there were those rapidly filling sketchbooks and the little bits and pieces about Cheryl's loss. Some of them seemed like they might be worth something to some reader who wasn't me, and so I began putting them together and cleaning them up, sanding off some of the rougher edges, finishing some of the half-thoughts, seeing what was there. And lo, a 32-page comic emerged, almost out of empty space.

When it came time to do a second issue, a year or so had suddenly passed again. I'd also published another book, *Don't Go Where I Can't Follow* (Drawn & Quarterly), intended as a sort of memorial to Cheryl that was more about our life together and the time leading up to her death. And I found my feelings about both books had shifted in the intervening time in a few ways. For one, I was beginning to feel less comfortable with inhabiting the material's mental and emotional space, or with having my fraught recent past on display for the world to see, to judge, and to pity. I'd just begun a new relationship as well, and the work seemed to create complexities as it sought stable footing. And then *Don't Go* began getting some unexpected press, and I began to wonder if the subject may be in danger of starting to define my work as an artist and author just as I was beginning to shape a career with other sorts of stories in mind. And so I decided to hold off. That first volume with its peculiar appellation of "#1" was left mutely unaccompanied on readers' bookshelves, its story unfinished.

And then more time passed. By 2012 I had begun to feel differently again. My life had changed further – the relationship had ended, I had moved to a new city, and I had finally published one of those other projects I'd been at work on the whole time, and it seemed to be successfully finding a new, respectable audience. And so an author's inherent impulse to put an unfinished story out of its misery finally began to outweigh the promised, but diminished, emotional toll that revisiting Cheryl's death was likely to take. And so I descended back into the material and in 2013 released the un-numbered *The End*, an eighty-page hardcover, combining most of the original material with a second half, what would have been *The End #2*, had it ever been completed, finishing the story. I thought. If the first comic had begun the story of grief and loss, this second, complete volume was meant to bring it to a close. To bring readers full circle, to resolution.

That previous version didn't cry out to me for explanation. I was content to let the material speak for itself, to connect with readers or not, on its own terms. It had its own life out in the world for the next few years, finally going out of print around 2017 or 18. This third volume does feel to me like it demands some explication. Time has again passed, as it seems stubbornly determined to do, and my view of the material from those sketchbooks and the period they describe, has continued to change. The prospect of a reprint sparked the idea of a new edition. In real life, of course, stories don't ever really end. We attach endings in the telling because we have lives to live and boundaries are a comfort and convenience to our meaning-making minds. Telling a story is therefore as much about what you leave out as it is what you put in. Whatever you put in focus, something else is left blurred or out of frame. What is your point of view? What is eclipsed by what? How far back do you travel to make a start, and how far forward to make an end?

The experience of grief does not trace a simple narrative arc. It's messy. I used to joke to prospective readers that there ought to be a warning label on the front of the book, declaring in bright orange letters: *VERY SAD*. Nevertheless as heavy as the subject matter was, the original edition always felt a little clean to me, a little bit of a simplification. It included the pieces – and therefore the subjects – that I could figure out how to finish.

For the present volume I have added some rougher punctuations, a few extra narrative eddies in the stream, a few misshapen rocks to break the current, a few of the unfinished thoughts that so powerfully characterized my experience of that period. With the distance of accumulated time the events may well get a little harder to see clearly, but from further away one's view is widened as well. And experience is, hopefully, a teacher.

One other thing that was left out of the two earlier books about Cheryl's death was that her departure was, like many deaths, complicated.

In the sixteen years since Cheryl died, I have known other deaths among friends and family. One thing I've come to realize in that time is that many – maybe most – people leave behind complications when they pass on, beyond just their loss. Sometimes grief must compete for a place with anger, or bewilderment. An acquaintance who lost his partner to suicide a few years after Cheryl died was the first person to make this clear to me. Suicide is, perhaps, singularly fraught. But there are other ways. The illness that kills you may first utterly change your personality. A caretaker might bear the brunt of a dying partner's rage or resentment. Carefully guarded secrets might come out at the wake or in the sorting through of belongings that follows. A mistress might show up at the funeral.

Cheryl's death was complicated for me. There are one or two gestures toward that fact in the original book, but just barely. In rereading my old journals in preparation for the present volume I realized that it took a year or more before I was even really able to feel much outside of grief. In my case the loss demanded about a year of sovereignty before it would give any ground to other, more tangled feelings. After that, they did begin to filter into the journals' pages. But I generally wasn't interested in, or capable of making the complications a full part of the book, whether they be feelings of anger or confusion, or a reaching out toward acceptance or forgiveness. For one thing, those feelings were much harder to describe, to picture, and it turned out to be an emotional place I didn't really want to spend a lot of time inhabiting. For another it wasn't a way I wanted Cheryl to be remembered – by me or the world at large. So those pieces never really got finished. But it was part of my experience. So those first two versions of *The End* will always feel in some small way incomplete for that absence.

A full accounting of both the grief and complexity together may be a bit too much for one small story. I would need many more pages, and a deeper well of resilience to tell that story completely and do it justice. The towering weight of grief and death really does seem to be more than enough as the subject for 100 or so pages of comics and a few scraps of text. But this book is not just a 'story', it's also a document, an archaeology. So some of those pieces have been left in this version. Take from them what you will.

In the years after the first two publications I heard from people for whom those books were, for lack of a better word, helpful. One reader wrote that he hadn't read anything else on grief that captured his experience, and he wanted other people in his life to read the book in order to understand what he was going through. If that is true, it feels like allowing some of the more fraught material into the book might likewise touch others who have passed over similar ground. When it happened to me it felt like I was the only one in the world. Now I know that isn't so. And that may be a useful thing to share.

II. Five Things I've learned About Loss

The material in the main body of the book is drawn from a little over two years worth of sketch-booking and journaling. But I didn't stop thinking about the experience when I closed the last notebook. Following, loosely numbered, are some other observations I have made about my own experience of loss fifteen years later that aren't really dealt with elsewhere in the book, and that may be of use, or at least, of interest.

1. Talking About Death is Weird

Sometime in the year after her death I assembled an exhibition of Cheryl's own artwork at Lula Cafe in Chicago, where we had both worked – she as a bartender, me as a cook – and where I regularly helped curate the artwork (this show is referenced on page 35). At some point in the weeks before the show went up, I was passing out postcards for the event at an opening for another show I was part of. On the front of the card was an image of one of Cheryl's photographs (see pages 156-157), on the back were the show's title and the words 'In Memorial'. At some point I came to a few people standing in a small group, talking in the convivial way people do at such gatherings, and passed out

the cards. An acquaintance looked at what he'd just been handed and said, in a slightly jokey way "'In memorial?' What, did she die or something?".

The group went suddenly silent. His girlfriend admonished him in a half-whisper that yes, she had indeed died or something. It was by most measures a crushing social faux pas. But to me it was incredibly refreshing. I laughed and just said that yeah, actually she died. To simply have the fact said aloud, to have the unspeakable, uncomfortable truth I carried around all day, every day, everywhere I went, just pushed over crashing onto the floor where everyone would have no choice but to turn and look... it actually made me very happy. He felt terrible, I was grateful. I explained that yes, it was a memorial show and there would be a chance to donate blood earlier in the day, since that was one of her last wishes – she had been the recipient of a tremendous amount of donated blood over the course of her illness. Suddenly we could all talk about it like it was just a real thing in the world and not avert our eyes uncomfortably and hope it would go away. I'm going to guess that to this day he probably tries not to think about that moment in his life if he can help it. I have memories like that myself, where I said exactly the wrong thing in a group of people and felt everyone cringe. I have a vague memory of him apologizing again later at Cheryl's show. I hope he believed me when I explained what it actually felt like on my end.

Despite having gone through a devastating loss myself, and having had to navigate other people's social discomfort, I still never know what to say to people in the position I once occupied. It's an impossible question, death is just too big. It's a cliche to say that our culture doesn't deal well with death, but that doesn't make it any less true. The thing I try to keep in mind, and at which I sometimes fail, is to say *something*. To not pretend nothing is wrong. And to ask about the story. For me an invitation – or just an opening – to tell some part of the story meant very much, and I've found that to be true of others. We make meaning from meaninglessness by putting events into the structure of story, and we cement it into reality in repeated tellings. For me the time and attention of my friends and family was a tremendous gift. That I have the resources to be that friend is nevertheless still something I occasionally have to remind myself of.

2. Grief is Sticky

In the many years following Cheryl's death it still sometimes feels awkward that our relationship and her death still have a place in my life. Both altered its course vastly. They do not rule my existence, but they have and will remain (I assume) present. After a while the anniversary of her death for several years in a row felt unremarkable to me. I might not even remember the anniversary until days later, or only be reminded when my mother asked how I was doing with slightly more concern in her voice than usual. And then for several years after that it carried a very heavy weight every year, and I could feel it coming days in advance like an approaching storm. And I don't think I've ever known quite what to do with that.

In this current age of extended serial monogamy into adulthood, there is a sort of socially acceptable shorthand for one's exes – as youthful blunders, indulgences, or as a kind of set of educational experiences on 'the path that led me to you'. Break-ups, however one-sided they might actually be, can be spun. It's harder to wrap a silver lining

around a cruelly untimely death and the shadow it might cast over the rest of one's life. For several years, without exactly realizing it, I think I expected the shadow simply to lift and disappear for good. And there have of course been times where it felt like it had. But it seems to come back eventually, sometimes stalling overhead for an extended stay. It can be easy to wonder if it's some weakness of character that keeps the cloud from moving on a little more quickly – why can I not summon a little breeze, a little sunlight?

FInding other examples can be helpful in this regard. In her book *Team of Rivals*, Doris Kearns Goodwin's tells the story of Abraham Lincoln's grief. He lost his first great love to death and spent some years in a deep depression over it, a mood that apparently came and went the rest of his life, long into his later marriage and presidency. And for some reason knowing that has occasionally helped me give myself a break. I would scarcely reproach Lincoln his grief, or put it down to some defect in his character. If anything it makes him a more interesting figure, adding depth and texture to the story of his life and career. As for myself, sixteen years in, I think it's safe to say that this is just the way of things. So, thank you Ms. Goodwin.

The fact that Cheryl's death is still part of my life nevertheless weirdly contrasts with the fact that people who have just read a book about it feel as though it has just happened. And so they will come up to me at book signings or comics festivals and express their sympathy. And I have to try and convince them I'm actually doing fine. It's hardly something I can complain about, having published two books on the subject – in a way I'm the one who keeps insisting on bringing it up by appearing at these things and continuing to keep the books in print. Probably this is just one of the weirdnesses of it. Death, being an awkward subject, seems to demand an apology for being brought up.

3. We Think Death is a 'Thing'.
    It's Not, It's the Absence of a Thing

Part of the strangeness of loss for me was trying to wrap my head around it and always feeling like there was nothing there for me to wrap my head around. And then trying again. And again, and not being able to stop. Our brains just don't know what to do with such a sudden and utter vacancy. In every other instance of absence in life the brain has something to do with the circumstance. If you go outside and your car is not there, it's because it's in the shop, or it's been stolen, or towed, or your girlfriend borrowed it to go to the store. Your car didn't stop existing. If a person you're used to having around is gone, your brain's explanation is that that the person is in another place. Physically. The idea that they are literally nowhere is just not something our brains know what to do with. I don't generally envy religious people their faith, but my guess is that believing in a place for your loved one to have gone to, a place you can later meet up with them again... that probably helps your brain relax about the conundrum a little bit. Not completely, but a little.

In her book *How Emotions Are Made,* the psychologist Lisa Feldman Barrett talks about the fact that people who live together unconsciously help regulate one another's physiological, emotional and hormonal states. Our partners are constantly there, playing certain predictable roles of talk and touch and timing that help the internal regulation of our bodies. We balance ourselves out with them as reliable physiological hand-holds. It's one of the reasons an abusive relationship can be so difficult to walk away from. When your partner dies, when they utterly disappear, it feels like you have lost a rather large important piece of yourself. Because in a very real sense you have.

Like many people in my place, even still, I have occasional dreams in which Cheryl shows back up in my life, with some explanation or other about where she's been all this time and why. Some of these, especially early on, have been a profound gift. I would get to see her again, and it sometimes felt very real. But as time went on it would more often be fraught. My life had moved on, maybe I had a new partner or a new life in a new city, but there would be some expectation that I should make room for her in some way. Or, worse, her absence is part of some sinister plot or betrayal. The mind grasps for an explanation.

My understanding of current dream theory is that for all their strangeness dreams are basically the experiential output of our brains running programs for dealing with various anticipated real-life problems. They are so often anxious because it is precisely the unpleasant experiences

that our brains are designed to help us handle. Being unable to accommodate Cheryl's disappearance, once every year or two my gray matter decides to run a scenario in which she shows back up and test various scenarios. Just so I'll be prepared... in case. It makes me think of my cat. Sometimes when I reach out my hand to pet her, her brain – despite two years worth of experience – guesses that I'm launching an attack and she runs out of the room. This is partly understandable: her brain is only the size of a walnut. Mine is the size of a cantaloupe, but it seems to be doing pretty much the same thing.

4. Grief Means You've Joined a Club.
   So You Might As Well Go to the Meetings

In the months after Cheryl's death, at the urging of someone or other, I joined a group for a while, at Gilda's Club in Chicago, founded in memory of Gilda Radner who also died of cancer. I had two choices. The first group I tried was populated by people my age. They had mostly lost parents. I could feel right away that we were not having the same experience. I instead joined one consisting of people twenty, thirty, forty years my senior, who'd lost partners. The age difference meant very little, whereas the particular flavor and dynamic of the absence meant very much.

For every important part of my life, I have found people to share it with, who can relate. I skateboard, and I have friends who skate, who know what I'm talking about when I talk about skating. Same for comics and art, same for my family. They are small communities of interest and care. Micro-cultures. And so of course having no one to talk with about the experience of loss would create a hole. They're called 'support' groups, which... is fine. I suppose I got support from those people, and hopefully I returned the favor. But mostly it just helped to be able to report the ways you were feeling, the profound strangeness of life after death... and be able to see real recognition in the eyes around the room. They knew exactly what I meant. I had other friends who listened and, again, that was a tremendous gift. But they didn't really know what I was talking about. The people in the group did. My skater friends are not a skateboarding support group, they're just fellow travelers who know what I'm talking about when I say the words "half-cab nose manual". The people in the group knew what I was talking about when I said "I started crying at the supermarket," or "I didn't get out of bed yesterday." We were all walking a long hard road. Having people to walk it with doesn't make it shorter, or less of a slog. But it is nice to have people who understand, and who might know if there is an accident ahead, or danger of falling rocks.

5. You're Not Always Grieving
   The Thing You Think You Are

One thing I learned in the group, from the moderator, is that two thirds of men will be in a new relationship 25 months after being widowed, compared with one fifth of women. It's depressing to be predictable. I was engaged to be married almost exactly 25 months after Cheryl's death. When your partner dies, the primary void, of course, is the loss of that person. But along with them, your future disappears. And the self that was one half of a pair and a partnership. At least for me there was a powerful impulse to be back in a stable, committed, long-term relationship with a future. I don't know what the statistics say about the longevity of those relationships, but mine lasted about three years. There were many reasons for its end, and along with the problems, there were wonderful times, too. But in retrospect I believe that my very strong drive to get back to the place I had so recently been in had helped me push past problems in the match that I might otherwise have recognized as flashing alarms. I wasn't interested in seeing them that way. I had a life to reclaim. And it created turbulence for both of us that probably could have been avoided if I had listened to some of the quieter voices in the back of my mind at the time.

In the years that followed I slowly became acquainted with myself again, eventually, as myself. And then I was lucky enough to find a partner who could completely know and understand and accept me as I am, whether I was flying above or below the passing clouds of my past. I guess that's the 'new life' I kept imagining and invoking in those notebooks. I knew it was coming. I didn't know how long it would take to arrive, or quite how to recognize it when it did.

· · · · · · ·

Maybe the next sixteen years will bring new observations. The view from this current point, of the planet that was once me, that was once Cheryl, that was once a vortex of loss, 16 years distant, is a little less crisp, perhaps, and most days the cut of it is less sharp. But I can still feel the gentle tug of its gravity, and I'm fine with that. That pull is a comfort in a way. A reminder that the connection to that time, and to Cheryl herself is still real, and that the time I spent there matters. And I can nevertheless be happy and whole on this new planet, in this new life, in this future where I have landed.

APPENDIX I:

Some Later Thoughts

I DID A READING FROM [redacted] DON'T GO WHERE I CAN'T FOLLOW YESTERDAY AT BONESHAKER BOOKS IN MINNEAPOLIS. THE BOOK IS A SORT OF MEMORIAL THAT I DID AFTER THE DEATH OF MY PARTNER CHERYL WEAVER IN 2005.
YOU CAN SET UP YOUR LAPTOP HERE.
WHAT CONNECTOR DO YOU NEED TO HOOK IT UP?
AS I SET THINGS UP FOR THE TALK I WAS PERIPHERALLY AWARE OF AN EARLY ARRIVAL WITH A COPY OF THE BOOK GLANCING OVER FROM TIME TO TIME, AS IF HE WANTED TO COME TALK BUT WASN'T SURE IF IT WAS AN APPROPRIATE MOMENT.
AS I FINISHED GETTING THINGS SET UP HE DID COME OVER. HE LOOKED AT MY PICTURE ON THE COVER, THEN UP AT ME. "ARE YOU THE AUTHOR?" HE ASKED
YEP, THAT'S ME. YOU WANT ME TO SIGN THAT FOR YOU?
SURE.
WHAT'S YOUR NAME?
SAME AS YOURS.
"OH, YEAH?" I SAID. "ANDERS? THAT'S FUNNY," [redacted]. AS I OPENED THE BOOK AND FOUND A PAGE TO SIGN HE GOT OUT HIS DRIVER'S LICENSE. LAST NAME, TOO.
OREGON
ANDERS [redacted] NILSEN
WHOA.
THAT'S CRAZY!
YEAH.
WOW. SO ARE YOU NORWEGIAN?

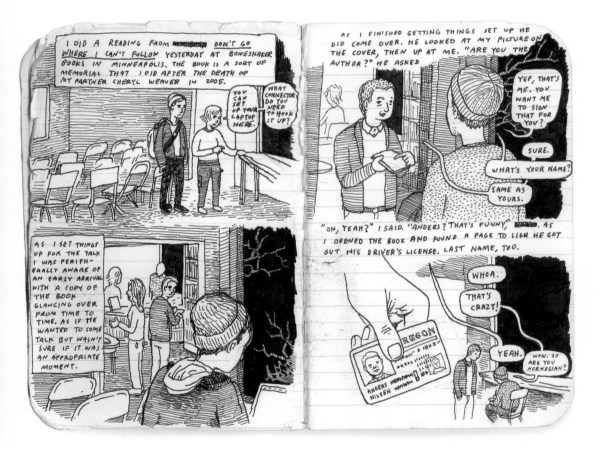

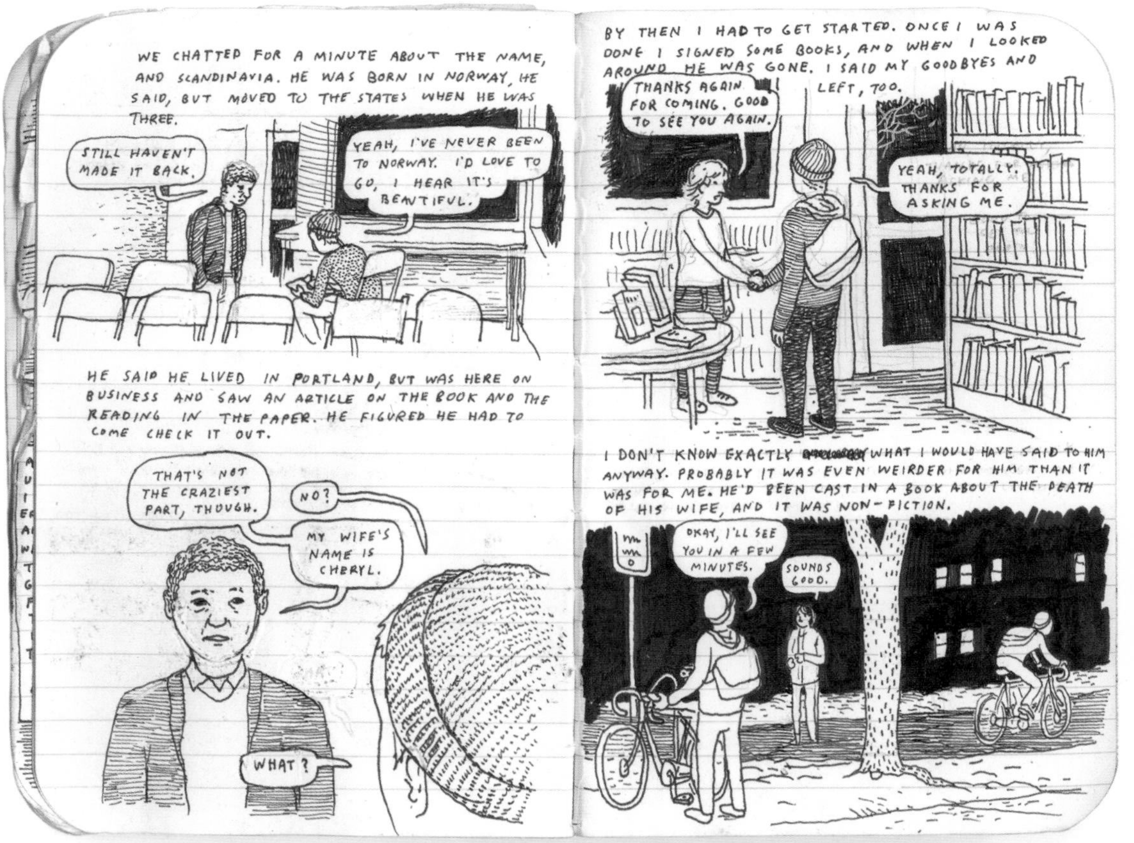
WE CHATTED FOR A MINUTE ABOUT THE NAME, AND SCANDINAVIA. HE WAS BORN IN NORWAY, HE SAID, BUT MOVED TO THE STATES WHEN HE WAS THREE.
STILL HAVEN'T MADE IT BACK.
YEAH, I'VE NEVER BEEN TO NORWAY. I'D LOVE TO GO, I HEAR IT'S BEAUTIFUL.
HE SAID HE LIVED IN PORTLAND, BUT WAS HERE ON BUSINESS AND SAW AN ARTICLE ON THE BOOK AND THE READING IN THE PAPER. HE FIGURED HE HAD TO COME CHECK IT OUT.
THAT'S NOT THE CRAZIEST PART, THOUGH.
NO?
MY WIFE'S NAME IS CHERYL.
WHAT?
BY THEN I HAD TO GET STARTED. ONCE I WAS DONE I SIGNED SOME BOOKS, AND WHEN I LOOKED AROUND HE WAS GONE. I SAID MY GOODBYES AND LEFT, TOO.
THANKS AGAIN FOR COMING. GOOD TO SEE YOU AGAIN.
YEAH, TOTALLY. THANKS FOR ASKING ME.
I DON'T KNOW EXACTLY WHAT I WOULD HAVE SAID TO HIM ANYWAY. PROBABLY IT WAS EVEN WEIRDER FOR HIM THAN IT WAS FOR ME. HE'D BEEN CAST IN A BOOK ABOUT THE DEATH OF HIS WIFE, AND IT WAS NON-FICTION.
OKAY, I'LL SEE YOU IN A FEW MINUTES.
SOUNDS GOOD.

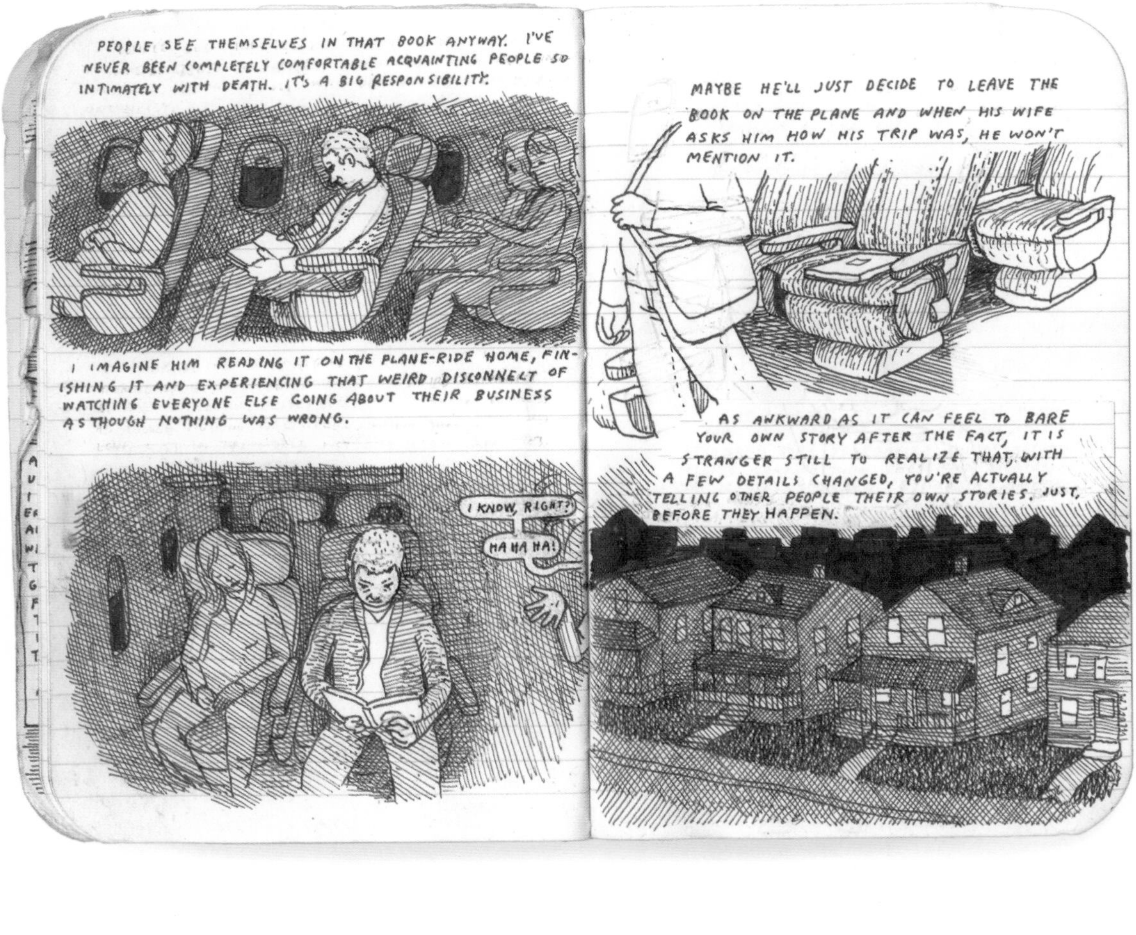
PEOPLE SEE THEMSELVES IN THAT BOOK ANYWAY. I'VE NEVER BEEN COMPLETELY COMFORTABLE ACQUAINTING PEOPLE SO INTIMATELY WITH DEATH. IT'S A BIG RESPONSIBILITY.
I IMAGINE HIM READING IT ON THE PLANE-RIDE HOME, FINISHING IT AND EXPERIENCING THAT WEIRD DISCONNECT OF WATCHING EVERYONE ELSE GOING ABOUT THEIR BUSINESS AS THOUGH NOTHING WAS WRONG.
I KNOW, RIGHT?
HA HA HA!
MAYBE HE'LL JUST DECIDE TO LEAVE THE BOOK ON THE PLANE AND WHEN HIS WIFE ASKS HIM HOW HIS TRIP WAS, HE WON'T MENTION IT.
AS AWKWARD AS IT CAN FEEL TO BARE YOUR OWN STORY AFTER THE FACT, IT IS STRANGER STILL TO REALIZE THAT, WITH A FEW DETAILS CHANGED, YOU'RE ACTUALLY TELLING OTHER PEOPLE THEIR OWN STORIES. JUST BEFORE THEY HAPPEN.

Eulogy for Helen

I want to talk a little bit about the idea of gifts, in a couple of different senses of that word. But before I start I want everyone to do something with me. Close your eyes... and take a deep breath.

[Give everyone time to do this. Do it yourself.]

Like probably everyone in this room I have been the recipient of gifts of one sort or another from Helen Nelson. On the one hand she sent me twenty dollar checks every year on my birthday and Christmas when I was a kid... and those were certainly gifts... but that's not really what I'm talking about. She also made me a very finely crafted needlepoint Christmas stocking when I was very small, along with all her grandchildren, and, eventually her own adult kids as well. And maybe that gets a little closer to what I mean.

I've been aware for many years of some of my deep debt to my grandfather Harold. As a minister he spent his life getting up in front of groups of people once a week to talk about stories, to tell stories, to interpret them, to ruminate on how they might help us think about how we ought to live our lives and how we ought to treat one another and to consider what in life is really important. He did it as a minister, I try to do it as an author and cartoonist, but I'm very aware that in some small way it's a similar vocation, and it's a gift that came to me, at least in part, through him.

It's only in the last few years that I've begun to realize that I probably received a similar gift through Helen. She was a craftsperson and an artist in her way as well, as evidenced by her needlepoint work, which was very fine. But she was also an appreciator and curator of fine objects more generally. Some of my strongest memories of visiting the home she kept in Morris, Illinois are of the arrangement of the space itself and of the objects in it. For one thing it was very clean.

No house I live in will probably ever be that clean and orderly. But it was also very thoughtfully and carefully arranged. I remember the commemorative plates arranged on the walls, the finely crafted spoons she had collected on travels in Norway and Sweden, and the little porcelain Hummel figures arranged on the end tables on either end of the couch. I loved those little figures. I related them to my own small toy figures, even then: my G.I. Joe and Star Wars figures. It was puzzling to me in a way, because they were clearly not meant to be played with — that would have been a very bad idea, and anyway their limbs didn't move and they couldn't hold a gun, so how fun could it really be? But they were clearly vehicles for a kind of storytelling and they were objects of beauty, carefully arranged.

My mother's house is similarly carefully curated. The kinds of objects are different, but the impulse is much the same. Both natural and crafted objects of meaning and beauty, thoughtfully arranged. The same impulse shapes the spaces in my house. And it's not an accident. You could say this sensibility is a gift that my mother and I received from my grandmother. But the truth is she got it herself from her own mother. One of my own most beautiful, most prized objects is the crocheted bedspread on my bed, made with meticulous care, by hand, by Helen's mother, Cecilia. This kind of gift has come through her, perhaps, more than from her. Where did she get it? How far back must we go?

And that brings us to the next, much larger sense of the word 'gift.' And it is all of this: the air you just breathed in and the sky and the light coming in the windows, and the thoughts in your head and the people sitting around you. The grass and the trees outside, the sound of the traffic. It is, on the one hand, life. Everything. Yourself.

It is so huge that it can be hard to really take in, or appreciate. And sometimes it doesn't feel like much of a gift. There were times in Helen's life when she probably struggled to appreciate it. She had dark moments when she was a child. I remember a story from later in her life, at a transitional time when Harold talked about sitting down to balance the checkbook, and she got so frustrated that she ended up throwing it at him across the table and stomping out of the room. It can be hard to appreciate at times. This gift we have is impossibly huge. But it's worth trying to wrap your head around it once in a while. And it is, for me, all the more profound because it is a gift with no giver. It is simply the universe, doing its thing.

The universe is made up of stuff. Dirt and ice and gases and dust. Stars and galaxies. And some of that stuff is us. We are made of the same material as everything else. We're only different in that we are aware of ourselves, and of the other stuff moving around us. We can feel it and see it and smell it and we can think about it, and talk about how weird it is. We can tell stories about it. We are aware. That is the gift. Our awareness. Our ability to take it in. We, in a sense, are a gift that the universe has given to itself.

So what does all of this have to do with Helen, and what we are all doing here? I've been using the word 'gift'... but 'gift' isn't a perfect word. It's a very good one, it gets very close to the mark, for example, a gift isn't something you earn or deserve and neither is all of this. But the word 'gift' falls short in one important respect, which is that we don't get to keep this thing. It is only lent. We borrow it for a while, and then we have to give it back. You might say my grandmother has been giving it back slowly, little by little for several years. But that process was made complete a few days ago. What was lent has now been returned. She got to hang onto it for 94 years, so it's hard to complain about that. And she had a remarkably full life.

As far as I can tell, the universe doesn't care if you say thank you, or are properly grateful. But I am human, and for me it feels very important to say thank you when someone gives me a gift. And to keep on saying it every time you think of how great it is, if the giver is around. And even if you are only borrowing a thing, to express your gratitude when the time comes to give it back. And that's what we are doing here, today.

So, on behalf of myself, and of my grandmother, and of the people who got to share a little in the gift of her life, to the universe:

Thank You.

APPENDIX II:

Some Work of Cheryl's

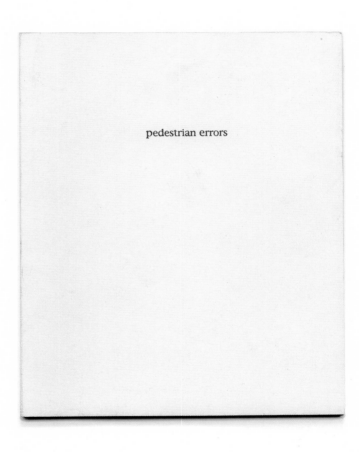

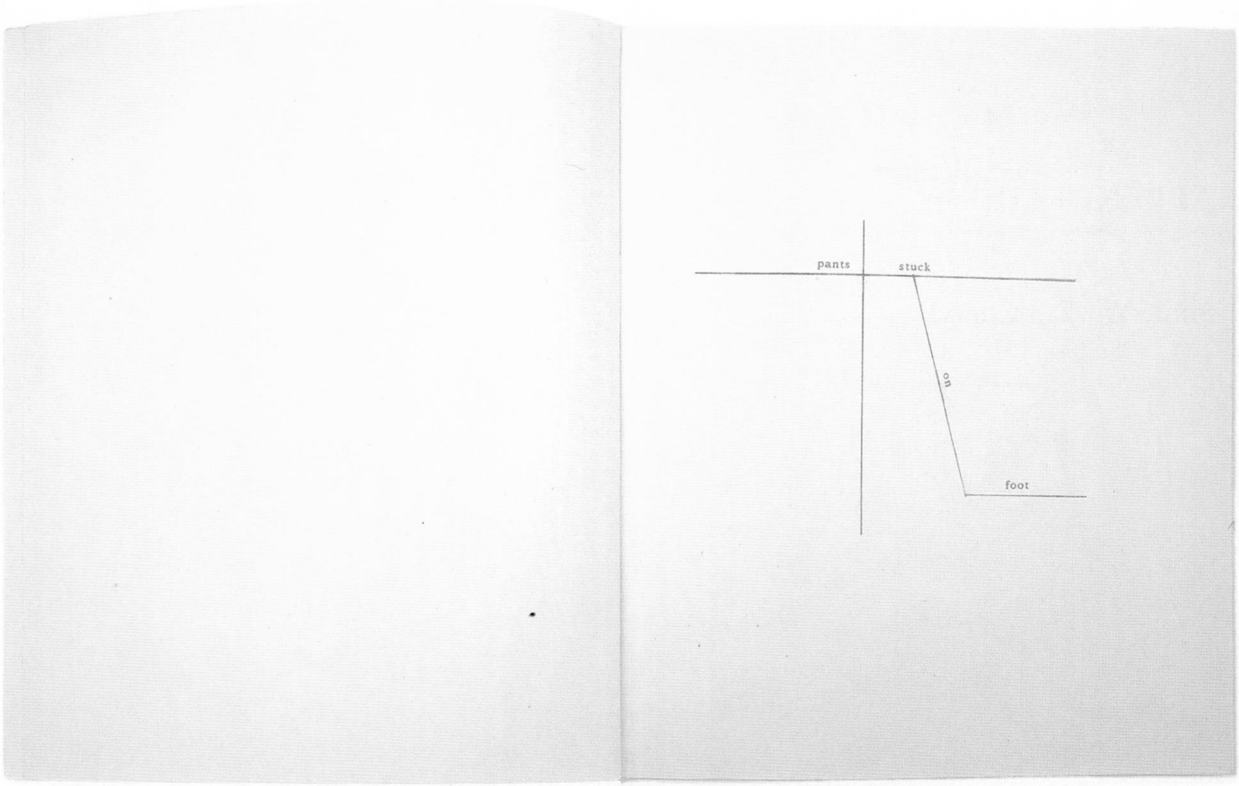
pants
stuck
on
foot

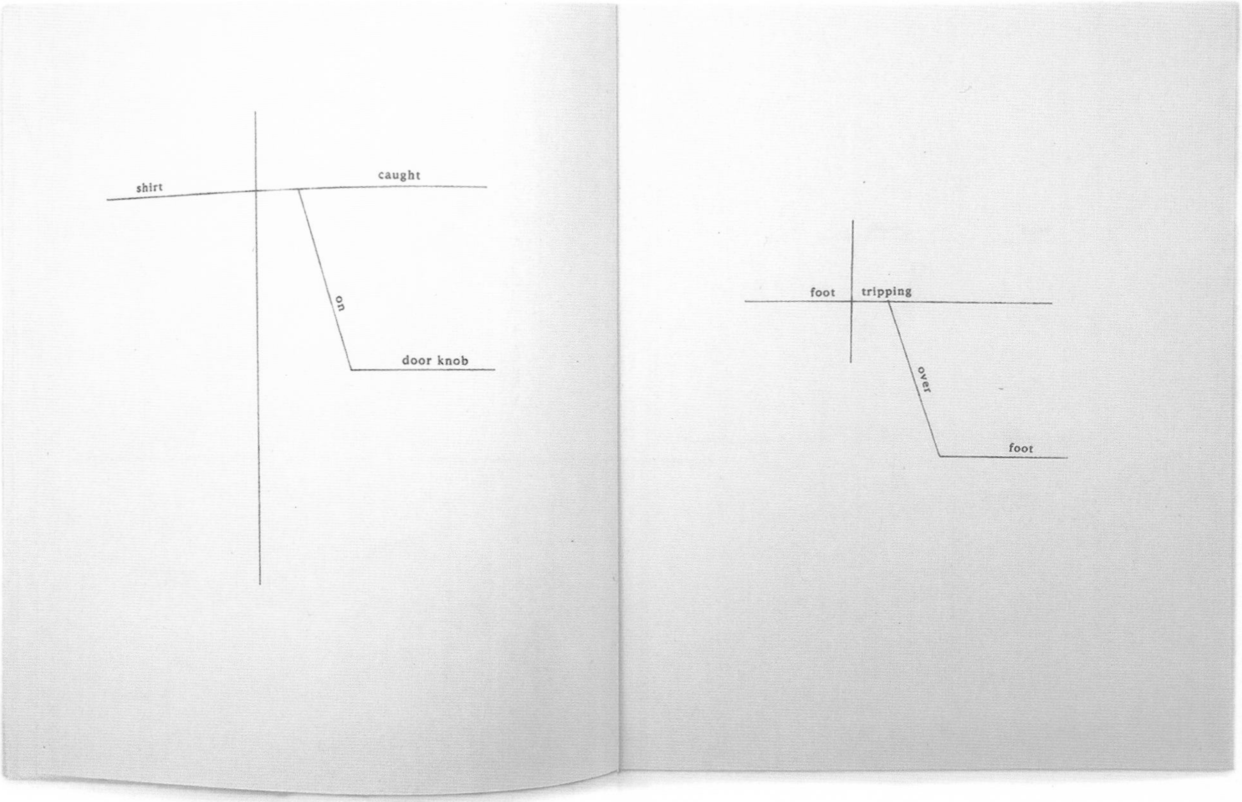
shirt
caught
on
door knob
foot
tripping
over
foot

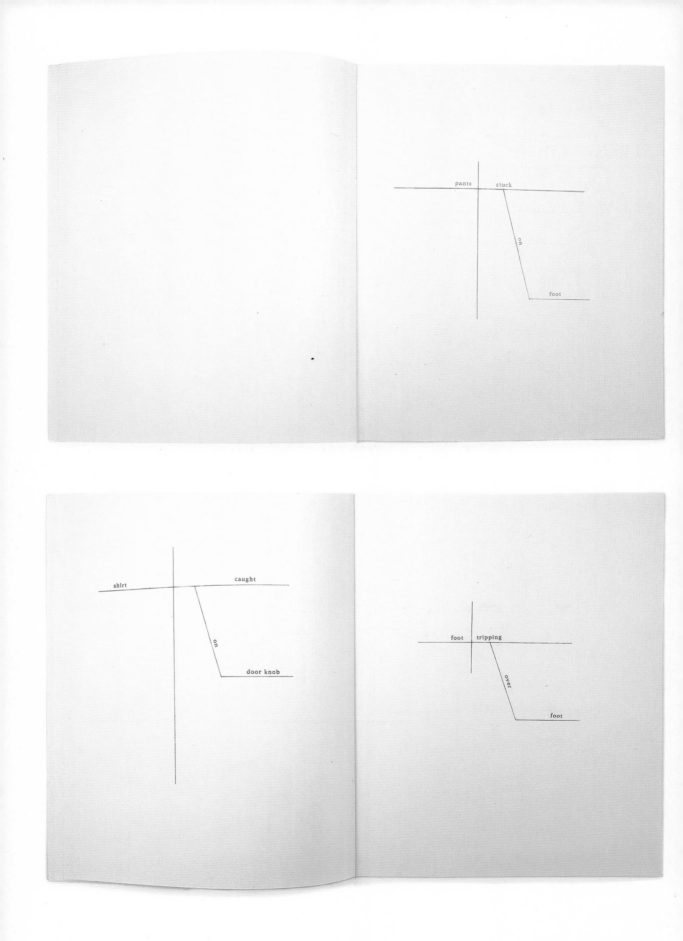

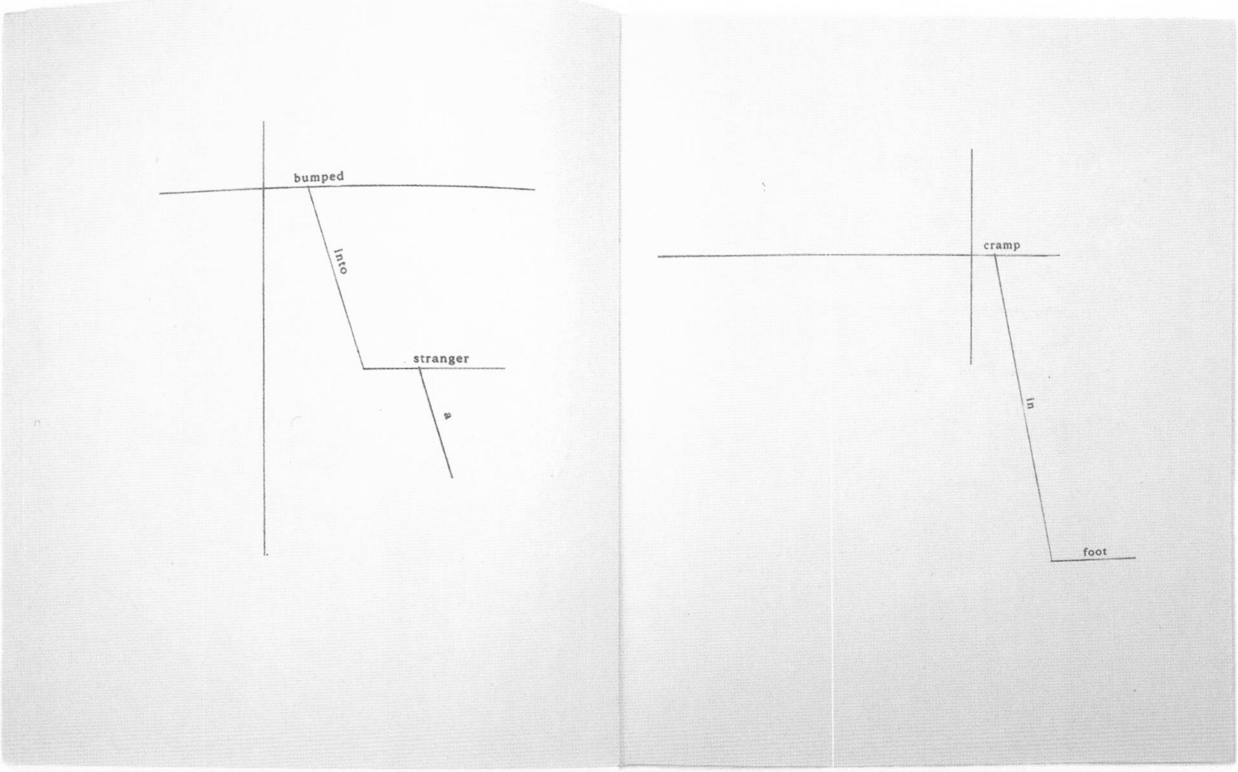
bumped
into
stranger
a
cramp
in
foot

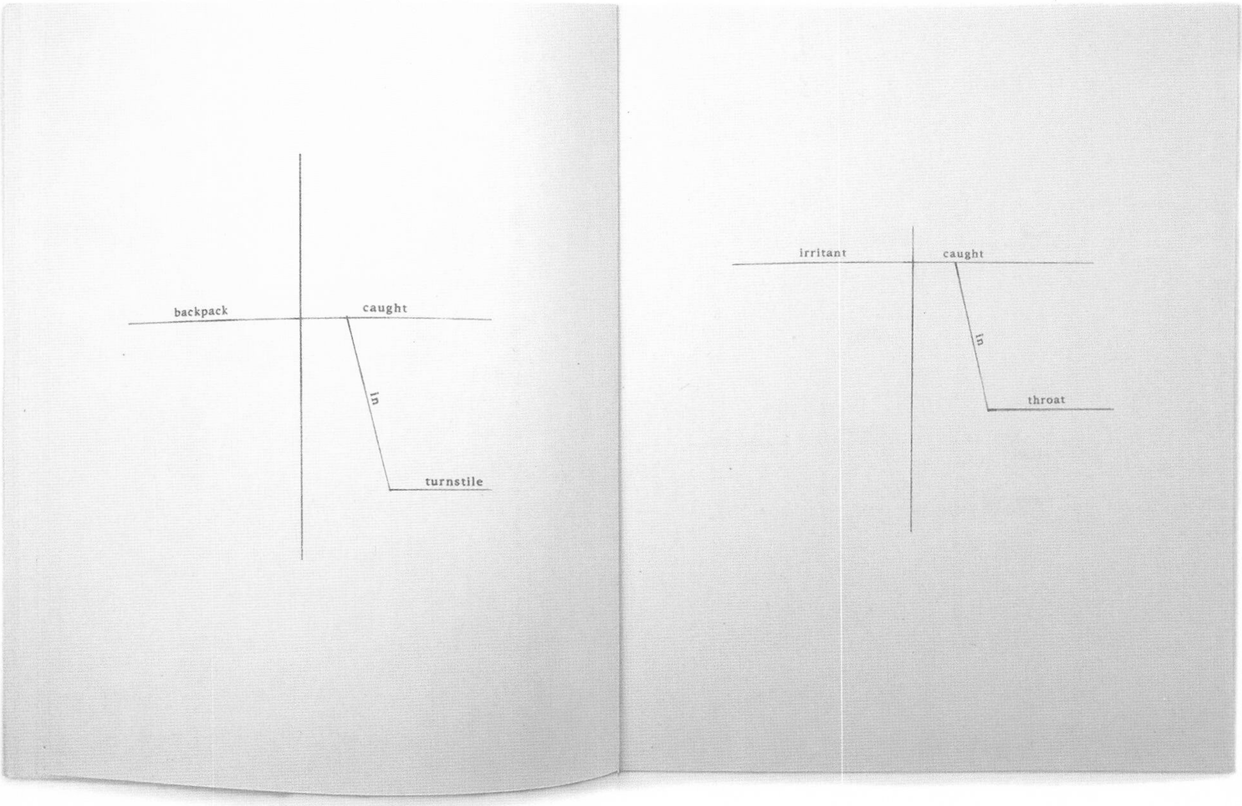
backpack
caught
in
turnstile
irritant
caught
in
throat

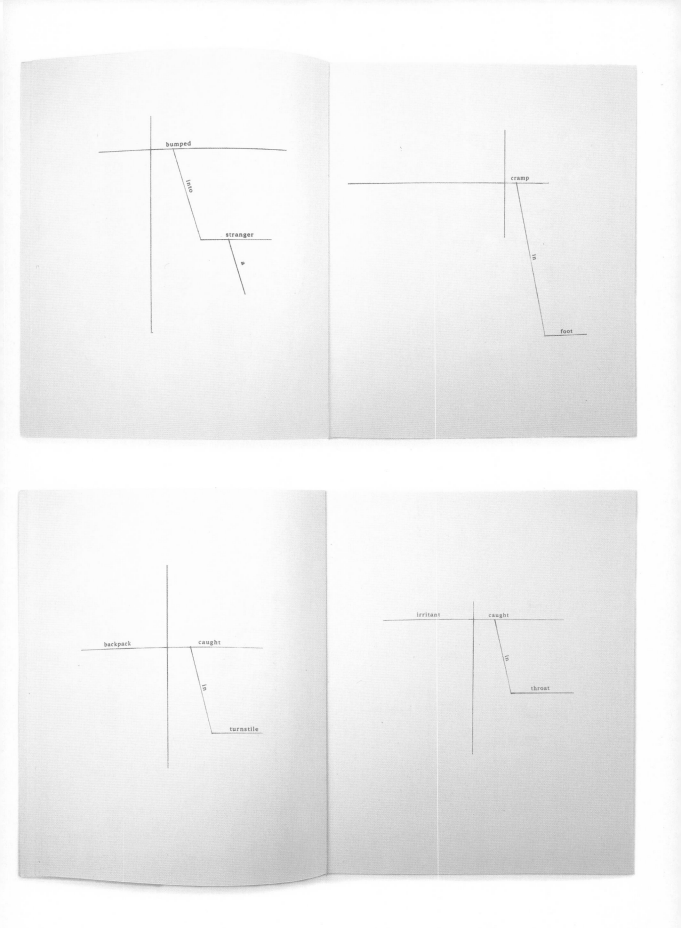

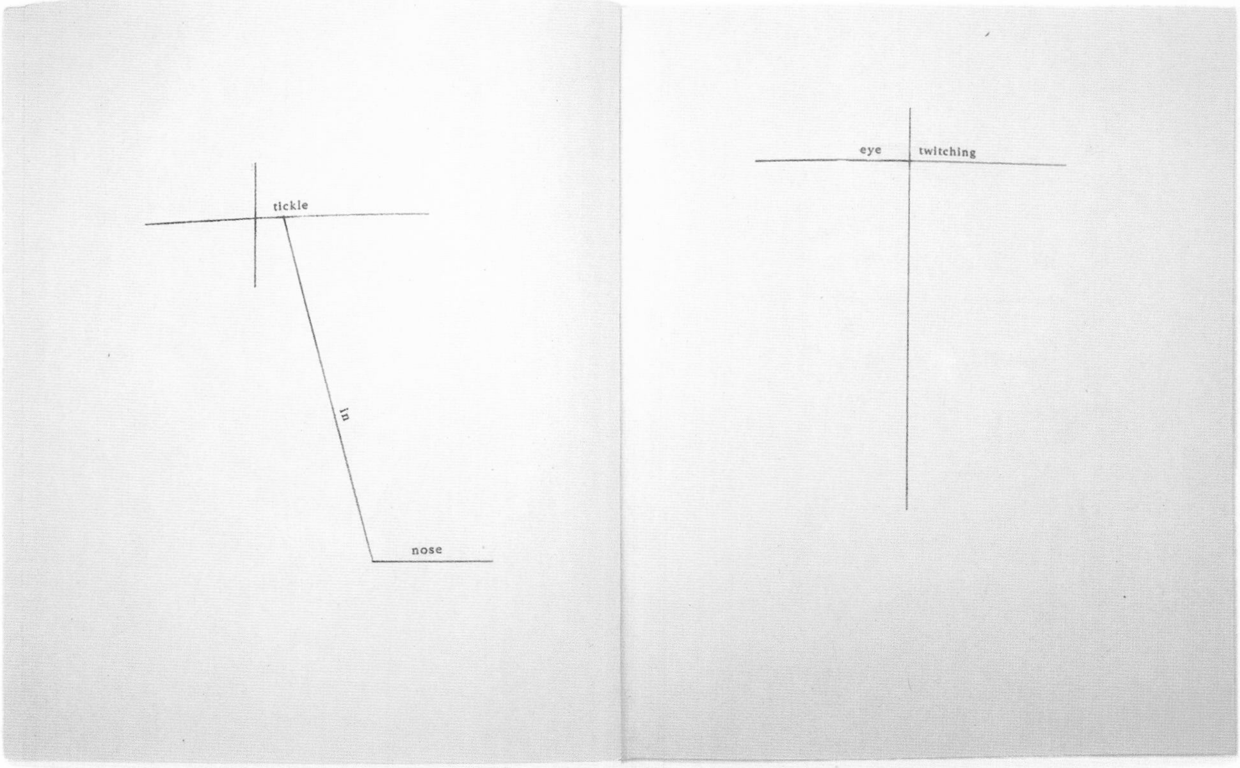
tickle
in
nose
eye
twitching

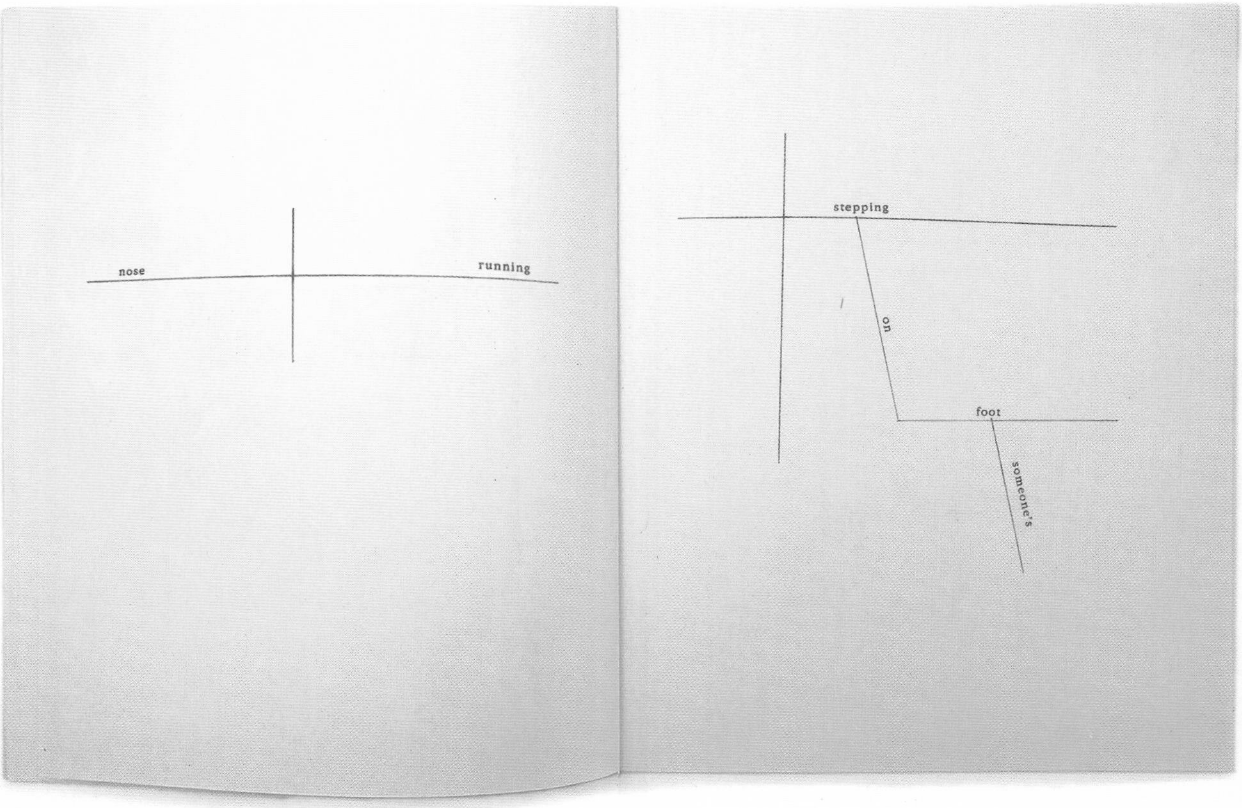
nose
running
stepping
on
foot
someone's

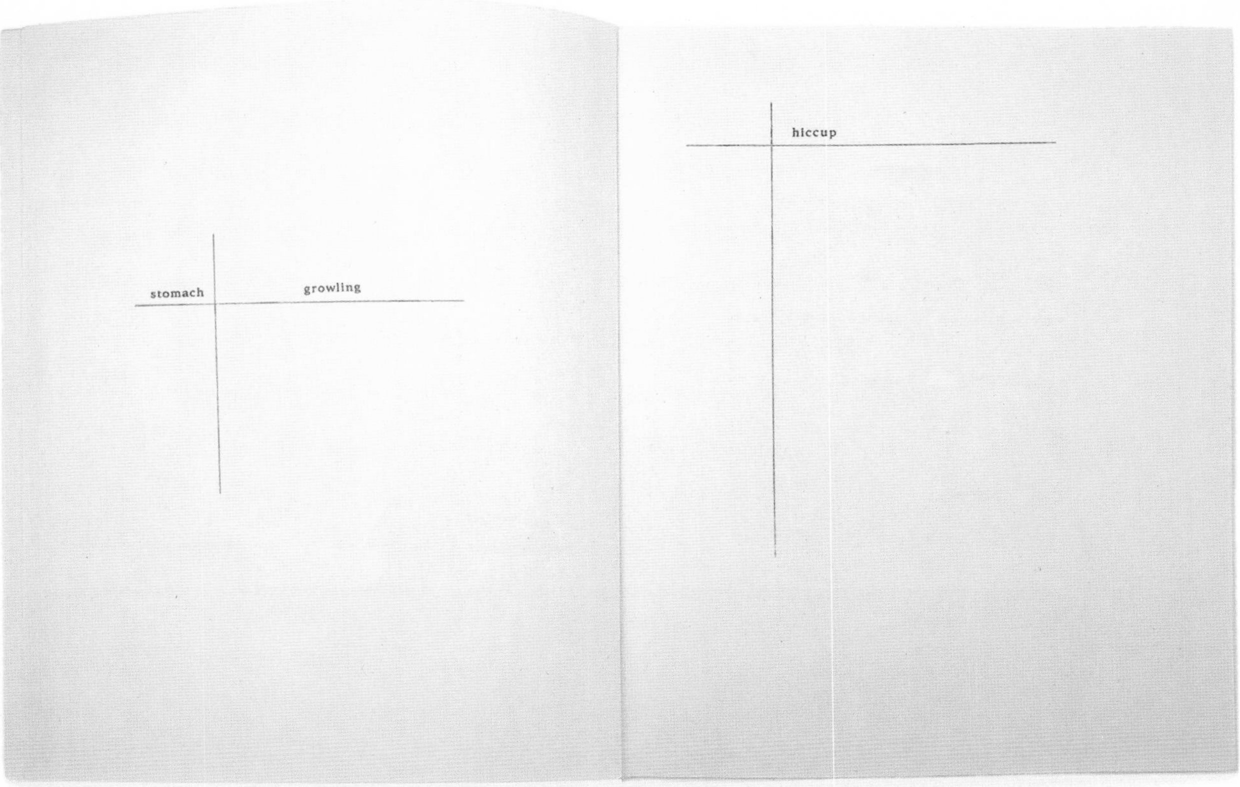
stomach
growling
hiccup

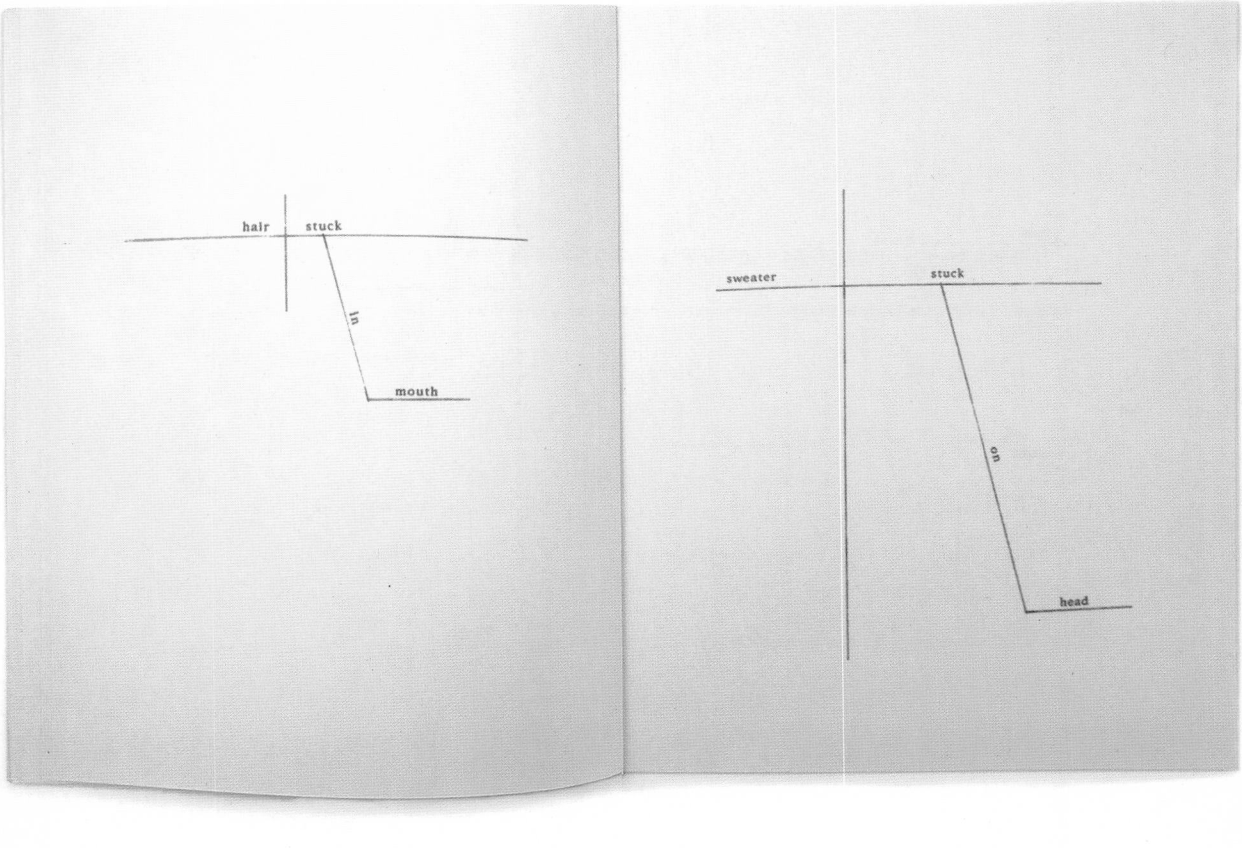
hair
stuck
in
mouth
sweater
stuck
on
head

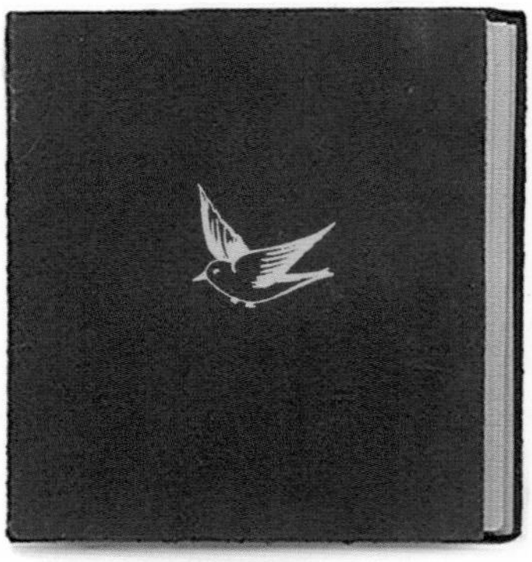

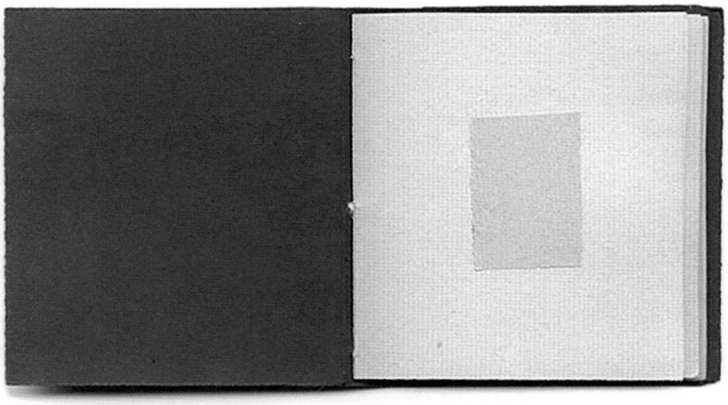

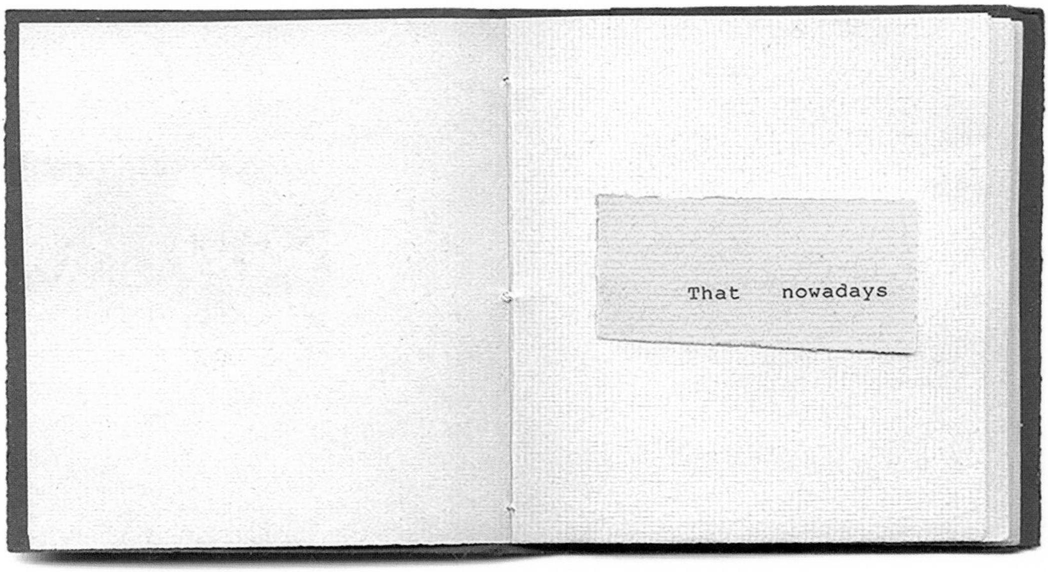
That nowadays

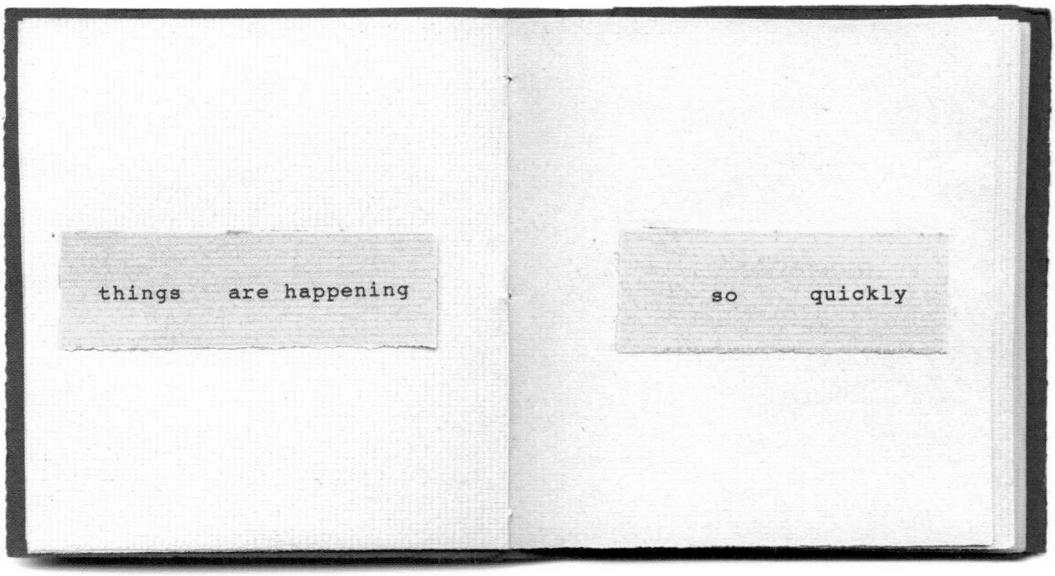
things are happening
so quickly

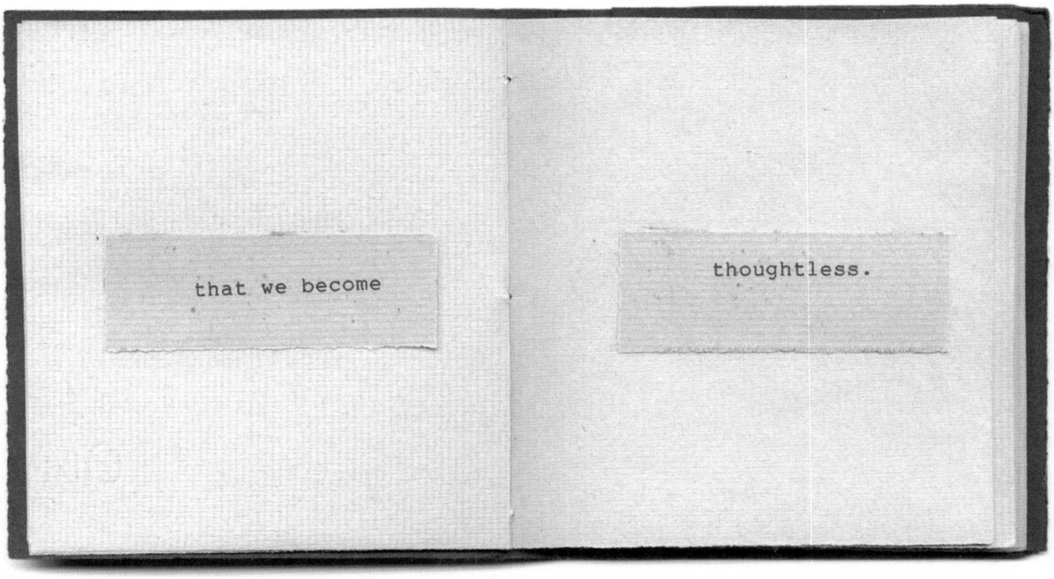
that we become
thoughtless.

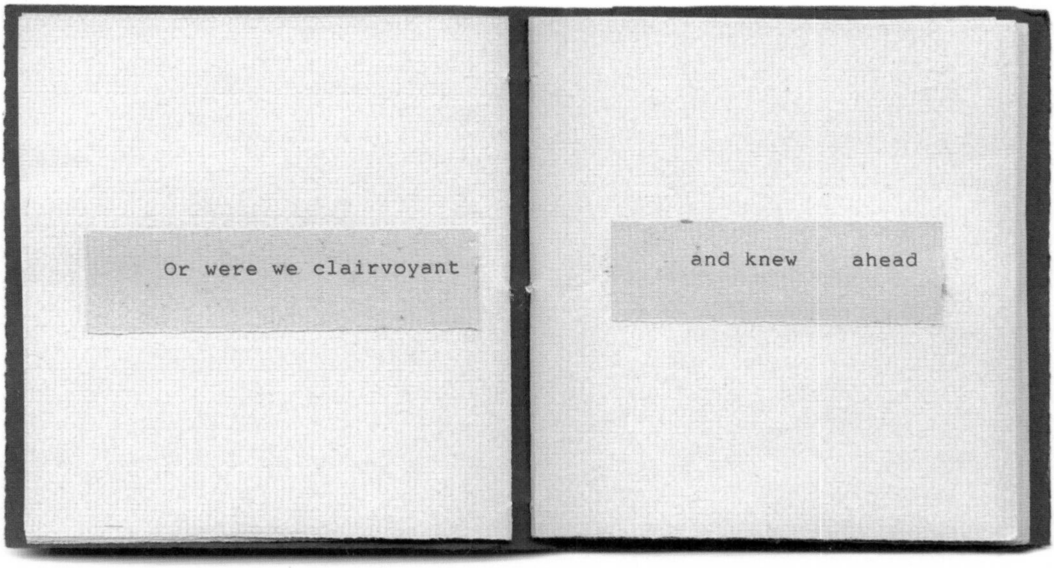
Or were we clairvoyant
and knew ahead

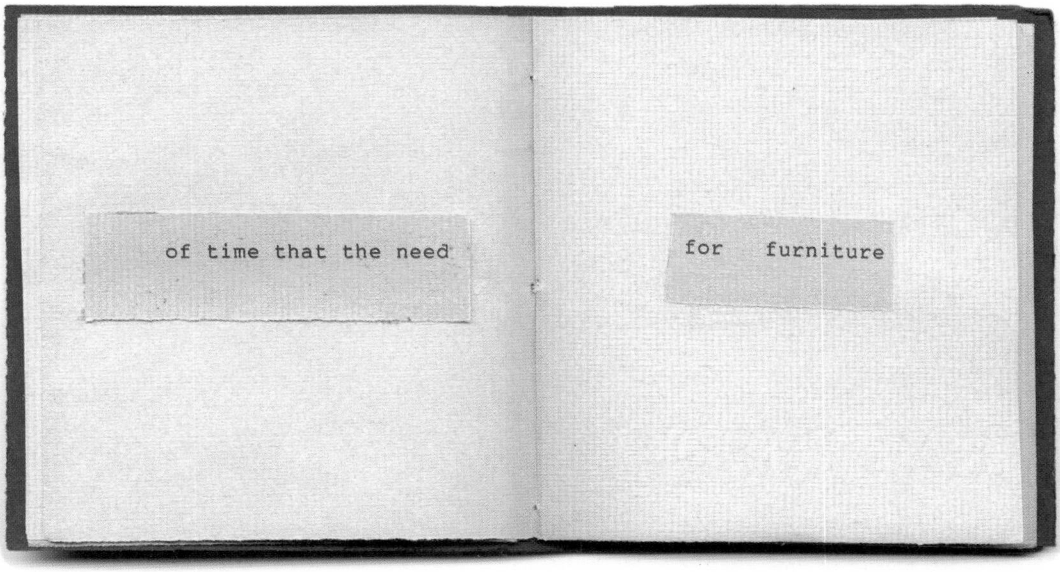
of time that the need
for furniture

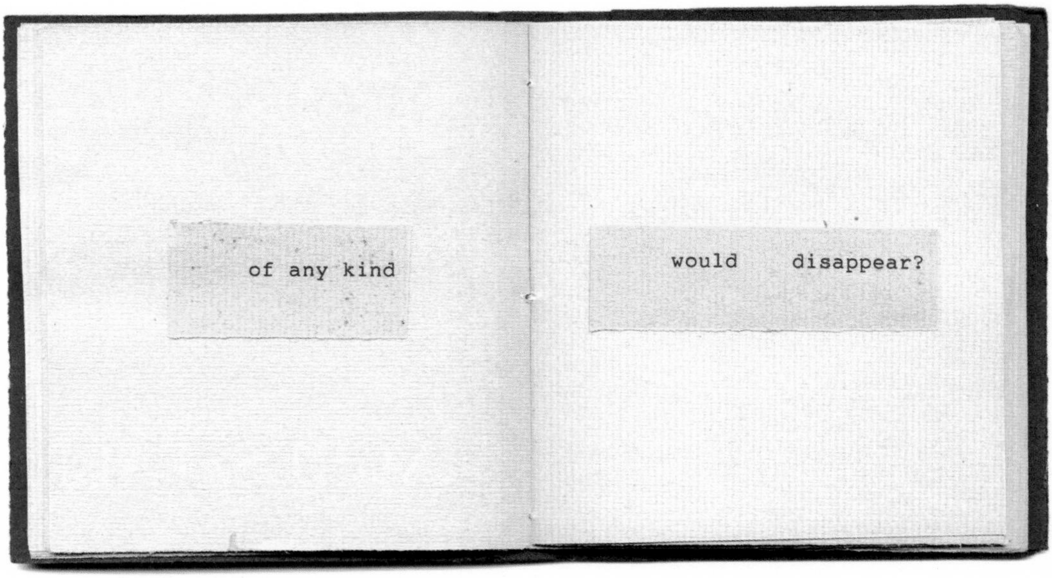
of any kind
would disappear?

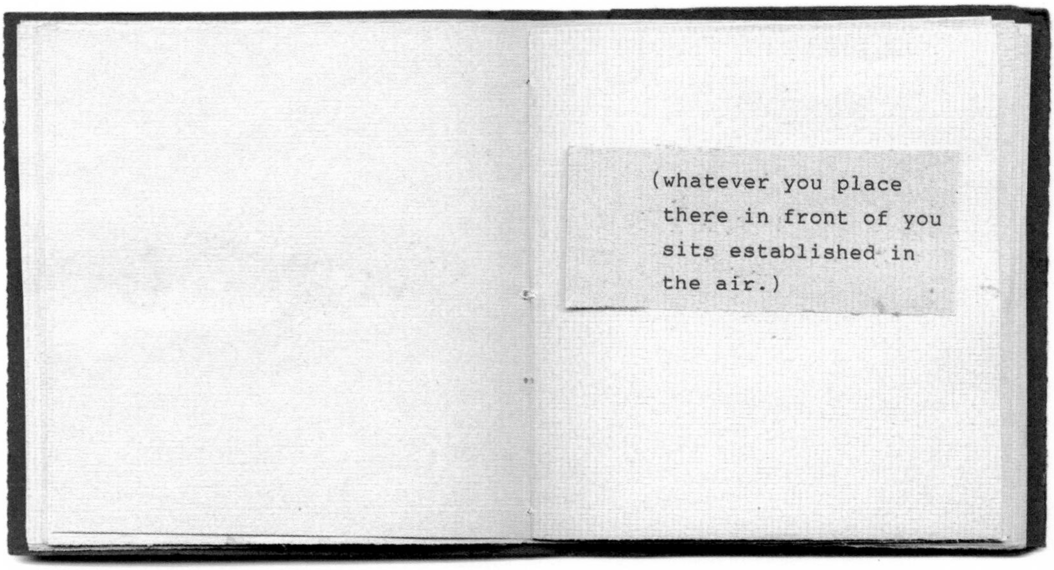
(whatever you place
there in front of you
sits established in
the air.)

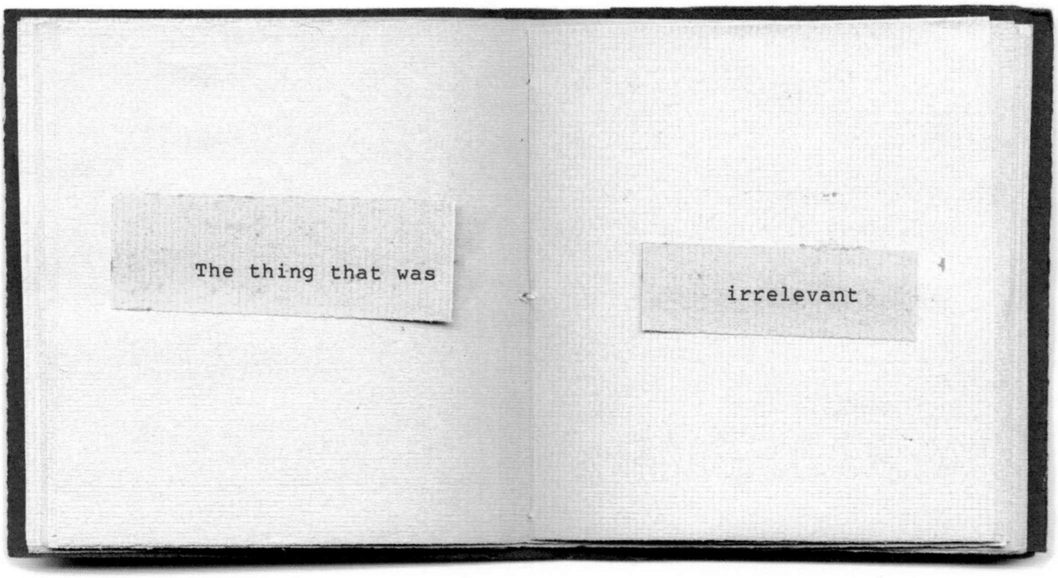
The thing that was
irrelevant

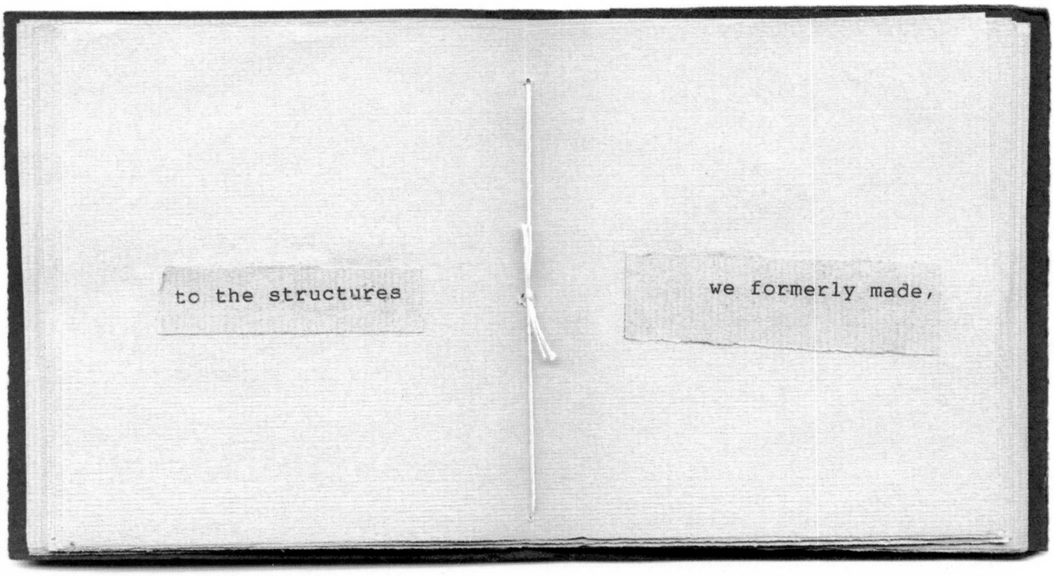
to the structures
we formerly made,

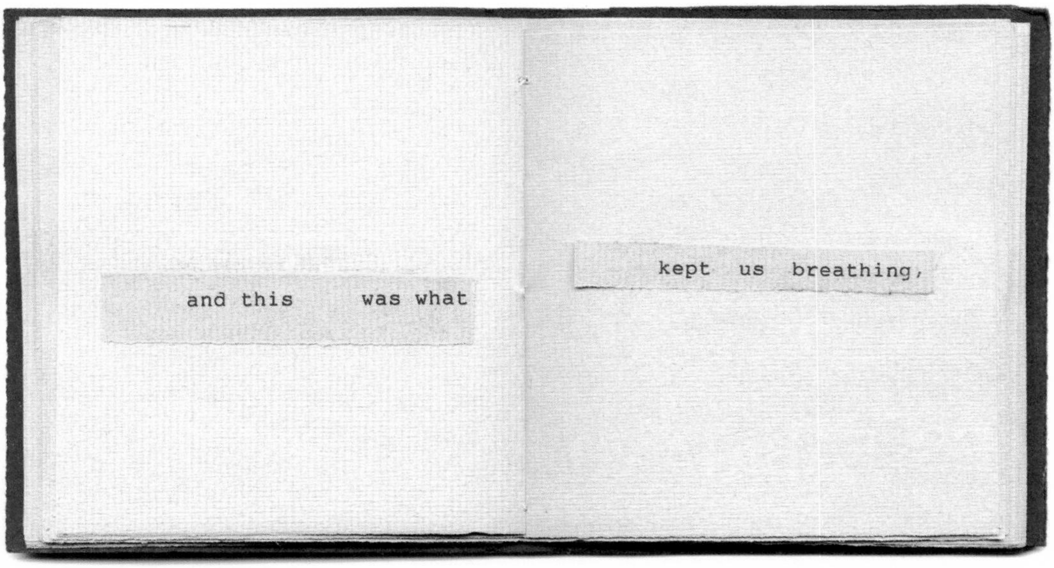
and this was what
kept us breathing,

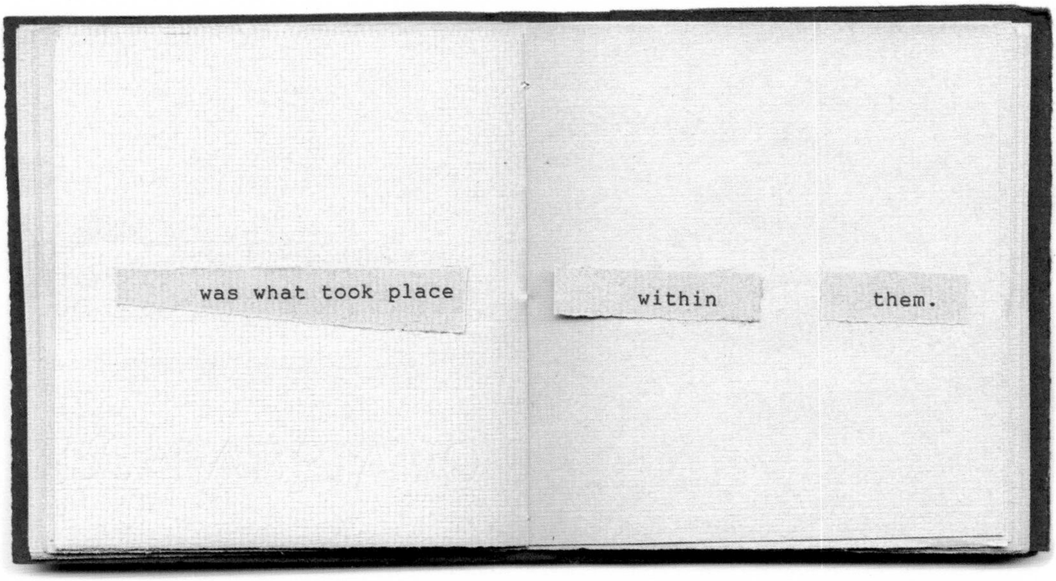
was what took place
within
them.

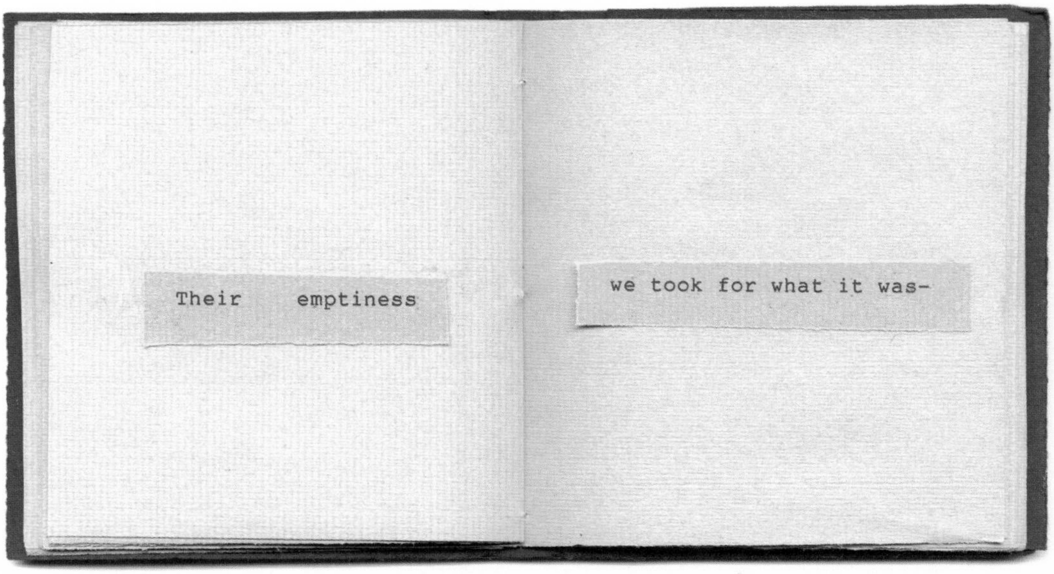
Their emptiness
we took for what it was-

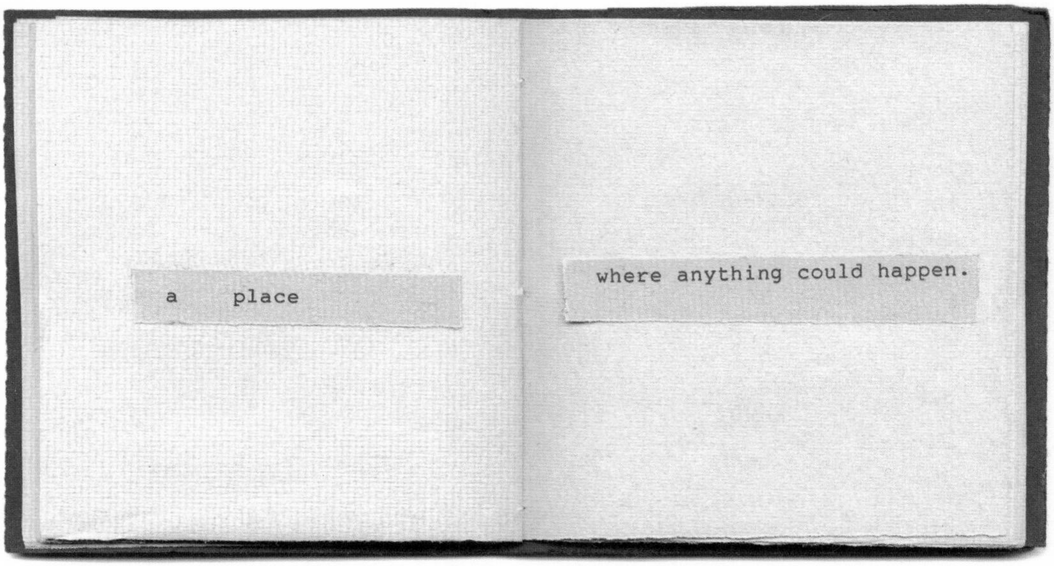
a place
where anything could happen.

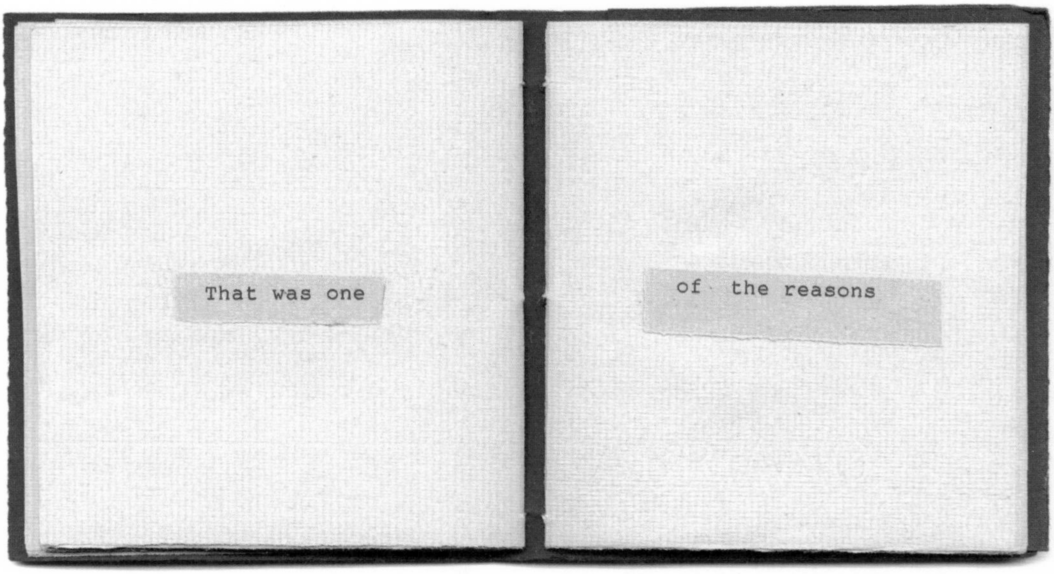
That was one
of the reasons

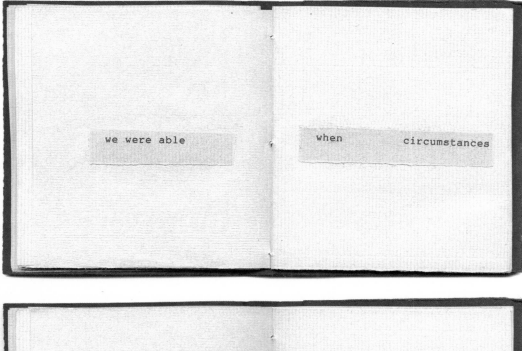

we were able

when   circumstances

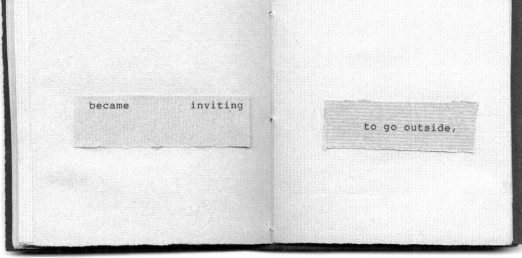

became   inviting

to go outside,

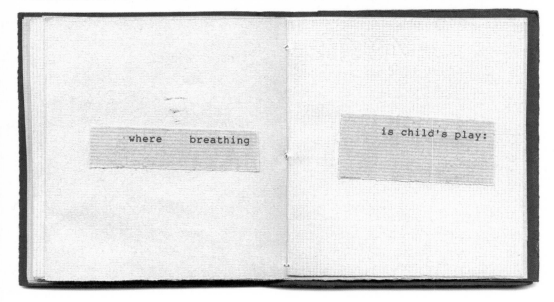

where   breathing

is child's play:

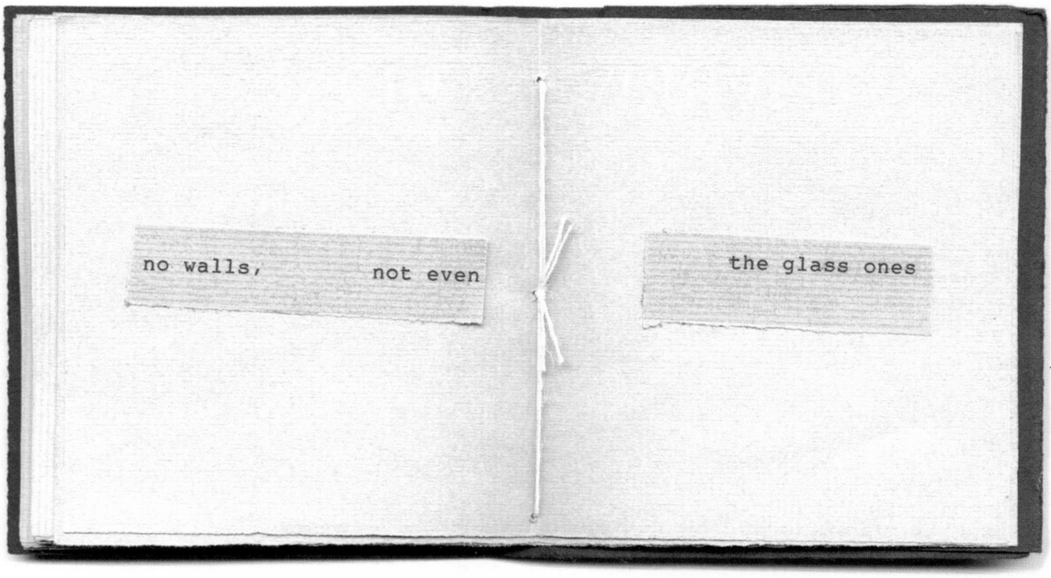
no walls, not even
the glass ones

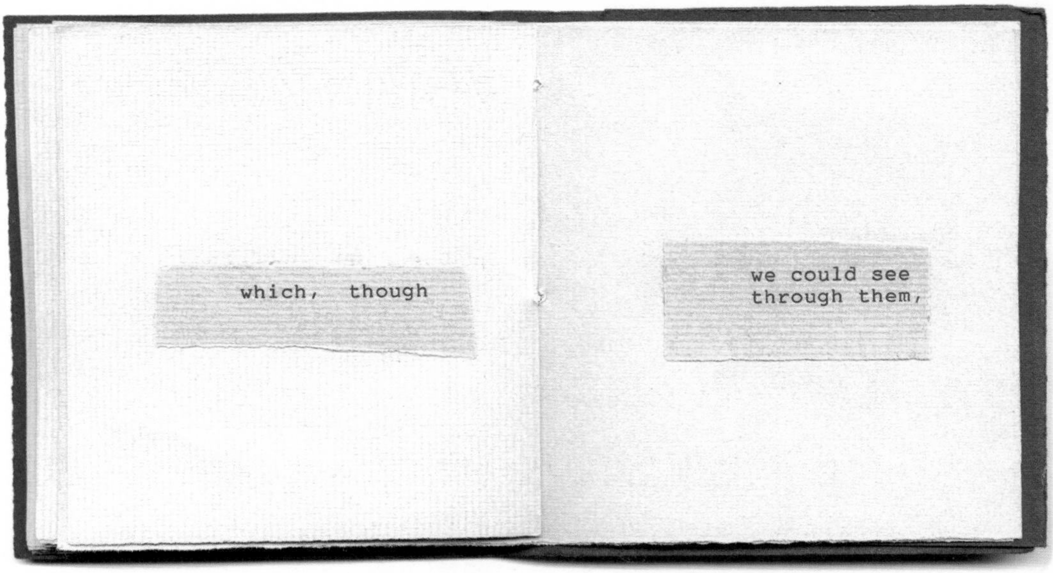
which, though
we could see
through them,

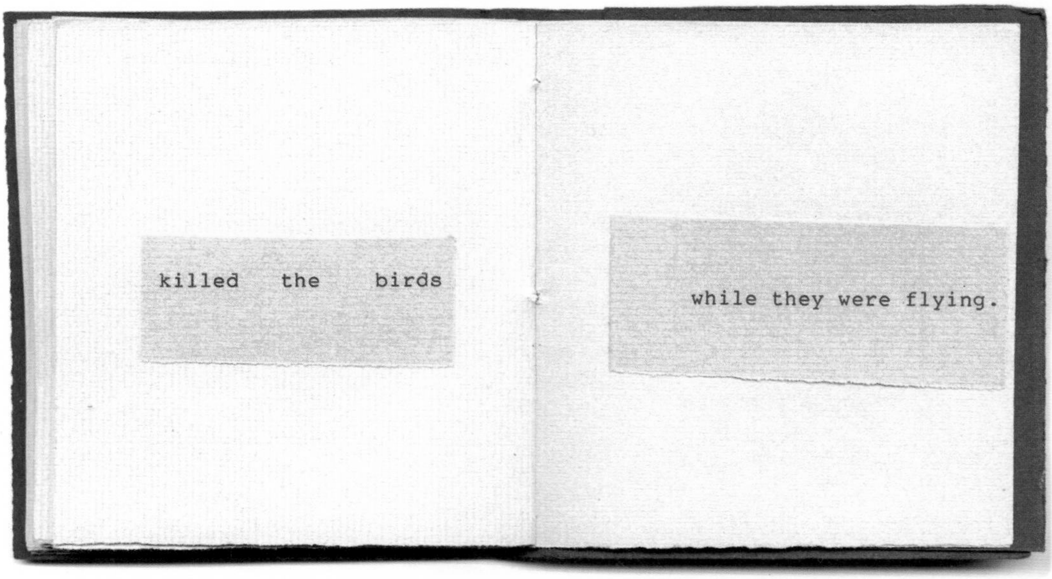
killed the birds
while they were flying.

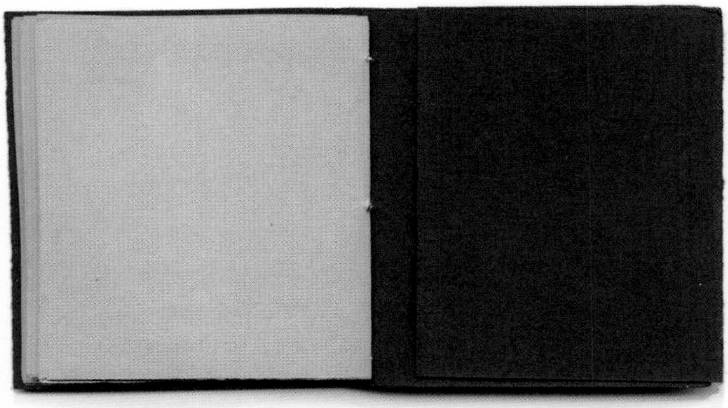

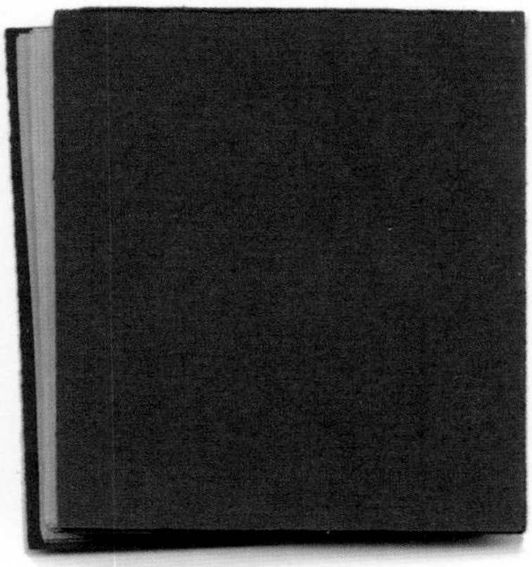

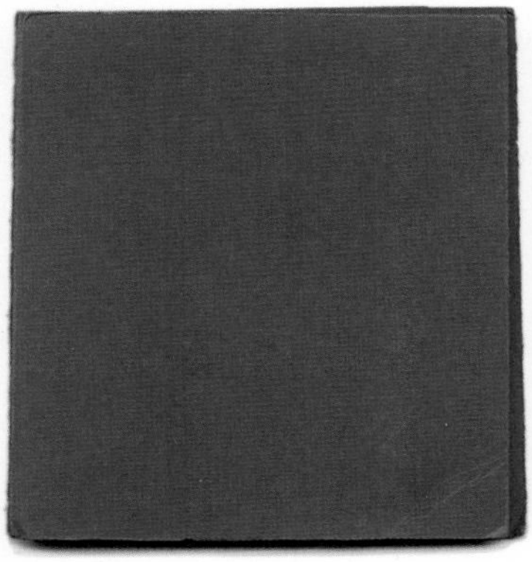

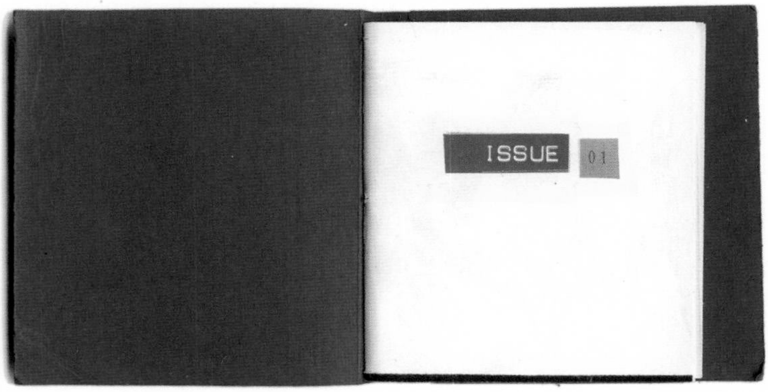
ISSUE
01

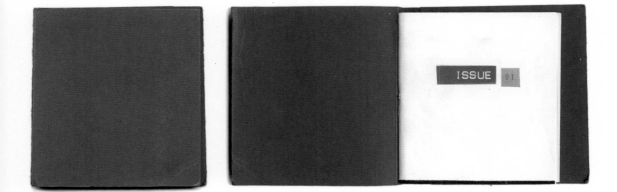

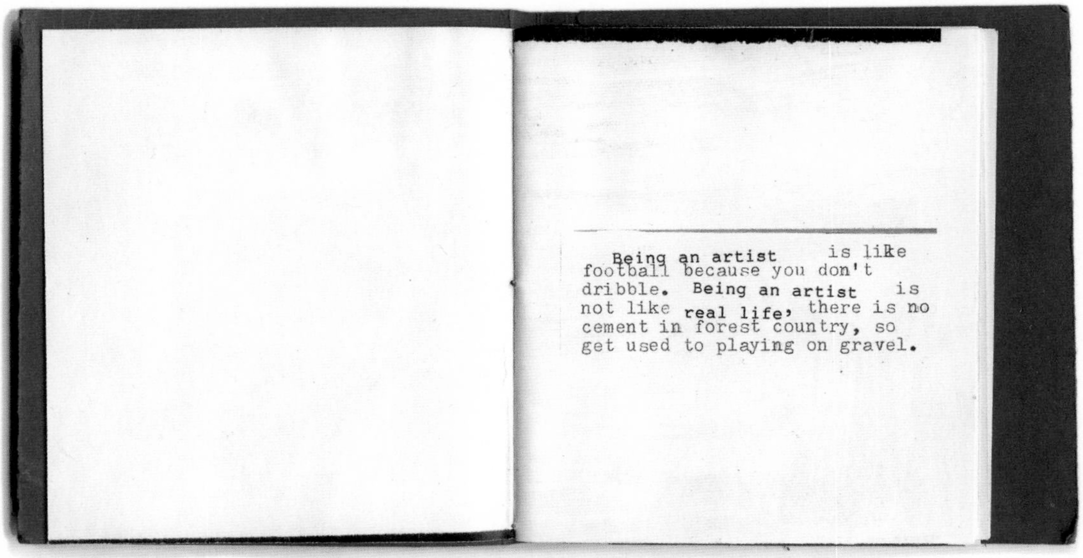
Being an artist is like
football because you don't
dribble. Being an artist is
not like real life, there is no
cement in forest country, so
get used to playing on gravel.

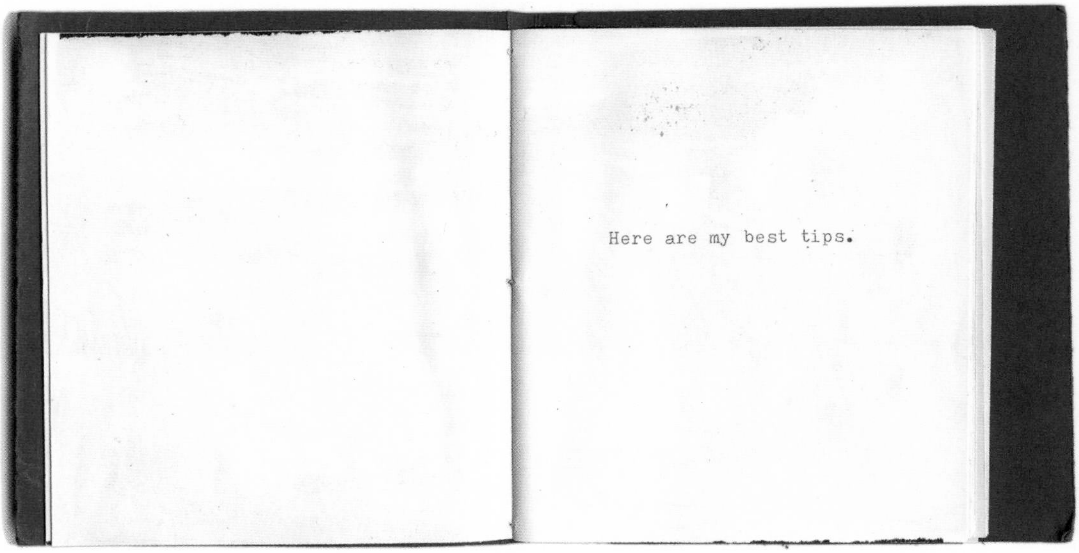
Here are my best tips.

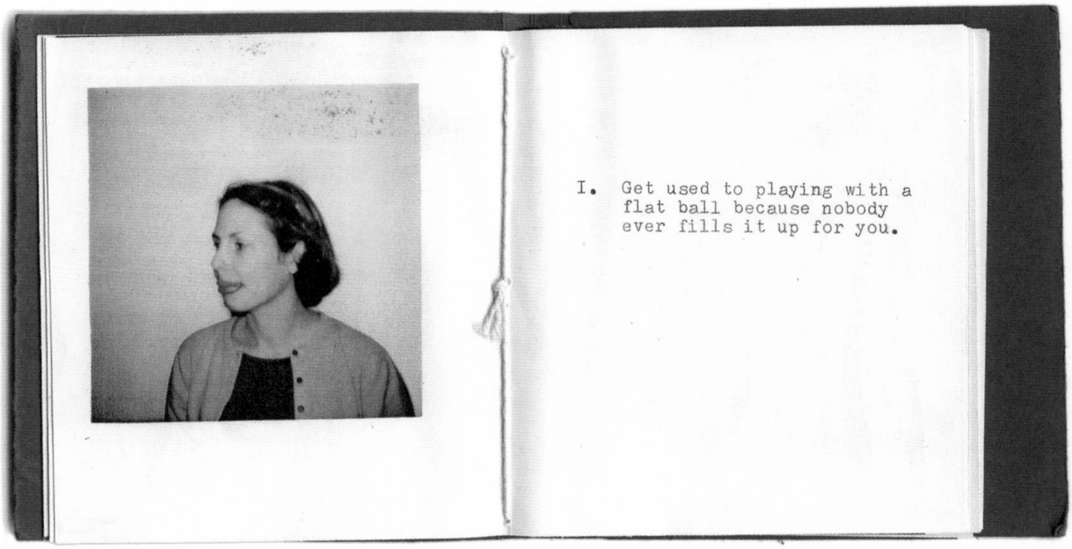
I. Get used to playing with a flat ball because nobody ever fills it up for you.

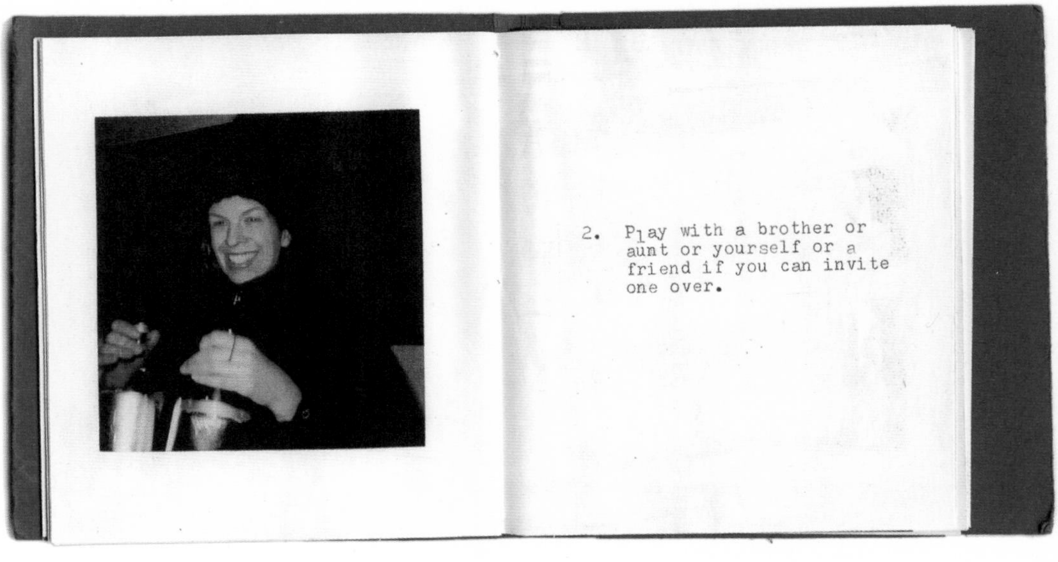
2. Play with a brother or aunt or yourself or a friend if you can invite one over.

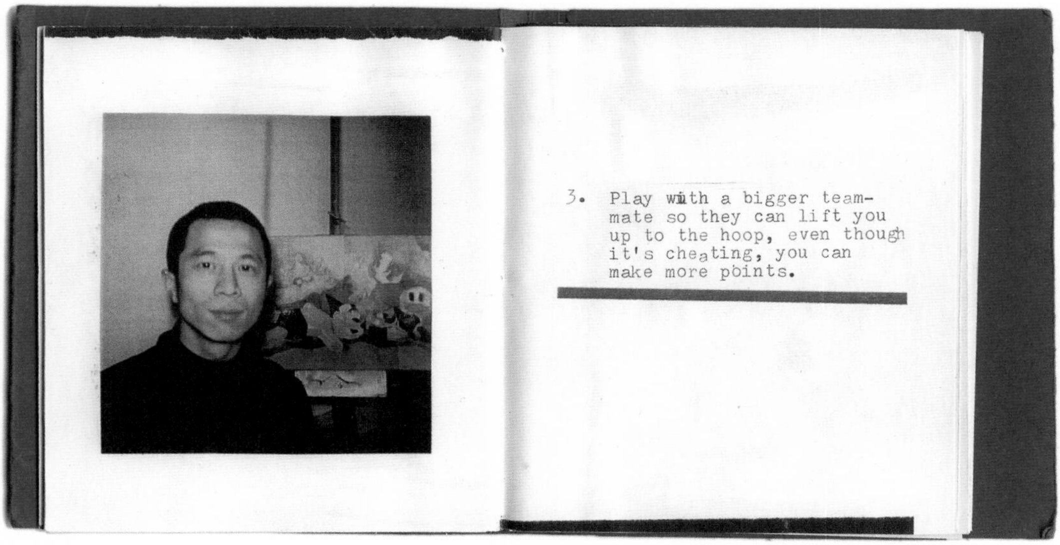
3. Play with a bigger team-
mate so they can lift you
up to the hoop, even though
it's cheating, you can
make more points.

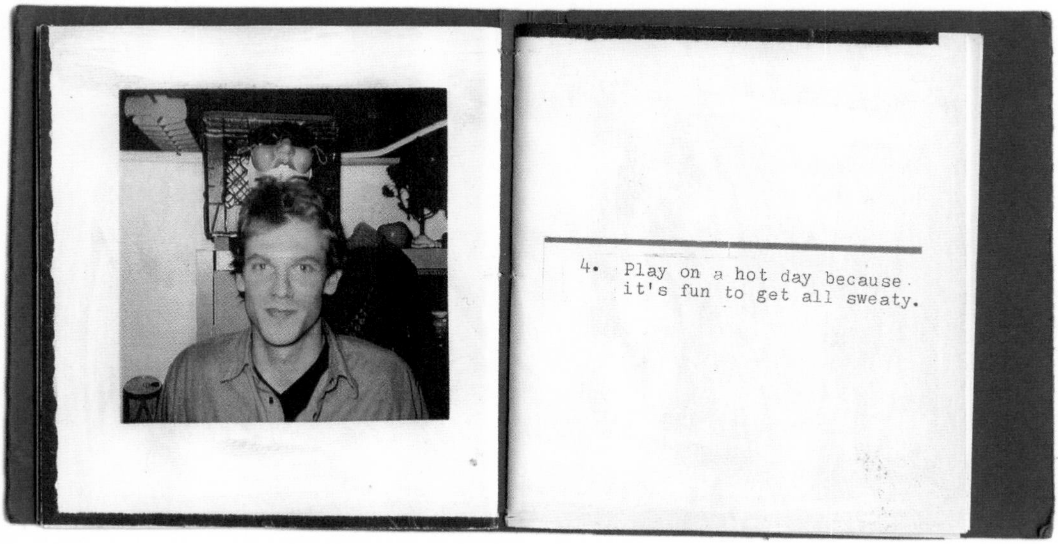
4. Play on a hot day because
it's fun to get all sweaty.

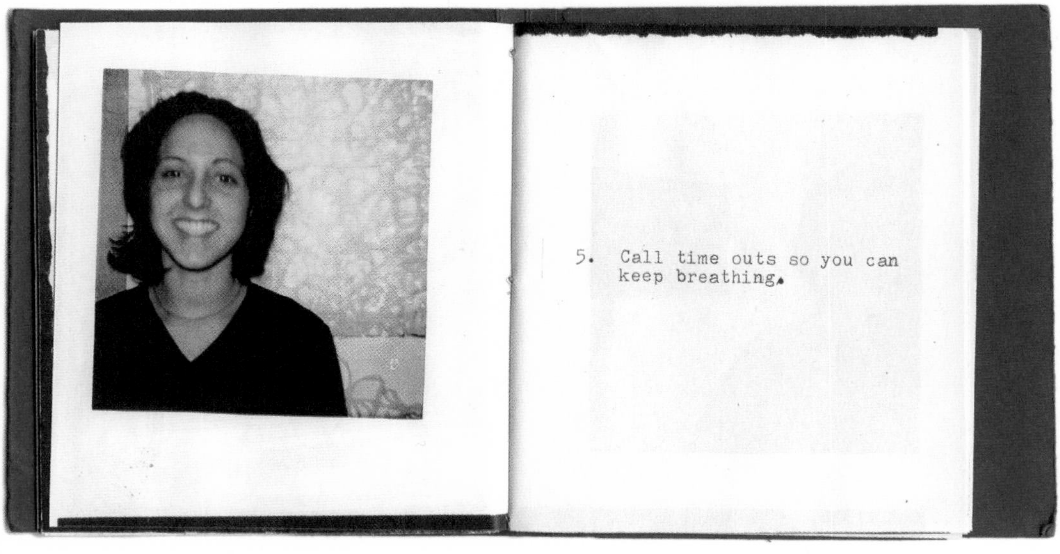
5. Call time outs so you can
keep breathing.

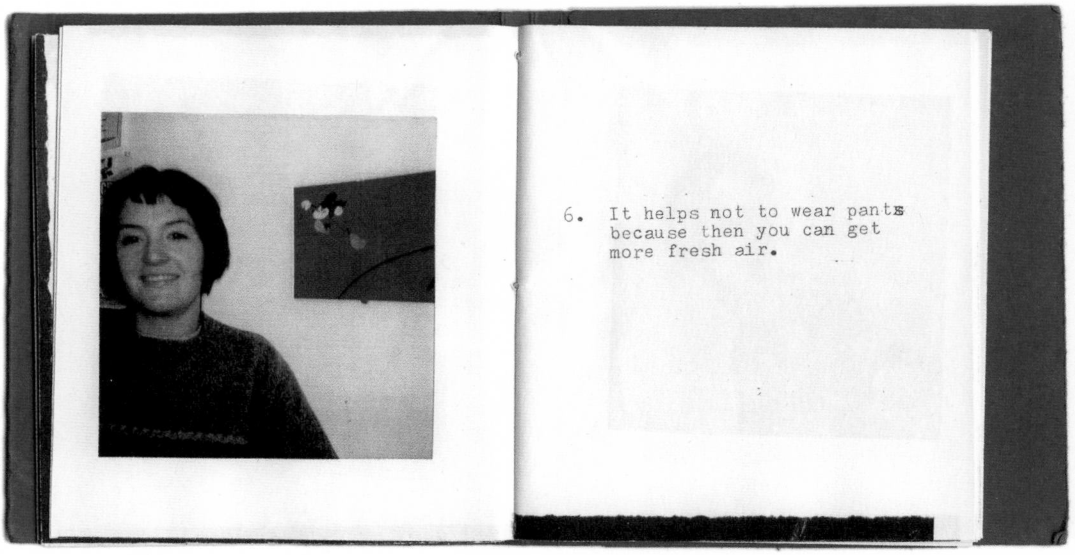
6. It helps not to wear pants because then you can get more fresh air.

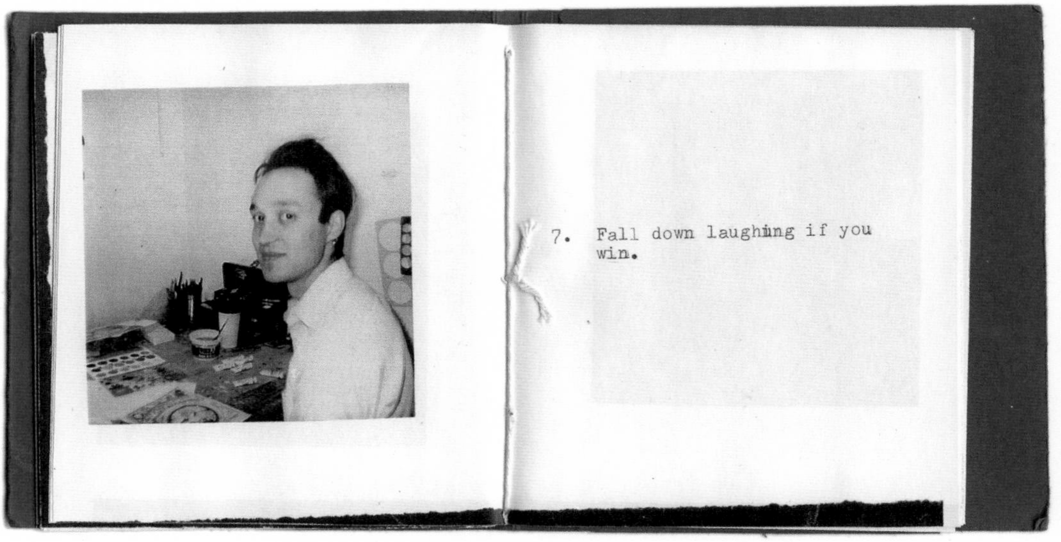
7. Fall down laughing if you win.

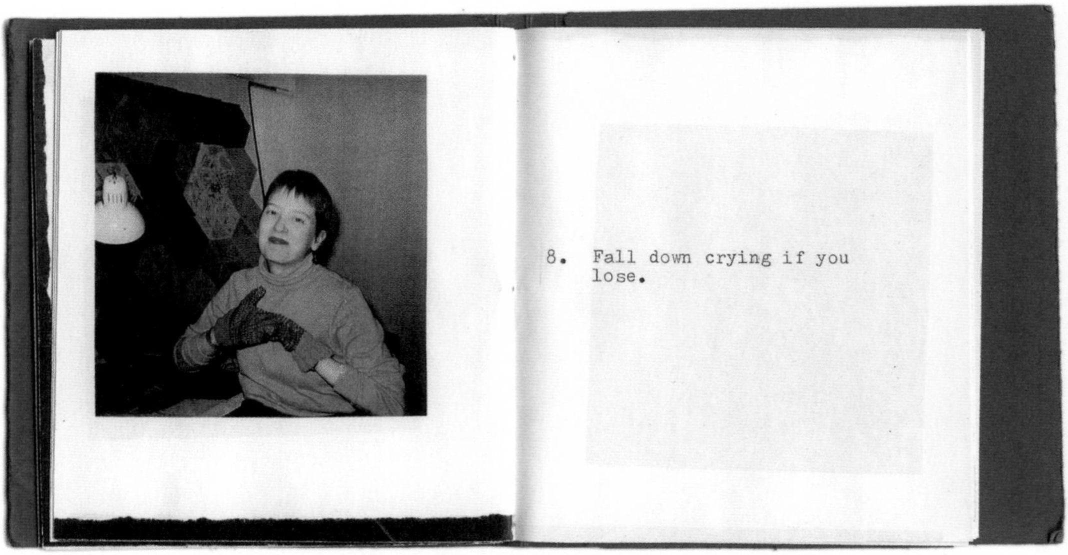
8. Fall down crying if you lose.

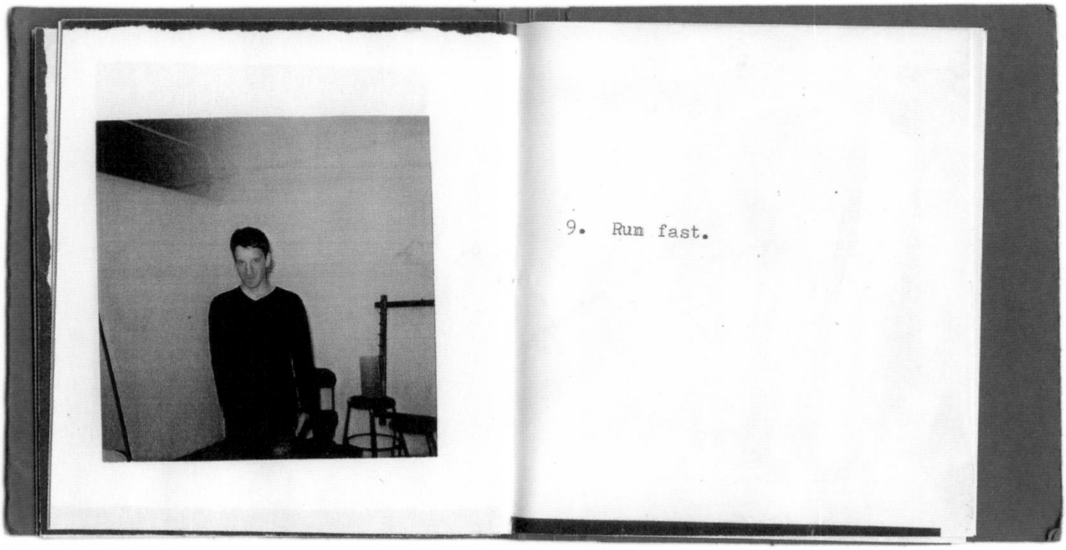
9. Run fast.

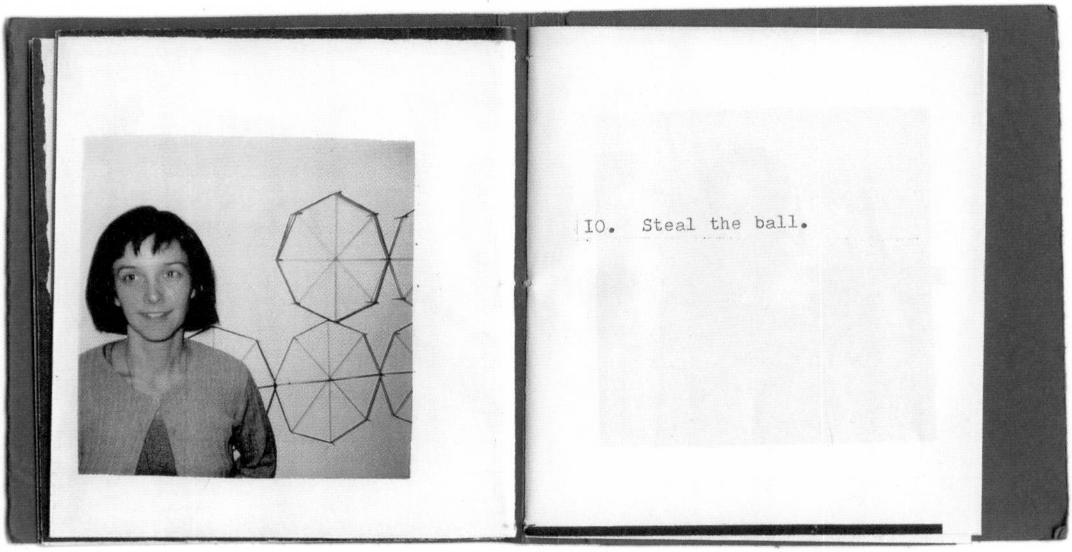
IO. Steal the ball.

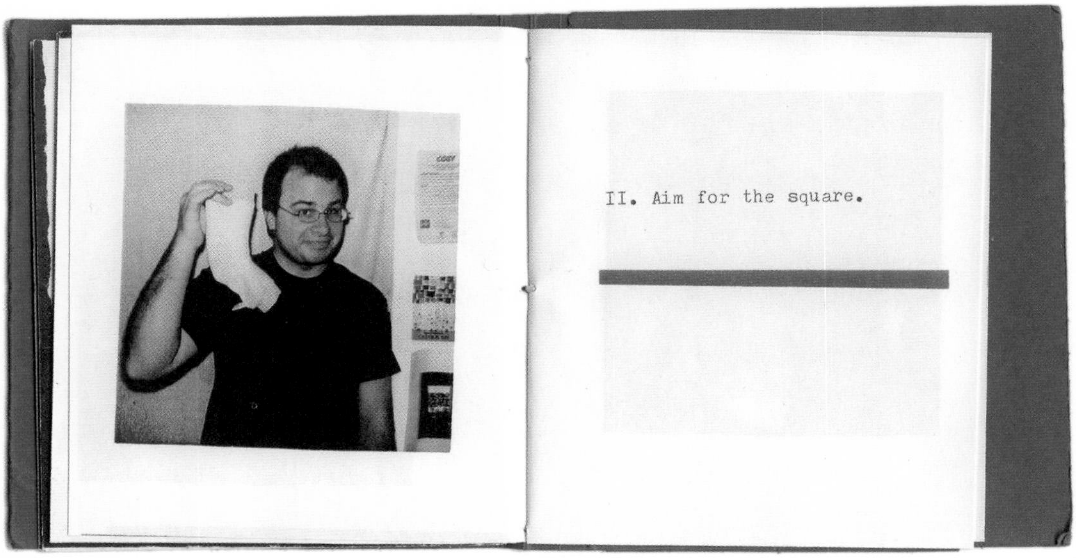
II. Aim for the square.

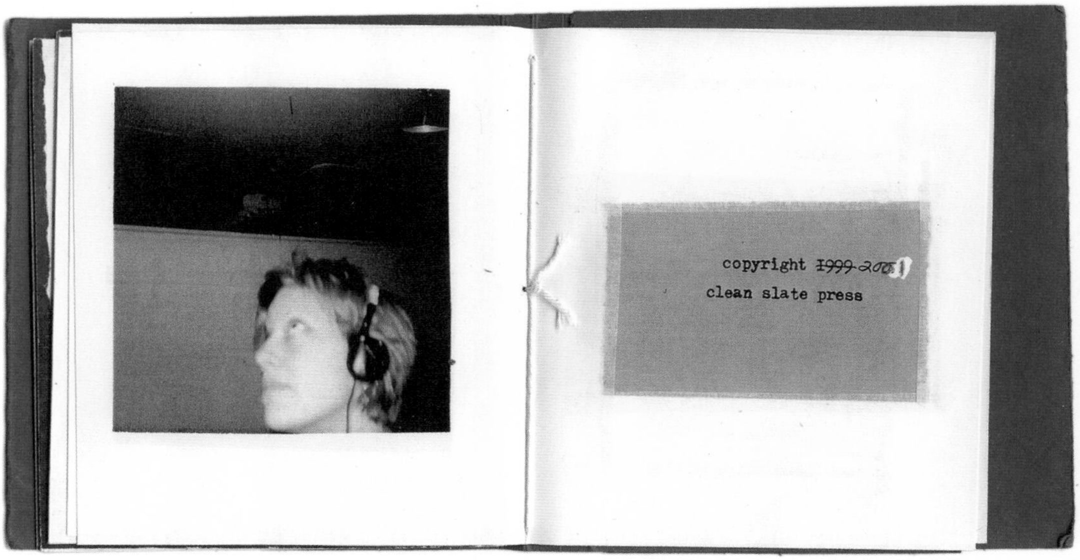

copyright ~~1999~~-2001
clean slate press

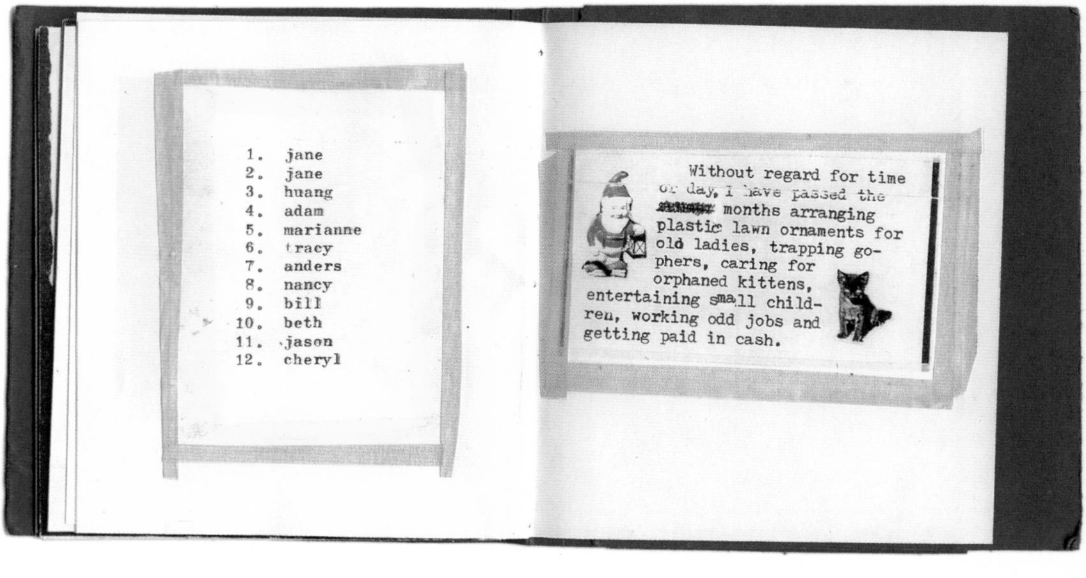

1. jane
2. jane
3. huang
4. adam
5. marianne
6. tracy
7. anders
8. nancy
9. bill
10. beth
11. jason
12. cheryl
Without regard for time or day, I have passed the [redacted] months arranging plastic lawn ornaments for old ladies, trapping gophers, caring for orphaned kittens, entertaining small children, working odd jobs and getting paid in cash.

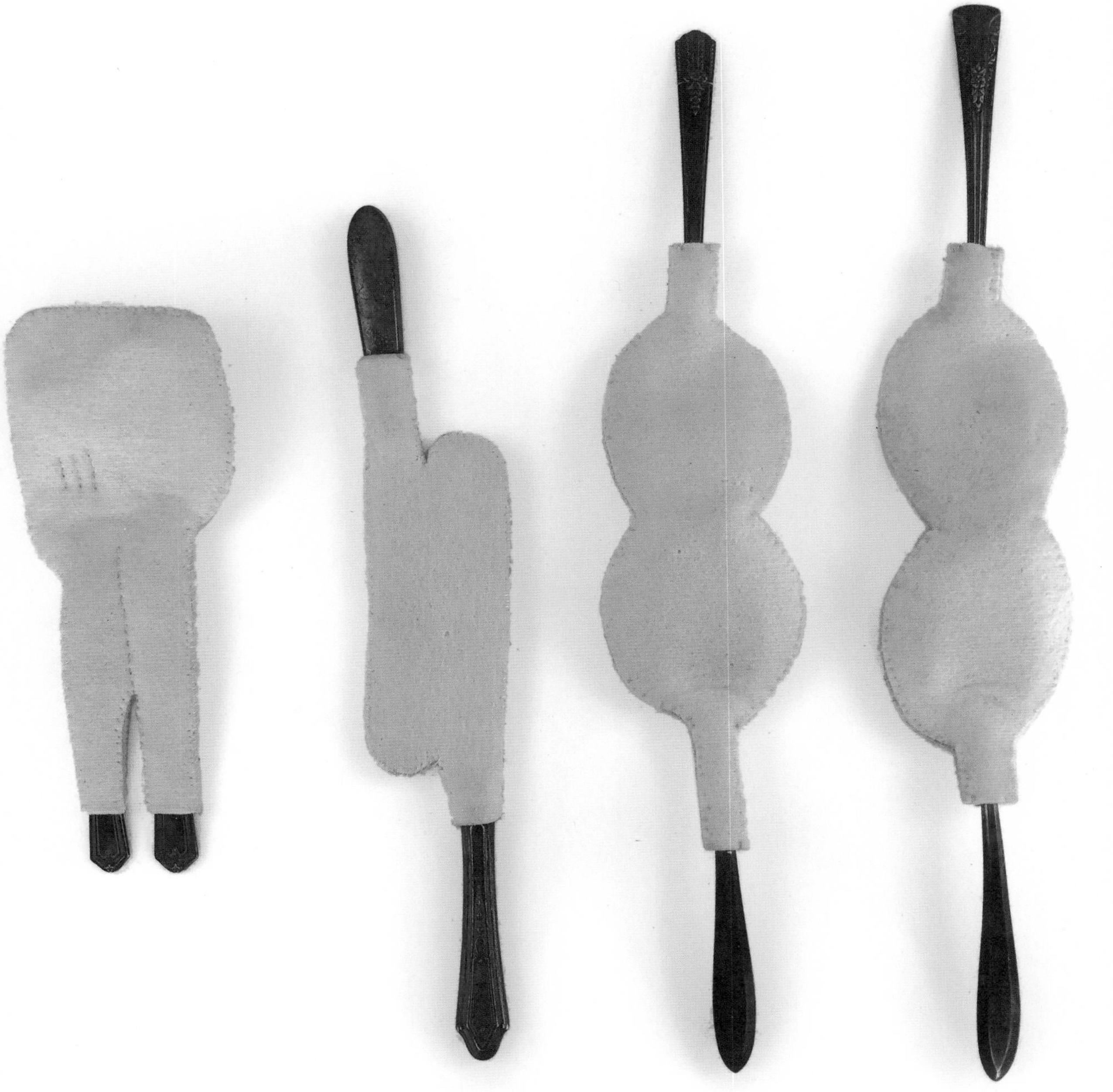

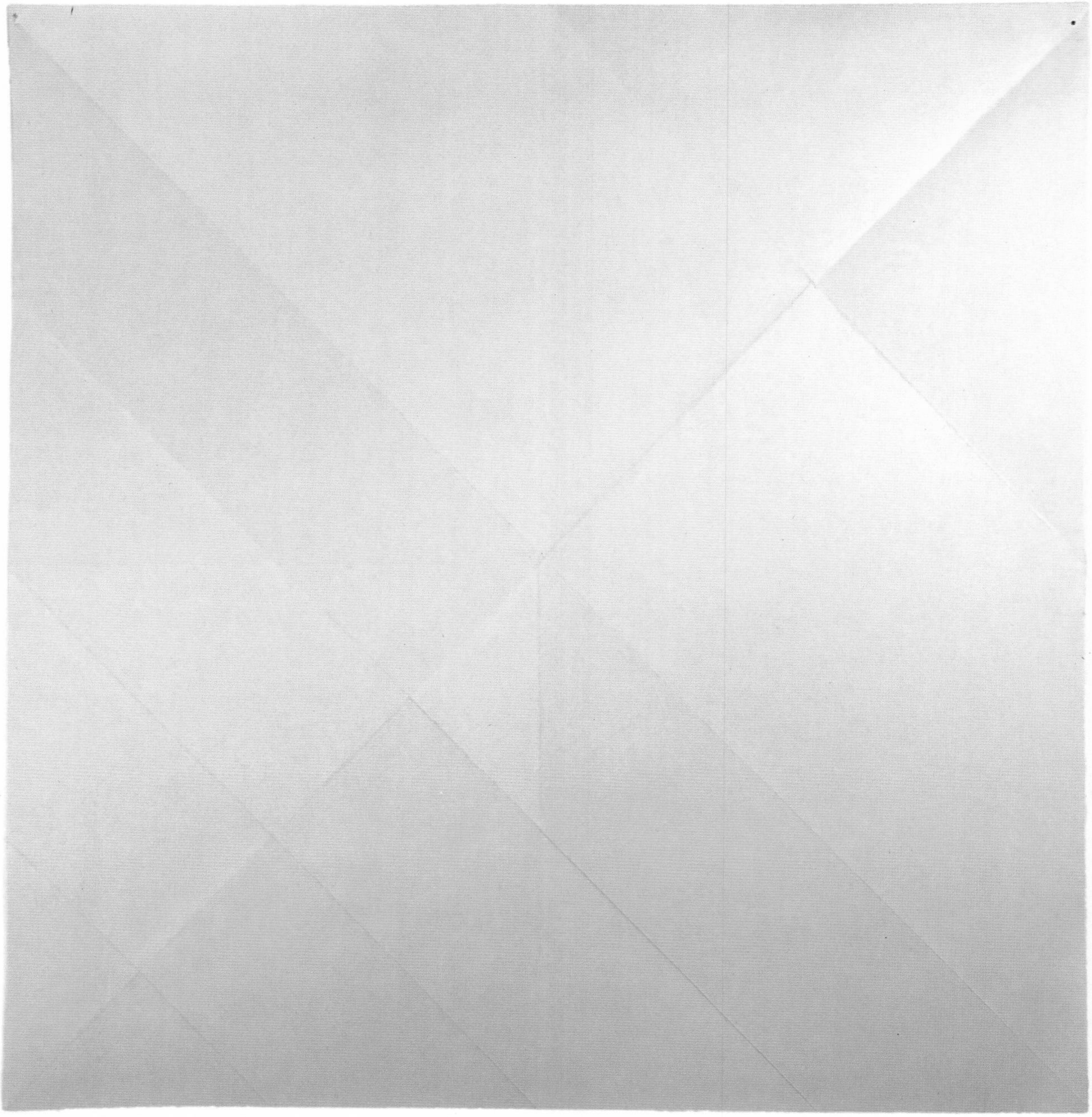

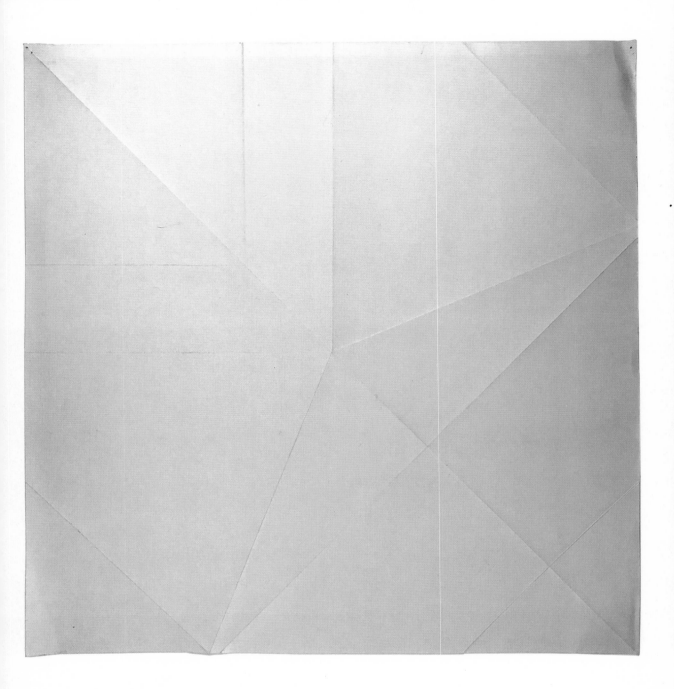

NOTES

Pages 3-15, 17-18, 20-33 and 36-37 originally appeared in *The End #1* (Fantagraphics, 2007) alongside some other material that has been cut from the present volume.

A rough, early version of *Solve for X* (PP. 20-33) was shown at Junc Gallery in Los Angeles in 2007 as part of an invitational accordion book/sketchbook show organized by Esther Pearl Watson and Mark Todd.

20 Dollars (PP. 38-47) was originally published in the anthology *Mome #7* (Fantagraphics, Spring 2007)

You Were Born and So You're Free (PP. 63-67) was originally produced as an edition of 2-color screenprints on a collection of topographical maps that had been collected by Cheryl before her death. The current book-friendly version originally appeared in the first edition of *The End* (Fantagraphics, 2013).

Talking to the Dead (PP. 70-83) originally appeared in a slightly abbreviated form in the first edition of *The End*.

How Can I Prepare You For What's to Follow (PP. 99-102) was originally designed as a five-color serigraphy print produced in collaboration with Nick Butcher and Nadine Nakanishi at Sonnenzimmer. The text was written on the occasion of my nephew Severin's birth in 2007. The version in the present volume originally appeared in the first edition in 2013.

Only Sometimes (PP. 112-117) originally appeared in the first edition in 2013.

Appendix I: Some Later Thoughts

Other People's Stories (PP. 125-126) originally appeared in my book *Poetry is Useless* (Drawn & Quarterly, 2015), a collection of drawings and strips from my sketchbooks. It's included here as an example of work I have continued to do relating to the subject of death and loss, years after the time period detailed in *The End*.

A Eulogy for Helen (PP. 127-128) is included for the same reason. My own non-belief in God or in an after-life is not really an explicit subject of this book – I even mention 'heaven' once or twice – it's a useful metaphor. But this would be a very different book if I was a believer. The widespread presumption of supernatural belief in American culture and media about death (and other things) is a simple fact, but it's meaningful to me to try and help expand the ways of thinking about the subject free of those hand-holds. *The End* is a gesture in that direction in a very small way (I once was pointed to a discussion on Facebook about *Talking to the Dead*, in which one believer took umbrage at the implication that the ghost of her husband might not actually be talking to her). The eulogy I wrote for my grandmother after her death in 2015 is another. Helen was the first person close to me to die after Cheryl's death in 2005. Because of my experience having dealt with and thought about death more than most of the people in my family in the intervening time – certainly more than anyone of my generation and younger, I felt a responsibility to say something about it at the gathering. I also knew I was not the only non-believer in the house. The piece doesn't belabor the point, but it is, I think, clear. Helen was a minister's wife for six-ty years, so it's safe to say she was a religious person, but she was never dogmatic in any way, at least not to me. She happily attended her daughter's church in her later years, which is more steeped in questions of social justice than in, say, debates about the literal truth of the bible, and which is where the funeral took place. But there were other people in the pews that day as well, including my grandmother's eldest nephew, who is a retired fundamentalist preacher in Iowa in the most conservative wing of the Lutheran church, the Missouri Synod. I would have been willing to hear his take, but I also wanted room to offer mine. Which I was very gracefully given. From comments afterward it was a welcome addition to the proceedings to several attendees. So this is a non-believer's eulogy, springing from a non-believer's cosmology. It meant a lot for me to give it, to get to honor my grandmother, and to have it heard in that place. There's nothing more relevant to our lives than their beginnings and endings. We need meaningful ways to talk about them that don't paper over the gaps in our understanding with distraction and invention. Metaphors and parables can be powerful tools – they are the building blocks of my own vocation after all – but pretending to certainty we can't have, in the words of Denis Diderot, "...explains nothing, confuses much and is unnecessary."

Appendix II: Some Work of Cheryl's

Pedestrian Errors is a book project Cheryl was working on when I met her in 1999 at the School of the Art Institute of Chicago (SAIC). She had a sort of ongoing semi-experimental micro-publishing project called Clean Slate Press at the time which included a small collaborative photo zine she did with a friend, several little hand-made books and other things. One of our original reasons for hanging out was her invitation to me to do something for it. For a while I worked on a very early version of the sketchbook strip that later became my book *Dogs and Water* for her, titled, at the time, *Nothing So Far*. *Pedestrian Errors* was one of only two Clean Slate Press projects that I know of that was actually offset printed in an edition of more than five or ten — I think there may have been around 500 copies printed originally. It was a companion to a video series she did around the same time with models acting out some of the 'errors,' filmed on Super 8 and then painstakingly re-filmed on video with the film being run slowly by hand through the projector. Some of these were shown in a showcase of experimental video work in New York in 2000, called *New Romantics*.

Bird/Cage is a hand-made book with text from John Cage's *A Year from Monday: New Lectures and Writings*. She made several versions of this in slightly different forms. After her death I made a screenprinted edition of the piece, based on her basic design and gave them to friends and sold some at comic shows.

Being an Artist is Like Football is the original of a little book she made a small spiral-bound edition of in 2000, featuring – and given out to – the other inhabitants of the 15th floor graduate studios of SAIC's Michigan building. We were not a couple when she made it.

Felted Objects – These sculptural/found object pieces pre-dated our meeting at SAIC. I believe she made them in Portland at the now-defunct Oregon College of Arts and Crafts in the late nineties, before coming to Chicago for graduate school. They are one of the (many) things in her studio that intrigued me and made me want to know more about her. These were part of Cheryl's posthumous show at Lula in 2006, titled *Views, Lakes, Foldings,* which is referenced on page 35 and in the Afterword.

Foldings – Also exhibited at the Lula show (and again in a group show in 2010) were some of her 'Foldings' – basically abstract, minimalist works-on-paper, on which the only 'marks' are the physical creases in the paper.

Sky Photos – For a little over a year over the course of 2002 and 2003 Cheryl placed a tripod and a 35mm film camera in the front window of our apartment in Humboldt Park in Chicago. She would periodically look outside and take a picture of the sky when the mood struck her. There are a couple of hundred photos total. Several of these were printed at large scale and exhibited at the 2006 show.